MW00812749

Documents of the Salem Witch Trials

Documents of the Salem Witch Trials

K. DAVID GOSS

Eyewitness to History

ABC-CLIO™

An Imprint of ABC-CLIO, LLC

Santa Barbara, California • Denver, Colorado

Copyright © 2018 by ABC-CLIO, LLC

All rights reserved. No part of this publication may be reproduced, stored in a retrieval system, or transmitted, in any form or by any means, electronic, mechanical, photocopying, recording, or otherwise, except for the inclusion of brief quotations in a review, without prior permission in writing from the publisher.

Library of Congress Cataloging-in-Publication Data

Names: Goss, K. David, 1952– editor.
Title: Documents of the Salem witch trials / K. David Goss.
Description: Santa Barbara, California : ABC-CLIO, an Imprint of ABC-CLIO, LLC, 2018. | Series: Eyewitness to history | Includes bibliographical references and index.
Identifiers: LCCN 2017032306 (print) | LCCN 2017035699 (ebook) | ISBN 9781440853210 (ebook) | ISBN 9781440853203 (alk. paper)
Subjects: LCSH: Trials (Witchcraft)—Massachusetts—Salem—History— 17th century—Sources. | LCGFT: Trial and arbitral proceedings.
Classification: LCC KFM2478.8.W5 (ebook) | LCC KFM2478.8.W5 D63 2018 (print) | DDC 133.4/3097445—dc23
LC record available at https://lccn.loc.gov/2017032306

ISBN: 978-1-4408-5320-3 (print)
     978-1-4408-5321-0 (ebook)

22 21 20 19 18   1 2 3 4 5

This book is also available as an eBook.

ABC-CLIO
An Imprint of ABC-CLIO, LLC

ABC-CLIO, LLC
130 Cremona Drive, P.O. Box 1911
Santa Barbara, California 93116-1911
www.abc-clio.com

This book is printed on acid-free paper ∞

Manufactured in the United States of America

Contents

Preface

The purpose of this publication is to provide the student of the Salem witch trials with a general overview of the entire documentary history of the Salem witch trial episode from some related events prior, through the actual tumult of 1692, to the concluding events that brought the trials to an end. Equally important, it seeks to expose the student of the Salem trials to a representative sampling of some of the specific and important primary source documents available, especially public court records, bringing those persons involved back to life once again through their verbatim testimonies.

In the telling of this tale of community fragmentation and interpersonal animosities, this work will also attempt to seek out some of the underlying reasons for the events of 1692, by placing the people of Essex County, Massachusetts, into their proper cultural and historical context. This, I believe, is an essential element in understanding the Salem trials, and it is perhaps the most difficult one to fully appreciate in our contemporary culture—so skeptical of the existence of things supernatural, or what Reverend Cotton Mather called "the wonders of the invisible world."

For this reason, this documentary history will attempt to highlight those primary sources that not only delve into the trial accusations and court proceedings, but also examine those instances where accusers and victims express mutual agreement about the unquestioned need to seek out Satan's influence on their godly society and destroy the minions of Satan wherever they may be found. In this, the student will discover that many of the alleged victims of the Salem episode were not in any way skeptical concerning the reality of witchcraft and the supernatural, but only differed on the question of who indeed might be guilty of spiritual wrongdoing—victims protesting their innocence in the face of execution, but never questioning the reality of witchcraft per se.

In this way, it is hoped that a more accurate understanding of life in 17th-century New England may emerge. Here the student will encounter a Puritan community, uniform in its religious beliefs and following a generally accepted standard of moral behavior grounded in Calvinist Biblical teaching. Even under the most stressful circumstances, this was a standard rarely, if ever, questioned. This united community consensus would, when combined with the intolerance of Chief Justice William Stoughton, help to sustain the trials in the face of an ever-increasing sense of public discomfort. In addition, these documents underscore the significance and negative influence of the so-called afflicted children and the use and acceptance of spectral evidence as a prime mover of events. In the final analysis, that public consensus would ultimately shift when outspoken, prominent, critical voices of common sense—such as Thomas Brattle and Robert Calef—would finally emerge to help sway public opinion after September 1692. After this, New England and the Puritan experiment would never be the same. These events, even when read through the documents of the time, present a fascinating story often difficult for contemporary readers to fully understand. It is hoped that the following historical documents will provide the reader with a balanced perspective of what took place in Salem in 1692, and why.

Concerning how this publication might be most effectively used, it should provide the researcher with the needed primary source material to describe the proceedings of the Salem court, and in particular, the general attitudes and testimonies offered that shaped the event. It would be inaccurate to imply that this work provides a comprehensive array of court proceedings, of which there are hundreds. Rather, this volume offers a representative sampling of that much larger collection, presenting a balanced offering of representative examples of various types of court documents available. In addition, in this documentary history, the reader will be exposed to the most essential verbatim testimonies concerning some of the trials' most significant cases, as well as a sampling of other official, trial-related sources. For the general reader, this volume should provide a solid, academic overview of the trials themselves: how they were conducted, how they came to an end, and their overall impact upon colonial New England.

It should be noted that persons wishing to conduct more intensive research beyond the scope of this publication should avail themselves of the University of Virginia's extensive website on the Salem witch trials, which contains a vast collection of unannotated court documents, manuscripts, contemporary publications, and miscellaneous records that have been made available to the general public. The following terms are essential in understanding the content of the witch trial documents. For this reason, I am including brief explanations to assist the reader.

1. Explanatory note: What is a *deposition*?

A *deposition* in 1692 was a formal, legal statement prepared by an individual claiming to have been hurt by another. Many such documents were submitted during the Salem witch trial episode. Each hand-written deposition would detail exactly what crime or crimes had been allegedly committed by the accused, then the statement would be signed by the alleged victim, and also by others who served as the victim's witnesses as to the truthfulness of the deposition document.

Having detailed the crime in writing, and having signed the deposition attesting to its accuracy, the deposition would then be presented to the court for review. If the proposed case, based upon the content of the deposition, had sufficient legal merit, the court would then issue a *warrant* (or court order) to the *County Sheriff* or *Marshall* to apprehend and arrest the person accused in the deposition, and have them brought before the court on a specific day for questioning.

2. Explanatory note: What does it mean to *cry out against* someone?

It should be noted that often but not always in the case of the Salem episode, a deposition would be preceded by informal, in-court testimony spontaneously offered to the court by the *afflicted children* whereby individuals would be "cried-out against." Such disruptive, accusative behavior was often instrumental in paving the way for the subsequent writing of depositions against those who were identified by the *afflicted children* as being responsible for their affliction.

3. Explanatory note: What is a *pretrial examination*?

After the apprehension and arrest of a suspected witch, the initial period of questioning in court was known as a *pretrial examination*. If insufficient evidence was presented during the pretrial examination, the case against the accused was dismissed with no further action taken. Conversely, if in the minds of the justices of the court sufficient evidence was presented to warrant a trial, the accused would remain under arrest, and be remanded to jail until the time of their trial at the next convenient session of the court.

4. Explanatory note: What is *spectral evidence*?

Unfortunately, during the Salem witch trials, the special Court of Oyer and Terminer responsible for trying the cases, allowed the *spectral evidence* offered by the afflicted children to be submitted as proof of witchcraft against the accused. The only persons in the court who were able to testify to seeing spectral evidence were the afflicted children. Such evidence, as described to the court by the "afflicted children," usually took the form of spiritual representations of individuals suspected of witchcraft who were invisible to all except those claiming to afflicted. Spectral evidence was, by far, the most common type of evidence presented against suspected witches during the trials. Interestingly, the Court of Oyer and Terminer had been warned against using spectral evidence in "The Return of Several Ministers" report submitted to them following the execution of the first victim, Bridget Bishop, in June 1692. Most ministers regarded it as too unreliable and untrustworthy, especially when coming from witnesses claiming to be under the power of the evil hand of witchcraft. Chief Justice Stoughton and his fellow justices, except for Nathaniel Saltonstall who wisely resigned from the court, chose to ignore this warning.

Evaluating and Interpreting Primary Documents

In historiography, which is the study of the writing of history and the employment of historical methods, a primary source is a document, recording, artifact, work of art or literature, or other information resource that was created at or near the time being studied, usually by someone with direct, personal knowledge of the particular past events, persons, or topics being described. Primary sources are original sources of information about the past, unlike secondary sources, which are works later historians create from a study, citation, and evaluation of primary sources. A modern textbook of American history, a modern biography, like Emerson W. Baker's *The New England Knight: Sir William Phips*; a modern monograph, like Laurel Thatcher Ulrich's *Good Wives: Image and Reality in the Lives of Women in Northern New England, 1650–1750*; a modern television series like PBS's *Colonial House* or *We Shall Remain*; or a modern film like *The Witch*, may be helpful in explaining New England colonial life in the 17th century to contemporary readers and viewers, but they are all secondary descriptions and depictions based upon firsthand experiences and recollections recorded and preserved in the primary documents of the period.

Primary documents—as illustrated by the document selections included in *The Documents of the Salem Witch Trials*—come in many forms and types, including letters, journals, polemics, speeches, literary works, and public records and documents. All these types of sources were written by a particular person at a particular time in a particular place for a particular reason. Some were written with no expectation that they would ever be read by anyone other than the original recipient; others were written for publication or at least with an eye to wider distribution. Some were meant to inform, some to persuade, some to entertain, and some to obfuscate. Each exhibits the political, religious, class, ethnic, or personal biases of their creators, whether those attitudes were consciously or unconsciously expressed. Some are the product of poor memories, bad information, or outright deception, but all are authentic voices of someone alive at the time, and can add at least a little to the information we have of an otherwise irrecoverable past age or person. Nonetheless, historians must carefully evaluate and test all primary sources to determine how much weight and credibility each should be given.

How to Read Primary Documents

When evaluating a primary source, historians ask the following questions:

1. Who wrote or produced it? What is known about this person's life or career?

2. When was the source written or produced? What date? How close or far was that date from the date of the events described?

3. Where was it produced? Which country, which region, which locality?

4. How was the source written or produced? What form did it originally take? Was it based upon any preexisting material? Does the source survive in its original form?

5. Why was the source written or produced? What was its creator trying to do, and for whom?

6. Who was the source written or produced for? Who was its audience, and why? What do we know about the audience?

7. What is the evidential value of its contents? How credible is it?

Readers of the document selections contained in this volume should apply these same questions to the selections they read or study.

When analyzing a primary document, scholars also seek to identify the key words and phrases used by the author and try to understand what the author meant by those terms. They will also try to summarize the main thesis of the source to understand what point the author was trying to make. Once the author's thesis is understood, historians evaluate the evidence the author provided to support that argument, and try to identify any assumptions the author made in crafting those arguments. Historians also examine the source within the context of its time period by asking if the document is similar to others from the same period, or how widely was it circulated, or what tone, problems, or ideas it shares with other documents of the period. Scholars will also seek to determine if the author agrees or disagrees with other contemporary authors on the same subject and whether or not the source supports what they already know or have learned about the subject from other sources?

Primary sources offer modern readers and researchers the actual words of people who lived through a particular event. Secondary sources, like textbooks, offer an interpretation of a historical person or event by someone who did not know the person or witness the period. Reading primary sources allows us to evaluate the interpretations of historians for ourselves and to draw our own conclusions about a past personage or events. Asking the questions listed earlier will help users of this volume better understand and interpret the documents provided here. Because of unfamiliar and archaic language or terminology, or very different modes of expression or styles of writing, some primary sources can be difficult to read and hard to understand.

However, an important part of the process of reading and using historical sources is determining what the documents can tell about the past and deciding whether one agrees with the interpretation offered, both by the author of the original source and by later creators of secondary works based on the original document. By using primary sources, modern readers become aware that all history is based on sources that are themselves interpretations of events rooted in the interpreter's own opinions and biases. This awareness allows modern students to recognize the subjective nature of history. Thus, reading primary sources provides modern readers with the tools and evidence needed to make informed statements about the world of the past and of the present.

Historical Introduction

Witchcraft before Massachusetts Bay Colony

The events generally known as the Salem witch trials did not occur in a cultural vacuum, but rather may be seen as an extension of many witch-related incidents that preceded them. Essentially, it is important to confirm that belief in witchcraft was, and in some places still is, a firmly held cultural norm. It is described as a punishable offense, if proven, in the ancient Babylonian *Code of Hammurabi* dating back to 1754 BCE, and ultimately finds its way into the Mosaic Law of the ancient Hebrews in the Book of Exodus 22:18, which reads: "Thou shall not suffer a witch to live."

The *Lex Romana* of the Roman Empire proscribed malefic witchcraft, and considered it a capital offense. Likewise, the law codes following in the wake of Rome, such as the *Code Justinian*, all considered witchcraft both a real threat and worthy of condemnation when and if discovered.

It should come as no surprise therefore that throughout the late medieval period, and well into the 17th century, witch trials were quite common occurrences in Europe, and after 1645, in colonial New England as well. During that 500-year period, prevailing legal codes regarded an act of witchcraft—especially malefic witchcraft—as a capital offense, always punishable by death if proven to the satisfaction of Church and State magistrates.

To help in this pursuit, in 1486–1487, Jacob Sprenger and Heinrich Kramer, two scholarly, German monks, actually produced a very popular and widely distributed, second only to the Bible, large volume, *The Malleus Maleficarum* (*Hammer of the Witches*). It proved to be a guideline text on witch-hunting—for both Protestants and Catholics—and further legitimized the practice of discovering, prosecuting, and condemning individuals suspected of acts of witchcraft. This work, together with a body of distinctly English scholarship on the subject, especially, George Gifford's *Dialogue Concerning Witches and Witchcrafts* (1593), William Perkins's *A Discourse on the Damned Art of Witchcraft* (1608), and John Cotta's *The Tryall of Witchcraft* (1616), looms menacingly in the background of the Salem trials and, to a degree, helps account for the serious and virulent attitude taken by the formally educated members of the Court of Oyer and Terminer, such as Deputy Governor William Stoughton. In other words, there were enough academic precedents to witch trial activity, documented by a sizeable body of recognized scholarly literature, that the outbreak of witchcraft in Salem was never considered a mere outgrowth of a superstitious and uneducated populace.

Witchcraft to the common yeoman farmer, as well as to the Massachusetts educated elite, was something to be taken seriously, and it always was.

Early Cases of New England Witchcraft Prior to 1692

The first documented case of execution for witchcraft in New England was that of Alice Young, who was convicted and hanged for witchcraft in Windsor, Connecticut, in 1647. The timing of this incident follows closely upon the establishment of two colonial legal codes—wherein witchcraft is identified as a capital crime—being first established in both Massachusetts Bay and Connecticut colonies in 1641 and 1642, respectively.

The Young case was quickly followed by that of Margaret Jones, convicted and hanged for witchcraft in Boston in 1648. While in neighboring Dorchester, Alice Lake was discovered, convicted, and hanged in 1651.

Not all such early cases resulted in conviction and death. Some instances—in fact the majority of cases—resulted in dismissal or a verdict of innocence. Despite this, often the negative collateral damage done to the lives and reputations of the victims of such accusations was unavoidable. In the case of Jane Walford of Portsmouth, New Hampshire, although she was exonerated of the crime of witchcraft in 1656, and again in 1669, her tainted reputation was sadly transferred to her daughter Hannah, who found herself accused of the same crime in 1682. Indeed, in New England witchcraft history, "at least three times a mother and daughter were accused together": Winifred and Mary Holman at Cambridge, Massachusetts, in 1659; Mary Staples, her daughter Mary (Staples) Harvey and her granddaughter Hannah Harvey, in Fairfield, Connecticut, in 1692; and Winifred Benham Sr. and Winifred Benham Jr. at Wallingford, Connecticut, in 1697 (John Putnam Demos, *Entertaining Satan*, p. 70).

Such multigenerational suspicion of witchcraft in 17th-century New England was not as common as "guilt by association" through marriage. Husbands of suspected witches were also often charged. Examples of this tendency, prior to the Salem outbreak, include Margaret and Thomas Jones of Charlestown (1648); Mary and Hugh Parsons of Springfield, Massachusetts (1651); Joan and John Carrington of Wethersfield, Connecticut (1651), Nicholas Bailey and his wife of New Haven, Connecticut (1655); Nicholas and Margaret Jennings of Saybrook, Connecticut (1661); Andrew and Mary Sanford of Hartford, Connecticut (1662); John and Elizabeth Blackleash of Wethersfield, Connecticut (1662–1663); Nathaniel and Rebecca Greensmith of Hartford, Connecticut (1662–1663); and Ralph and Mary Hall of Setauket, Connecticut (1665), all of whom were jointly suspected of witchcraft acting in collaboration with each other. Salem would produce several more married witchcraft suspects (Goss, *The Salem Witch Trials*, pp. 4–9).

Altogether, *outside* of the Salem episode, the residents of New England between 1628 and 1688 would produce approximately 140 known cases of witchcraft accusations; leading to 61 trials, resulting in 16 executions—consisting of two males (both husbands of accused witches) and fourteen females (Demos, *Entertaining Satan*, pp. 401–409). The Salem outbreak would result in a total of 25 deaths.

These include five individuals to die under poor prison conditions, 19 persons hanged, and one individual pressed to death for his unwillingness to cooperate with the court (Baker, *A Storm of Witchcraft*, pp. 288–292).

However, always the most vulnerable to witchcraft accusations and prosecution were those single women lacking the protection of a spouse. One of Boston's most celebrated cases involved Anne Hibbens who, although the wife of a prominent Boston merchant, suffered excommunication from the Boston church in 1640. However, the death of her husband in 1654 left her open to accusation for witchcraft in 1656, resulting in her arrest, trial, and execution.

Even more notorious and influential in the witchcraft history of Boston was the widely publicized 1688 case of the widow "Goody" Glover immortalized in Reverend Cotton Mather's book *Memorable Providences Relating to Witchcrafts and Possessions* (1689). The primary purpose of Mather's book was to stem the growing tide of skepticism among a minority of puritan clerics and other more sophisticated colonists, and conclusively demonstrate the validity of witchcraft as a real and present danger to the godly community (Richard Weisman, *Witchcraft, Magic and Religion in 17th-Century Massachusetts*, pp. 65–66). When published in 1689, just four years before the Salem outbreak, *Memorable Providences* became a colonial bestseller, with a wide and diverse Massachusetts readership.

In this account, Mather chronicles the incident of the Goodwin family of Charlestown, Massachusetts, wherein the four children of John Goodwin, in 1688, suffered physical ailments and afflictions very similar to those later claimed by the so-called afflicted children of the Salem episode of 1692. The alleged perpetrator of these afflictions was a lowly, Irish washerwoman known only as Goody Glover, who, when formally accused, confessed to the crime of harming the Goodwin children with malefic witchcraft. Mather himself bears witness to this in his personal conversations with Glover in prison. The torments of the Goodwin children ended when Glover is finally convicted and hanged in Boston.

A possible connection between Mather's vivid published account and the Salem outbreak's similar character was recognized as early as 1764 by former royal governor Thomas Hutchinson in his three-volume work, *The History of the Colony and Province of Massachusetts Bay*, in which he observes: "the conformity between the behavior of Goodwin's children and most of the supposed bewitched at Salem . . . is so exact as to leave no room to doubt the stories had been read by the New England persons themselves, or had been told to them by others who had read them." Thus, it seems possible that Reverend Cotton Mather's popular narrative description of the Goodwin case may have unwittingly paved the way for the Salem episode in providing a generally accepted paradigm of what constituted a "typical witch episode."

The Salem Witch Trials

The Salem witch episode, in reality, has its origins in the life and career of Reverend Samuel Parris, a Harvard-educated son of a West Indies plantation owner who, upon the death of his father, Thomas Parris, in 1673, left his position as a

Harvard student to assume the management of his father's estate and business interests in Barbados. This choice of career, in Parris's view, did not prove satisfactory, and by 1680, he had returned to Boston. Upon his arrival, he sought to return to business and got engaged to Elizabeth Eldridge, an attractive and well-connected daughter of a prominent Boston merchant. In spite of this shift, Parris decided to pursue a career in the ministry, seeking a position as the pastor of a Boston-area congregation.

In 1689, he was invited to serve as the minister of a humble, though contentious congregation of Salem Village (now, known as Danvers, MA). It was at the time a struggling, rural community located on Boston's North Shore about three miles north of the large, prosperous seaport town of Salem. Despite the location and modest status, Parris accepted the offer, managing to keep his status as a gentleman and his two West Indian slaves—Tituba and John Indian—to assist his wife Elizabeth maintain a well-ordered household and care for his family.

It should be noted that, while Parris maintained, until the time of his dismissal in 1695, that his negotiated contract with the leaders of the Salem Village congregation included a modest, but adequate salary, the ownership of the Salem Village parsonage, and an annual supply of firewood, a sizeable segment of the congregation did not agree. Consequently, from nearly the beginning of Parris's ministry, the Salem Village community was divided into two rival factions concerning their new pastor.

Immediately following Parris's arrival in 1689, attendance at the village meeting house nearly doubled, but by the following year it had leveled off as controversy and hostility increased. This was due to in part Parris's demanding contractual expectations and, in part due to his theological conservatism—especially his unwillingness to accept the more liberal, "Half-way Covenant"—which was a new, but generally accepted doctrinal policy of allowing new members into the congregation without requiring a personal testimony of the transformational indwelling of the Holy Spirit. Parris rejected what he considered an unacceptable compromise in allowing unregenerate sinners into church membership. In other words, Parris was a conservative, traditional puritan, taking a firm stance on who was, according to Calvinist theology, truly a member of the elect. Only the confirmed elect, the chosen people of God, in Parris's view, should be allowed to become members of the Salem Village congregation and participate in the partaking of the sacrament of communion. In his sermons, Parris stressed the realities of the unseen spiritual world where in reality "here are but two parties . . . the Lamb (Christ) and his followers and the dragon and his followers . . . here are no neuters (neutrals). Everyone is on one side or the other" (Reverend Samuel Parris, *Sermon Book*, September 11, 1692).

It was during the winter of 1691/1692 that the first suspicious behavior on the part of Reverend Parris's family began to manifest itself at home. His nine-year-old daughter Elizabeth—commonly referred to as Betty—and his 11-year-old niece Abigail Williams—began to act in strange and bizarre ways. According to the testimony of Parris's friend and colleague, Reverend John Hale of Beverly, who was asked to visit the Parris home during these fits, "these girls were (being) bitten and pinched by 'invisible agents.'" At first, Parris called in a local physician, Dr. William Griggs, to conduct a physical examination to determine if their behavior was a result of illness or fever. Griggs's diagnosis indicated no physical malady, but suggested that Betty and Abigail were suffering "under an Evil Hand" (Reverend John Hale, *A Modest Inquiry into the Nature of Witchcraft*, 1702, p. 23). Parris's neighbors, upon being informed of this, circulated the rumor that the girls were bewitched. One local woman, Mary Sibley, suggested to John Indian and Tituba, that they might effect a solution by baking a "witch's cake," comprised of oat meal and the girls' urine, and feed it to the Parris's dog. This practice was a traditional act of common folk magic to determine the positive identity of a witch suspected of bewitching someone. When this well-intentioned, act of "white magic" was done, according to Reverend Hale's account, Betty and Abigail "cried out of the Indian woman, named Tituba." The afflicted girls claimed "that she did pinch, prick and grievously torment them and that they saw her here and there, where nobody else could." Hale concludes that "these afflicted persons were so wracked and tormented so as might move a heart of stone" (Hale, *A Modest Inquiry*, p. 24).

It should be noted parenthetically that when Reverend Parris discovered from Tituba who was ultimately responsible for providing her with the recipe for the witch's cake and how it might magically reveal the culprit responsible for the malefic spell upon the afflicted girls, he publically rebuked Mary Sibley in the Sabbath service stating that she was equally guilty of practicing witchcraft, and that it was unacceptable and unjustifiable to use the Devil's devices, that is magic, even when the ultimate purpose is to fight against him.

Perhaps not surprisingly, John Hale observed that as he studied the afflicted girls' behavior, he was struck at how similar it was to the symptoms exhibited by the Goodwin children described in Reverend Cotton Mather's book: *Memorable Providences*, or as he said, "I will not enlarge in the description of their cruel sufferings, because they were in all things afflicted as bad as John Goodwin's children in Boston, in the year 1689" (Hale, *A Modest Inquiry*, p. 24).

After the application of the witch's cake remedy, Parris brought a gathering of some "worthy Gentlemen of Salem and some Neighbor Ministers to consult together at his house; who when they came and inquired diligently into the sufferings of the Afflicted, concluded they were preternatural, and feared the Hand of Satan was in them" (Hale, *A Modest Inquiry*, p. 25).

This point marks the start of the Salem episode since immediately after this meeting, Tituba was questioned concerning her involvement in acts of witchcraft—admitting her guilt in making the "witch's cake." Local ministers initiated private "fasts" and periods of "Public Humiliation" and petitioned for "A general Fast by order of the General Court observed throughout the Colony." All these efforts resulted in a continuation of the afflicted girls' aberrant behavior, and a general agreement of the need for more stringent measures.

By late winter, the Parris household girls had attracted two other adolescent females, Elizabeth Hubbard and Ann Putnam Jr., who joined them in displaying bizarre afflicted behavior, and blaming new suspects besides Tituba. Among the newly accused suspected witches were two unpopular and marginalized women: Sarah Good and Sarah Osborne.

The Pretrial Examinations: February to May 1692

At this point, the Salem Village selected a delegation of four male citizens to petition the Town of Salem, on February 29, 1692, to send out local magistrates—justices of the peace—to investigate the possibility that three local women might be in league with Satan and committing acts of malefic witchcraft upon young, innocent members of the local community. In response to this, Justices John Hathorne and Jonathan Corwin were sent to set up a series of pretrial examinations at Salem Village, investigating Tituba, Sarah Good, and Sarah Osborne under suspicion of witchcraft. The initial hearings took place in Ingersoll's Tavern, a popular gathering place in the heart of Salem Village, at 10:00 A.M., the following day, March 1, 1692.

The crowd of local residents at this hearing was so large that, in order to accommodate the number of interested attendees, the examination was relocated to the Salem Village Meeting House. One can only speculate how the Salem episode might have developed if the initial hearings had been handled in a more private and far removed location instead of being initially treated as a public spectacle.

The first pretrial examination, largely handled by the intimidating inquisitor, John Hathorne, was not successful in drawing a confession from the first victim, Sarah Good, who steadfastly maintained her innocence in the face of judicial badgering and the outcries and bizarre behavior of the four afflicted girls, all of whom accused Good of tormenting them during the hearing. This was also the first demonstration of "spectral evidence" whereby those giving evidence, testified to seeing the specter or spirit of an accused person performing malefic acts of witchcraft. The problem was the inability of the officers of the court to verify this type of evidence or corroborate it by personal observation since it was only visible to the afflicted children.

The use of spectral evidence as the primary proof against virtually all of the victims accused during the Salem episode was certainly one of the most controversial and unjustifiable positions taken by Hathorne and Corwin during the pretrial examinations. It would be later used by Deputy Governor William Stoughton and the Court of Oyer and Terminer throughout the trials from May through the end of October 1692. The end result of the first days' examination was that both Good and Osborne were to be held for further questioning and were placed in jail with the likelihood of being tried in the future for witchcraft when it was possible.

The reason usually given by historians as to why capital crimes could not be tried was that in 1684 the Province of Massachusetts had its royal charter revoked by England's King James II, as a preliminary step to the establishment of the short-lived Dominion of New England and the appointment of Sir Edmund Andros as its royal governor. When King James II was finally overthrown during the Glorious Revolution, Massachusetts, in the absence of a charter, was technically without the legal authority to try and execute capital offenders from 1689 through May 1692. This legal technicality apparently ended with the arrival of Reverend Increase Mather with the newly appointed royal governor of Massachusetts Colony, Sir William Phips in May 1692. Phips brought with him a newly issued Massachusetts charter, issued in 1691 by King William and Queen Mary, establishing the justice of the newly crowned monarchs. This new colonial charter unified Massachusetts Bay Colony and Plymouth Colony under one government, making Massachusetts henceforth a *royal colony* to be administered by a royally appointed governor.

Parenthetically, it should be pointed out that the remarkable Sir William Phips was a native New Englander, born in the Province of Maine, who came to Boston as a young apprentice shipbuilder, rose to sea captain, and plundered gold and silver from a sunken Spanish treasure ship in 1687. His total fortune from this salvaging venture amounted to "more than 200,000 pounds sterling" and would be worth, in today's currency, approximately $20,000,000. As a loyal subject of the newly crowned English sovereigns, William and Mary, young Captain Phips shared his fortune with his monarchs and in return received a knighthood, making him "the first man born in America to receive such an honor" (Baker, *A Storm of Witchcraft,* p. 202).

Thus, after May 1692, in Massachusetts Colony, with the installation of a new, royally appointed governor and a new colonial charter, land-based capital crimes could be tried and death sentences could be legally carried out—if not according to the old legal code of Massachusetts Bay Colony, at least according to the prevailing statutes of *English Common Law*, more specifically, the *Witchcraft Act of 1604*. This English statute "called for the death penalty for anyone convicted of invoking evil spirits or a familiar of the devil" (Baker, *A Storm of Witchcraft*, p. 26).

As to what sorts of activities or experiences might have preconditioned the so-called afflicted girls—either emotionally or psychologically—to experience physical affliction or feelings of spiritual oppression, some Salem area residents had their personal opinions. One such contemporary opinion was provided by Reverend John Hale: "I fear some young persons, through a vain curiosity to know their future condition, have tampered with the Devil's tools so far that hereby one door was opened to Satan to play those pranks in the year 1692. I knew one of the afflicted persons who, as I am credibly informed, did try with an egg and a glass to find her future husband's calling; 'til there came up a coffin, that is a specter in likeness of a coffin. And she was afterward followed with diabolical molestation to her death; and so died a single person" (Reverend John Hale, *A Modest Inquiry*).

Thus it was, at least in Reverend Hale's view, that at least some of the local young girls had unwisely demonstrated a dangerous fascination with the occult and fortune-telling through the use of what was then called "a Venus glass," seeking to tell the future. Reverend Hale and all puritan clerics would have regarded this recreational activity as unintentional sin on the part of the participant, leaving an immature young woman open to satanic influences. That spiritual vulnerability, pastor Hale felt, might have initially opened the door to the malefic actions of suspected witches like Osborne, Good, and Tituba (Hale, *A Modest Inquiry*, pp. 132–133).

While Sarah Good and Sarah Osborne steadfastly maintained their innocence in the face of mounting spectral evidence from the afflicted children and the virulent questioning of Justice Hathorne, on March 1, the third witch suspect—Tituba Indian—provided the magistrates and court observers with a detailed confession of witchcraft complete with descriptions of satanic activity capable of igniting a firestorm of fear for the spiritual safety of the local Christian community.

During her arraignment, the line of judicial questioning, as recorded in the surviving Salem court documents, followed the same basic format as the two cases preceding hers. Throughout the exchange, Justice Hathorne seems clearly convinced of the suspect's guilt. The only significant difference between Good and Osborne's response and Tituba's response was her answer:

HATHORNE: Why do you hurt these poor children? What harm have they done unto you?

TITUBA: They do no harm to me. I no hurt them at all.

HATHORNE: Why have you done it?

TITUBA: I have done nothing. I can't tell when the Devil works.

HATHORNE: What doth the Devil tell you? That he hurts them?

TITUBA: No, he tells me nothing.

HATHORNE: Do you never see something appear in some shape?

TITUBA: No, never see anything.

HATHORNE: What familiarity do you have with the Devil? Or, what is it that you converse withal? Tell the truth. Who is it that hurts them?

TITUBA: The Devil for ought I know.

HATHORNE: What appearance, or how doth he appear when he hurts them? With what shape, or what is he like that hurts them?

TITUBA: Like a man, I think. Yesterday, I being in the lean-to chamber, I saw a thing like a man, that told me to serve him and I told him no, I would not do such a thing. ("The First Examination of Tituba as Recorded by Jonathan Corwin," March 1, 1692)

Tituba proceeded to elaborate on her private conversation with Satan, stating that Good and Osborne were in reality "those that hurt the children, and would have her done it."

She next expands the size of the known group of female witches from two to four, adding "two of which she knew not." Finally, she concluded that altogether "there was five of them with the man" and that while Good and Osborne were from Salem Village, "the others were of Boston" ("The First Examination of Tituba," as recorded by Jonathan Corwin, March 1, 1692).

What Tituba reveals in her testimony is indeed a detailed description of a wide variety of witchcraft activities including malefic threats of bodily harm to her and the afflicted children; physical descriptions of the witches themselves and of their demonic familiars—some bizarre in their appearance; other familiars more conventional in the shape of two cats, a wolf and a yellow bird; night flying on sticks;

secret witch gatherings and plans to commit murder; or as Tituba finally noted, "they would have me killed Thomas Putnam's child."

At last, Hathorne inquires of her: "Did you never practice witchcraft in your own country?," and Tituba responds: "No, never *before now*" ("First Examination of Tituba as Recorded by Jonathan Corwin," March 1, 1692).

There can be little doubt that the Salem witch episode would have followed a very different course had not Tituba's colorful and elaborate testimony and accusations—offered at this precise time—provided Hathorne and Corwin with everything they needed to expand and intensify the search for more practitioners of witchcraft. Several noted historians have advanced the plausible idea that Tituba had been physically coerced into providing this incriminating evidence by her master, Reverend Samuel Parris. The presence of bruises and cuts upon her body are mentioned by trial observer Robert Calef in his 1697 negative critique of the Salem trials, *More Wonders of the Invisible World*. The importance of Tituba's confession therefore cannot be overstated. Had she not confessed and expanded the number of suspects, it is quite possible that "the Salem witchcraft outbreak might conceivably have been limited to three people" only (Baker, *A Storm of Witchcraft*, p. 156).

Indeed, by the end of her second examination on March 2, Tituba had implicated a total of nine possible suspects. In this way, Tituba Indian was an essential, first ingredient to the volatile formula that was about to explode across New England. After hearing her tale, in the opinion of the magistrates and the many witnesses present, there now appeared to be a real and serious supernatural threat requiring further intensive investigation. Reverend John Hale, a contemporary observer, supports this idea in his *A Modest Inquiry into the Nature of Witchcraft* stating: "And the success of Tituba's confession encouraged those in authority to examine others that were suspected, and the event was that more confessed themselves guilty of the crimes they were suspected for. And thus was the matter driven on" (Hale, *A Modest Inquiry*, p. 27).

Hale's assessment that Tituba's confession benefitted the trials in that, as a result "more confessed themselves guilty of the crimes they were suspected for," is one of the most profoundly ironic remarks made by any of the trials' contemporary observers. While it is true that after Titutba's confession, 54 other suspects would also confess, indeed fully *one-third of all those accused*, it should also be noted that her confession was precisely the reason why the Salem witch trials expanded to become arguably the greatest miscarriage of justice in American history.

An important final point concerning the future treatment of Tituba after her court appearance is that she is removed from Salem Village and sent to jail in Boston on March 7, 1692. She would never again testify or provide a single deposition against any of the future suspects. She would not even be indicted until May 9, 1693, long after the Court of Oyer and Terminer was disbanded by Governor Phips. Her case was finally reviewed by the Superior Court of Judicature and rejected.

Immediately following March 1–2 Salem Village Meeting House examinations, the group of four afflicted children expanded again. More people were beginning to feel the afflictions of the "invisible world." Others, not previously cried out against, would be accused.

Ann Putnam Jr. continued in her accusations, claiming torment at the spectral hands of Rebecca Nurse and Martha Corey, respectively. The latter of these, Martha Corey, was also identified as a source of spectral suffering by 20-year-old Mary Warren, a maid-servant of a local yeoman farmer, John Proctor. Added to the growing society of afflicted were Tituba's husband, John Indian, and Thomas Putnam's serving girl, Mercy Lewis.

It was during this sensitive and expansive period, on Sunday, March 20, 1692, that Parris's predecessor Reverend Deodat Lawson was invited to return to the Salem Village Meeting House to preach to the village parishioners. During the afternoon service, the afflicted girls struck unexpectedly during Reverend Lawson's sermon when Abigail Williams, Samuel Parris's niece, pointed upward crying, "look where Goodwife Cloyse [Rebecca Nurse's sister] sits on the beam suckling her yellow bird between her fingers!" This spectral disruption of Lawson's sermon and the Sabbath meeting only served to further heighten the community's sense of anxious desire to search out more likely witchcraft suspects.

By the last week of March 1692, Martha Cory was arrested, examined, and jailed pending her trial. And interestingly, the youngest person to be accused of witchcraft, Sarah Good's four-year old daughter Dorothy Good was also sent to jail to await trial along with elderly and infirm Rebecca Nurse. Some of this new wave of afflicted witnesses were middle-aged, such as Bathsheba Pope and Ann Putnam Sr., both of whom claimed to be under the hands of witchcraft.

It should be noted that, in general, it was the Putnam family and their circle who became, in association with the afflicted girls, important players in the drama of the witch trials, Ann Putnam Jr., "assuming a starring role." Other prominent accusers from among this group included: Thomas Putnam (Ann Jr.'s father), his brother Edward Putnam, and his brother-in-law Joseph Hutchinson, all of whom were responsible in the beginning for signing a deposition before Magistrates Hathorne and Corwin against Sarah Good, Sarah Osborne, and Tituba. Added to the Putnam group as accusers would also be Ann Putnam Sr. (wife of Thomas), Mary Walcott, a niece, and Mercy Lewis, a servant in the Putnam household.

By April, news of Salem's problems was becoming widely known throughout the colony, and a subcommittee of the Governor's Court of Assistants—supplemented by Magistrates Jonathan Corwin and John Hathorne—visited Salem to hear some of the evidence and to interrogate some of the accused. At this meeting also appeared a full contingent of the afflicted children who impressed the visiting dignitaries with the extent of their affliction. The result was that two more individuals, John and Elizabeth Proctor, were jailed.

By April 19, 1692, a new slate of accused persons, Mary Warren, Abigail Hobbs, Bridget Bishop, and Giles Cory, were brought in for questioning. Of these four, both Mary Warren and Abigail Hobbs would, after some initial prodding, confess to being witches. By taking this course, they, like Tituba, would ultimately save their lives. Both would be expected to provide the magistrates with additional details about how they were converted to the Devil's service and submit more names of their accomplices. Both girls readily cooperated with the court.

Abigail Hobbs, although currently a resident of Topsfield, claimed to have become a witch four years earlier at the tender age of 10 when she lived with her family in coastal Maine, then under the jurisdiction of Massachusetts Bay Colony and engaged in a frontier war with the French and their Native allies. Her pretrial examination and confession, unlike that of Tituba, was remarkable in its simplicity:

Q—You are brought before Authority to answer to sundry acts of witchcrafts, committed by you against and upon the bodies of many, of which several persons now accuse you. What say you? Are you guilty, or not? Speak the truth.

A—I will speak the truth. I have seen sights and been scared. I have been very wicked. I hope I shall be better, if God will help me.

Q—What sights did you see?

A—I have seen dogs and many creatures.

Q—What dogs do you mean? Ordinary dogs?

A—I mean the Devil.

Q—How often, many times?

A—But once.

Q—Tell the truth.

A—I do tell no lie.

Q—What appearance was he then?

A—Like a man.

Q—Where was it?

A—It was at the Eastward at Casco Bay.

Q—What did he say to you?

A—He said he would give me fine things, if I did what he would have me.

Q—What would he have you do?

A—Why, he would have me be a witch.

Q—Would he have you make a covenant with him?

A—Yes.

Q—And did you make a covenant with him?

A—Yes, I did, but I hope God will forgive me.

Mary Warren, the other self-confessed witch, had once been one of the afflicted girls, and participated with them "until Proctor (her master) threatened to whip her. She then defected from the accusers and was herself accused" (Rosenthal, *Salem Story*, pp. 46–47). She was formally charged on April 19, while her master and his wife, John and Elizabeth Proctor, were now both in jail and awaiting trial for witchcraft. Sadly, Warren would become one of the most cooperative providers of testimony against the Proctors, but would not be a completely reliable witness until after the examinations held in May.

Of the remaining two victims—Bridget Bishop and Giles Corey—brought in for pretrial examinations on April 19, both would be condemned to die, but in different ways and at different times. Bridget Bishop would be the first to be hanged, and the only victim to be executed on Friday, June 10, 1692. As a precedent for what was to come, her case is deserving of a careful review.

The Witch Trials

The first session of the newly created Court of Oyer and Terminer presided over by Deputy Governor William Stoughton was held in Salem at the Town House on June 2, 1692. By that time, the trials had already claimed the first victim, Sarah Osborne, ill at the time of her arrest in late February, who had been moved to the Boston jail and lingered there for over two months where she finally died on May 10 as a combined result of her illness and very unhealthy prison conditions. Her guilt or innocence was never determined by the Court of Oyer and Terminer.

It was the primary task of this court to hear and determine the likelihood of guilt concerning each of the growing number of persons then being held in prison under suspicion of witchcraft. The initial court membership included: Bartholomew Gedney, John Richards, Nathaniel Saltonstall (who would soon resign), Wait Winthrop, Samuel Sewell, John Hathorne, Jonathan Corwin, and Peter Sargeant. To help the court in this difficult assignment, the court charged Sheriff George Corwin—nephew of magistrate Jonathan Corwin—to "canvas the towns" of Essex County "for eighteen men for a grand jury to consider indictments" and also select a "pool of forty-eight 'honest and lawful men' for trial juries" (Baker, *A Storm of Witchcraft*, p. 26). Often, the grand jury would hear indictments and listen to testimony against the accused, and if both were determined to be valid, it would proceed to hold the trial of the accused on the same day. Justice during the Salem episode was swift.

The First Execution

Bridget Bishop was brought into court during the first day of session, June 2, chosen to be the first case to be examined by the prosecution's attorney, Thomas Newton. Newton was an experienced legal appointee personally selected by Governor William Phips, whose primary task was to generally administer the operations of the Court of Oyer and Terminer, choose the sequence of cases, and oversee the drafting of all legal documents. The interrogation of those accused and those giving testimony against the accused was the exclusive responsibility of the magistrates sitting on the bench. The argumentative Bishop, who had already been acquitted for witchcraft in 1679, would not fare well during the initial questioning on June 2 in part due to her unrepentant and defiant attitude. It is worth noting that Bridget was "the only person tried at the first session of the Court" (Charles Upham, *History of Witchcraft and Salem Village*, Vol. 2, p. 256). As such, her case set the precedent for all future sessions. She was condemned to be hanged at the end of the trial of that first day.

Records show that during the pretrial exchange with the magistrate, Bishop claimed that not only was she not a witch, but that she did not even know what a witch was. In response, magistrate John Hathorne logically posed that "if you do not know what a witch is, how do you know you are not one"? To which Bishop responded that, if she were one, Hathorne "would certainly know it." This was correctly perceived by those on the bench as a thinly veiled threat against the court in general and against the interrogator in particular. Such answers did not help Bridget's case.

On that occasion, a long list of depositions presented by neighbors and community residents formed a body of data for years past testifying to the suspicious behavior of Bridget, depicting her as a spiteful and vengeful woman. The evidence presented in Bridget's case was extensive yet was not always entirely of a spectral nature. A Quaker couple, Samuel and Sarah Shattuck, testified that in 1680 their previously normal son had been cursed by Bridget directly after they had had "a falling out with her," and that the bright youngster was now reduced to the mental level of an imbecile, "having to be watched by day and by night" for fear of falling into the well or into the flaming fireplace. This condition, they claimed, was Bridget's doing. And when in due time they had the boy brought to Bridget to effect a cure, she responded by scratching the child's face with her fingernails.

Even more damning was the testimony of John Bly Sr., who testified that he and his son, while employed by Bridget to take down the cellar wall of her house, had found several "poppets made up of rags and hogs' bristles with headless pins struck through them with the points turned outwards." Bridget was unable to provide a satisfactory explanation to why such suspicious items had been found in her basement.

Evidence of this sort was, though circumstantial, more convincing than the more typical spectral testimony presented by afflicted witnesses, so difficult to corroborate. Furthermore, upon being physically examined in private by a court-appointed committee of one physician and nine women, Bridget's body was found to bear several of what were generally known as "witch's teats." These were also called "Devil's marks," and were unusual, fleshy, and often discolored patches of skin, thought to be used by witches to suckle their demonic familiar with their own blood. All of this when combined with Bridget's longstanding reputation as an enemy to the peace of the community, and someone who had been repeatedly charged with domestic abuse, resulted in a verdict of guilty, and she was hanged on June 10, 1692, becoming the first victim of the episode.

In terms of procedure, this Bridget Bishop's trial establishes a pattern seen in virtually all future trials through 1692. Despite all the accumulated, historical evidence against Bridget, "the death warrant emphasizes only the harm done to the accusers, primarily *on the day of her examination*, as legal justification for the execution. Bridget Bishop died because the law said she afflicted Abigail Williams, Ann Putnam, Jr., Mercy Lewis, Mary Walcott and Elizabeth Hubbard, described in the death warrant as 'Salem Village single-women.'" This fact underscores the importance of spectral evidence, not only in Bridget's case, but in the cases of all other Salem witch trial victims. All the condemned appear to have been judged and executed based upon the spectral evidence described in formally prepared, written depositions and presented in court by the afflicted persons. Historian Bernard Rosenthal summarizes this important legal precedent in *Salem Story*.

"At her precedent-setting trial, almost certainly without legal counsel, Bridget Bishop thus found herself in the following situation: Accusers confronted her who had previously accused her of having spectrally afflicted them in public on the day of her examination; yet in trying to defend herself against those charges, the same accusers presented her and the court with *new* fits in response to *new assaults by her specter*, which *only they could see*." The problem with this process was simply that, her alleged victims appeared to be hysterical but otherwise in good health. Thus, "Bridget received her sentence of death for 'pining, consuming and wasting a group of accusers who did not manifest symptoms of such affliction . . .'" (Rosenthal, *Salem Story*, p. 69). This process was followed in virtually all future trials resulting in death warrants and executions. The justification for the execution of the alleged witch was almost always physical harm being done to the afflicted deponents, yet although the death warrant described these afflictions, none of the afflicted actually displayed any physical signs of affliction. All that might be said is that they claimed to be afflicted spectrally, but such evidence was only visible to those making the claim, but never to the members of the court. This fact caused some to reflect and urge caution following Bishop's execution. Magistrate Nathaniel Saltonstall took this opportunity to resign from the court entirely, giving the sheer distance from his home in Haverhill as the primary reason, although "he was very much dissatisfied with the proceedings." In truth, the trials had drawn first blood, and participants were unsure as how best to proceed.

At this juncture, on June 15, 1692, a select group of Boston clergymen, at the request of Governor Phips and the Governor's Council, issued an important advisory document entitled: "The Return of Several Ministers." This important discourse was strongly impacted by Reverend Cotton Mather who took the lead role in writing the report, while the elite committee of Boston clergy tried to provide wise guidance to the Court of Oyer and Terminer as to how best to proceed in the face of the mounting numbers of accused. "The Return" was clearly skeptical of use of spectral evidence that was regarded as suspect in condemning individuals for the crime of witchcraft. The several ministers also strongly urged that caution be exercised "particularly in connection with complaints against people 'formerly of an unblemished reputation'" (Rosenthal, *Salem Story*, p. 69). The report also condemned and warned against the use of any other superstitious or spiritual forms of evidence that might prove unreliable, such as "the touch test," whereby an afflicted victim might prove the guilt of an alleged witch by touching them during a fit, and thus be returned to normal as a result of passing the spirit or spell of affliction back into the body of the individual witch guilty of tormenting them. The ministers encouraged the court to limit the size and noise of the courtroom in order to minimize the influence of public outcries and emotion on the evidence and deliberations.

In short, this important cautionary report, issued immediately after the execution of Bridget Bishop, and prior to the execution of the 18 additional victims, warned that the basis for condemning individuals "as guilty of witchcraft, ought to be more considerable than barely the accused person being represented by a specter unto the afflicted." Unfortunately, at the end of this document, which could have been a thorough condemnation of the May-to-June court proceedings that ended in the conviction and death of Bridget Bishop, appeared an equivocating statement to the Court of Oyer and Terminer urging the court officials of "the Government the speedy and vigorous prosecution of such as have rendered themselves obnoxious, according to the direction given in the laws of God, and the wholesome statutes of the English nation, for the detection of witchcrafts" ("The Return of Several Ministers of Boston"). As a result of this concluding statement of support and endorsement, the warnings of the several ministers to the court concerning the dangers of spectral evidence and witch tests went largely ignored, and the tribunal continued to move into the summer season making effective use of the spectral evidence now being presented by the afflicted witnesses.

In terms of direct impact upon the behavior and procedure of the Salem court, it was almost as if "The Return of Several Ministers" had never been written. Interestingly, the only individual among the several Boston ministers to remain outspoken in his guarded skepticism of the court's tendency to depend upon the use spectral evidence was Reverend Cotton Mather's father, Reverend Increase Mather who, in his 1693 book *Cases of Conscience Concerning Evil Spirits* remarked pointedly that: "It were better that ten suspected witches should escape than that one innocent person should be condemned." Despite this belief, the senior Mather did not go so far as to publically condemn the actions of the court itself. As a result, both he and his famous son remain complicit in the actions of the Court of Oyer and Terminer and the deaths of those that were condemned by that infamous body.

The July Executions

During the course of the month of June, Justice William Stoughton and the Court of Oyer and Terminer proceeded to process the cases of more suspected witches, and ultimately on June 30, would condemn five—Rebecca Nurse, Sarah Good, Elizabeth How, Sarah Wildes, and Susannah Martin—all of whom would hang on July 19, 1692. The prosecution process followed by them with this group of victims was essentially the same as that in the case of Bridget Bishop, but with some slight deviations. Most notable among these procedural exceptions was the case of Rebecca Nurse.

Rebecca Towne Nurse had been first accused by Ann Putnam Jr. among a *second small group* of alleged witches including Elizabeth Proctor and Martha Corey, as early as the second week of March 1692. Altogether, there were at that time a total of seven suspected witches including, Tituba, Sarah Good, Sarah Good's four-year-old daughter Dorothy Good, Sarah Osborne, Rebecca Nurse, Martha Corey, and Elizabeth Proctor. Whereas the first accused group of four—Tituba, Sarah Good and her daughter, and Sarah Osborne—were on the outer periphery of Salem Village society, the members of the *second small group*—Elizabeth Proctor, Rebecca Nurse, and Martha Corey—were well-respected, middle-class, church members, now under suspicion of witchcraft (Norton, *In the Devil's Snare*, p. 44).

On March 13, young Ann Putnam claimed that she was afflicted by the specter of a woman who at first "she did not know" though she "knew where she used to sit in our meeting house." Within 24 hours of her first accusation, Ann Putnam Jr. had narrowed the field of suspects down to one individual, Rebecca Towne Nurse, "the seventy-year-old wife of Francis Nurse." While the accusation of a respected and elderly member of the Salem Village community represented a dramatic departure from the previous actions of the afflicted girls, several contemporary historians strongly suggest that it might well have been the result of 0over the boundaries of their respective lands." This ulterior motive is certainly possible (Norton, p. 47).

Regardless of the motives for the initial accusation, one point is certain, Ann Putnam Jr. was largely responsible for initially involving Rebecca Nurse and bringing her into that second group of witch trial victims that would—with help from the testimony of her mother Ann Putnam Sr.—later be condemned and executed on July 19, 1692. For this act, Ann Jr. would, on August 25, 1706, express profound regret in her confession read before the Salem Village congregation by their minister Reverend Joseph Green:

> I desire to be humbled before God for that sad and humbling Providence that befell my father's family in the year about 1692; that I, then being in my childhood, should by such a Providence of God be made an instrument for the accusing of several persons of a grievous crime, whereby their lives were taken away from them, whom now I have just grounds and good reason to believe they were innocent persons; and that it was a great delusion of Satan that deceived me in that sad time. ("The Public Confession of Ann Putnam," August 25, 1706)

In particular, Ann Putnam Jr. narrows her confession of guilt to focus squarely upon the direct damage done by her to the Nurse family by concluding "as I was a chief instrument of accusing of Goodwife Nurse and her two sisters (Sarah Cloyce and Mary Esty), I desire to lie in the dust and to be humbled for it, in that I was a cause . . . of so sad a calamity to them and their families; for which cause I desire to lie in the dust, and earnestly beg forgiveness of God, and from all those unto whom I have given just cause of sorrow and offense" ("The Public Confession of Ann Putnam," August 25, 1706). Of the three accused sisters mentioned in the confession, only Sarah Cloyce would escape with her life.

What makes the case of Rebecca Nurse so different from the majority of Salem witch trial cases—apart from her age and respectability—is the degree of support she received from both her community, as well as some persons of authority, none of whom would prove successful in saving her life. Among the evidence presented in her favor was a testimonial attesting to her good character as a long-time resident of Salem Village, signed by 39 friends and neighbors. Somewhat surprisingly, even one prominent member of the Putnam family, Nathaniel Putnam Sr. submitted a brief testimonial on Rebecca's behalf where he stated:

> I have known this, the aforesaid woman forty years, and what I have observed of her, human frailties excepted, her life and her conversation have been according to her profession; and she hath brought up a great family of children and educated them well, so that there is in some of them apparent savor of godliness. I have known her differ with her neighbors; but I never knew or heard of any that did accuse her of what she is now charged with. ("Testimonial of Nathaniel Putnam, Sr.," quoted in Upham, *The History of Witchcraft and Salem Village*, p. 272.)

Despite the best efforts of the Putnams and other afflicted persons to the contrary, Rebecca's trial, on June 30, 1692, initially ended in a verdict of innocent. This was the first such verdict produced by the Court of Oyer and Terminer, and as such "might have reached far beyond her own case" setting a positive legal precedent for other accused persons "of unblemished reputation" (Peter Charles Hoffner, *The Salem Witch Trials: A Legal History*, pp. 104–105).

However, the virulent and unsympathetic Chief Justice William Stoughton, according to the recollection of jury foreman Thomas Fisk, "directed the jury's attention to Nurse's words about Deliverance and Abigail Hobbs, two confessed witches, who had turned informants." Nurse supposedly said, "What do these persons give in evidence against me now, they used to come amongst us." Stoughton claimed that Nurse was thus tacitly admitting that she had also been in league with these two witches, and that she therefore must be guilty. The question was put to Nurse as to what she meant by the comment, and she did not respond. The jury reconvened, and reversed their verdict to guilty (Hoffner, p. 105).

The unusual action of Chief Justice Stoughton in working to change the verdict was unprecedented, "behaving more like a prosecuting attorney than a magistrate" (Emerson W. Baker, *A Storm of Witchcraft*, p. 193). After this, members of the Nurse family petitioned Governor William Phips, requesting a stay of execution order, "which he initially granted," but, according to Robert Calef's narrative in *More Wonders of the Invisible World*, "the accusers renewed their dismal outcries against her and some Salem gentlemen then persuaded him to rescind it" (Robert Calef from *More Wonders . . .* quoted in Mary Beth Norton, *In the Devil's Snare*, p. 225). All things considered, the case was unusual in many respects, but ended up in the same place as all the other cases tried up to that time. A final note to the case in Rebecca Nurse's summing up of her situation: "I can say before my eternal Father I am innocent, and God will clear my innocency [*sic*]" (SWP II: p. 584, quoted in Rosenthal, *Salem Story*, p. 92).

Concerning Sarah Good, the second victim listed among those condemned to hang on July 19, we have an interesting contrast to the Nurse case. The best-known facet of her case is the famous exchange between her and Reverend Nicholas Noyes, then a pastor of the Salem First Church. Charles Upham, the famous Victorian historian of the Salem witch episode, recounts the incident: "Mr. Noyes, at the time (July 19) of her (Sarah Good's) execution, urged her very strenuously to confess. Among other things, he told her 'she was a witch, and she knew she was a witch.' She could not bear in silence the cruel aspersion; and although she was about to be launched into eternity, the torrent of her feelings could not be restrained, but burst upon the head of him who uttered the false accusation. 'You are a liar!,' said she. 'I am no more a witch than you are a wizard; and if you take away my life, God will give you blood to drink'" (Charles Upham, *History of Witchcraft and Salem Village*, Vol. 2, p. 270).

Governor Thomas Hutchinson added a curious, possibly mythical addendum to this account in his *History of Massachusetts*, when he observed that "there was a tradition among the people of Salem, and it has descended to the present time [1764], that the manner of Mr. Noyes' death strangely verified the prediction thus wrung from the incensed spirit of the dying woman [Sarah Good]. He was exceedingly corpulent, of a plethoric habit, and died of an internal hemorrhage, bleeding profusely from the mouth."

The case of Sarah Good is noteworthy in yet another respect, the general public opinion concerning her character, which appears to have been generally negative. To be sure, she was impoverished, often begging support from local residents and living among the Salem community as a homeless indigent. However, it should be noted that, contrary to popular myth, she was not—as she is often described—an old woman in ill health, or as Thomas Hutchinson described her, "an old woman who was bed-rid." Sarah Good was in actuality relatively young, that is, about the age of 38 years old and pregnant at the time of her accusation in March 1692. She was also a mother of a four-year-old daughter.

She had been married twice. Her first husband, about which little is known, was Daniel Poole, but her second husband, William Good, did little to defend his wife. Indeed, he essentially confirmed the accusations of the deponents in that, during the pretrial examination, he testified that "she was a witch, or would be one very quickly," suggesting that she was "an enemy to all that is good" (Testimony of William Good v. Sarah Good). Such negative testimony concerning Sarah was abundant, especially concerning her tendency to take hospitality from families willing to provide her and her daughter temporary shelter, followed by her resentment and open hostility when they would, after a lengthy stay ask her to leave the household. In this respect, Sarah Good's case makes an interesting contrast to that of her fellow victim, Rebecca Nurse.

The August Executions

Between July and August, a second group of five victims were tried and condemned. These were hanged on Gallows Hill in Salem on August 18 and included: John Proctor, George Jacobs, Sr., Reverend George Burroughs, Martha Carrier, and John Willard. Of these five, John Proctor was probably the most strenuously defended by his friends and neighbors. His wife Elizabeth had been first complained against on April 4, "along with Sarah Cloyce, sister of Rebecca Nurse." By April 11, Elizabeth

Proctor's husband John would become implicated as "the first man in 1692 to be examined for witchcraft" (Rosenthal, *Salem Story*, p. 109). His initial examination was attended by a group of influential Massachusetts citizens, anxious to hear the testimony of an alleged "wizard." Among Proctor's hearers on the day of his examination were: Deputy Governor, Thomas Danforth, Samuel Appleton, Samuel Sewell, Isaac Addington and James Russell (SWP, Vol II: p. 661).

As in the case of Rebecca Nurse, it was the prevailing belief that if a sufficient number of respectable residents, long-acquainted with the accused, could testify to the high moral character of the accused, it might so influence the court as to dismiss the case, or at least consider the accused more favorably in the face of spectral evidence. This tradition of testimonial support was reinforced by the injunction favoring persons of an unblemished reputation evidenced by the "The Return of Several Ministers" in June, following the execution of Bridget Bishop.

Toward that end, as with Rebecca Nurse case, two testimonial petitions were drawn up in support of John Proctor. He had been a prosperous, yeoman farmer, whose land stretched from Salem Village to Ipswich. His pregnant wife, Elizabeth, although accused by the afflicted girls, would ultimately escape execution as a direct result of her pregnancy. Unfortunately, her husband, as merely the father of the unborn child, would not be able to avoid the hangman's noose.

John Proctor's first testimonial address was conceived, written, and first signed by the minister of the Ipswich congregation aptly named, Reverend John Wise, and is addressed to the "Honorable Court of Assistants Now Sitting in Boston." The Court of Assistants was *not* the Court of Oyer and Terminer, hearing the witch trial cases in Salem, but rather a select group of educated and elite leaders of the commonwealth, which traditionally, under the old Massachusetts Bay charter, had played the role as assistants to the governor and still served generally as a "supreme court" of the Colony of Massachusetts. It was hoped that the arguments of Proctor's address would therefore fall upon a fresh and less-biased set of ears. This document is formally entitled: "The Humble and Sincere declaration of Us, Subscribers, Inhabitants in Ipswich, on the Behalf of our Neighbors, John Proctor and his Wife, now in Trouble and under Suspicion of Witchcraft."

Such documents underscore the character and moral courage of many local individuals during the trials who were willing to take a public stand against the actions of the Court of Oyer and Terminer as well as the testimony of the afflicted girls. The document declares boldly that "as to what we have ever seen or heard of them, upon our consciences, we judge them innocent of the crime . . ." ("The Humble and Sincere Declaration . . . on behalf of John Proctor and his Wife"). The petition was signed by 32 Ipswich citizens, all males.

A second petition on behalf of John Proctor from the Salem Village side of Proctor's extensive property was also submitted, protesting that: "having for several years known John Proctor and his wife, . . . we never heard or understood that they were ever suspected to be guilty of the crime now charged upon them; and several of us, being their near neighbors, do testify that, they lived Christian-like in their family." This second petition was signed by 13 men and 5 women. Both petitions were passed by the Court of Assistant, which took no action, back to the Court of Oyer and Terminer. Doubtless, they succeeded in planting seeds of doubt in the minds of some of the assistants as to the wisdom and effectiveness of the Salem court's procedure. By October, such seeds would ripen into a growing harvest of negative public opinion against Stoughton, his court, Cotton Mather, and Governor Phips.

Added to these documents of support was evidence that some of the girls had lied to the court and falsely testified against John and Elizabeth Proctor. One deponent publicly admitted that she "had done so falsely," another witness claimed that "she must, at the time, have been out of her head," while another admitted to have "sworn falsely" and tried to explain her testimony in court by "acknowledging that what the girls said was 'for sport'," for as she said, "they must have sport." Despite all this questionable and unreliable testimony, John Proctor and his wife were both condemned, pregnancy being the only rationale for the saving of Elizabeth's life.

Utterly frustrated, John Proctor, now languishing condemned and awaiting execution in the Salem jail, wrote a desperate letter on behalf of the August 18 victims, to a select group of influential ministers in Boston where he stated his belief that: "The innocency [sic] of our case with the enmity of our accusers and our judges and jury, whom nothing but our innocent blood will serve, having condemned us already before our trials, being so much incensed and enraged against us by the Devil, makes us bold to beg and implore your favorable assistance . . ., that if it be possible our innocent blood may be spared, which otherwise will be shed, if the Lord doth not mercifully step in; . . . (for) we know in our own consciences, we are all innocent persons."

Clearly, as some scholars have pointed out, if a respectable male could be condemned for witchcraft—as unusual and rare as that might be—Proctor's case opened the door for more esteemed male suspects.

Of such more esteemed suspects included in the August group, two men stand out prominently, George Jacobs Sr. and Reverend George Burroughs. Jacobs Sr., like John Proctor a prosperous yeoman farmer, was arrested and examined on May 10 and condemned by the Court of Oyer and Terminer on August 12, 1692. Reverend George Burroughs was examined through July, and finally condemned and hanged with the four other victims on August 18. Both of these men, at least at the outset of their courtroom examinations, were incredulous that they would be even suspected of a crime such as witchcraft.

The skeptical Jacobs, when first accused by his servant girl, Sarah Churchill, and a cousin of Ann Putnam Jr., Mary Walcott, quipped his utter disbelief to the magistrates by boldly responding to the charge "you tax me for a wizard, you may as well tax me for a buzzard [sic], I have done no harm." What most hurt Jacobs's case significantly was the accusation of his granddaughter Margaret Jacobs, who together with her mother, had been also arrested under suspicion of witchcraft. Shortly following her arrest, young Margaret confessed to being a witch and then identified her grandfather as a fellow-practitioner of the dark arts. This, combined with the spectral evidence offered against him, was enough. Not dissuaded by either his granddaughter's condemnation or the testimony of the afflicted girls,

Jacobs famously stated, "Well, burn me or hang me, I will stand in the truth of Christ!" (Charles W. Upham, *Salem Witchcraft*, Vol. 2, p. 168).

It is to Margaret Jacobs's credit that, upon careful reflection, she decided to rescind her *confession of witchcraft* and also withdraw her testimony against both her grandfather and Reverend George Burroughs, both of whom she had vehemently testified against. The court quickly re-arrested her on the charge of witchcraft and committed her to the Salem jail. While in prison, on August 20, two days after the hanging deaths of both her grandfather and Reverend Burroughs, Margaret put her thoughts concerning her conscientious decision into a letter to her father explaining her reasons for her actions:

> Honored father (George Jacobs, Junior), I enjoy, though in abundance of affliction, being close confined here in a loathsome dungeon; The reason for my confinement is this; I having, through the magistrate's threatenings [*sic*], and my own vile and wretched heart, confessed several things contrary to my conscience and knowledge, . . . to the wounding of my own soul, but oh! the terrors of a wounded conscience, who can bear? But blessed be the Lord, He would not let me go on in my sins, but in mercy, I hope, to my soul, would not suffer me to keep it any longer, but I was forced to confess the truth of all before the magistrates, who would not believe me, but it is their pleasure to put me in here, and God knows how soon I shall be put to death. Dear father, may I beg your prayers to the Lord on my behalf, and send us a joyful and happy meeting in heaven. Your dutiful daughter, Margaret Jacobs.

This candid narrative from a self-confessed, yet now recanted witch, who was overwhelmed by a sense of guilt and remorse for her perjury, explains a great deal about the psychological and social pressures faced by those persons who found themselves being badgered by the magistrates to confess and give the names of their satanic accomplices. Of her sincerity, there can be little doubt inasmuch as she is aware that she presently stood upon then threshold of eternity, one that held for her eternal punishment for unrepentant sin.

In Margaret Jacobs's formal retraction, addressed to the magistrates of the witch trial court, she expresses her remorse and vindicates her deceptive behavior during her trial:

> They told me, if I would not confess, I should be put down into the dungeon, and would be hanged, but if I would confess, I should have my life; the which did so affright me, with my own vile, wicked heart, to save my life, made me make the confession I did, which confession, may it please the honored Court, is altogether false and untrue.

"The Lord, I hope, in whom I trust, . . . will forgive me for false forswearing myself. What I said was altogether false against my grandfather (Jacobs Sr.) and Mr. Burroughs, which I did to save my life and to have my liberty." As to why her change of heart, she offers the most basic of reasons: "but the Lord, charging it to my conscience, made me in so much horror that I could not contain myself before I had denied my confession, which I did, choosing rather death with a quiet conscience, than to live in such horror, which I could not suffer" (Margaret Jacobs, "The Humble Declaration of Margaret Jacobs unto the Honored Court Now Sitting at Salem"). In this manner, Margaret Jacobs, as a case study of both an accused and confessed witch, clarifies and explains the underlying rationale for at least some of the accusations, depositions, testimony, and confessions. Clearly, not all persons involved in the episode were, in the final analysis, as self-reflectively conscientious and articulate as Margaret Jacobs.

The day before his execution, Reverend George Burroughs was visited by Margaret Jacobs, who had already retracted her witchcraft confession to the court. She asked the minister's forgiveness for having falsely testified against him, a request that was freely given "and he prayed with her and for her." Charles Upham, in his study of the trials, further notes that "it is probable, that, at the same time, she obtained an interview with her grandfather for the same purpose. At any rate, the old man heard of her heroic conduct, and forthwith crowded into the space between two paragraphs in his will, in small letters closely written, a clause giving a legacy of 'ten pounds to be paid in silver' to his granddaughter, Margaret Jacobs" (Charles Upham, *Witchcraft at Salem Village*, Vol. 3, p. 319).

It was the hanging death of Reverend George Burroughs on August 18 that proved to be the most memorable incident on that tragic occasion. The prevailing folk-wisdom of that time held that an individual guilty of the crime of witchcraft could not recite sacred scripture accurately, and that in particular, they would not be permitted by their master, Satan to intone the words of "The Lord's Prayer" without making an error. Reverend Burroughs, a former minister of the Salem Village congregation and a person well-acquainted with many in the crowd of witnesses to his public execution, decided to take the opportunity to address the audience.

Robert Calef, a contemporary observer, in his *More Wonders of the Invisible World*, provides an eyewitness account of the condemned pastor's dramatic end: "Mr. Burroughs was carried in a cart with the others, through the streets of Salem to the execution. When he was upon the ladder, he made a speech for the clearing of his innocency [sic], with such solemn and serious expressions as were to the admiration of all present. His prayer (which he concluded by repeating the Lord's Prayer) was so well worded, and uttered with such composedness and such (at least seeming) fervency of spirit, as was very affecting, and drew tears from many, so that it seemed to some that the spectators would hinder the execution." Seated upon his horse, taking in the scene, was Reverend Cotton Mather, who put the crowd at ease after Burroughs's hanging, by reminding them that Burroughs had never been properly ordained a minister, and that the Devil "often had been transformed into an angel of light; and this somewhat appeased the people, and the executions went on" (Robert Calef, *More Wonders of the Invisible World*, p. 213).

The September Executions

The largest number of victims claimed by the Salem witch episode were executed in September 1692, seven being hanged on September 22 and one, Giles Corey, crushed beneath the weight of rocks on September 19, 1692, the only known case of death-by-pressing in American history.

Both Giles Corey and his wife, Martha, had been accused of witchcraft, being charged with tormenting some of the afflicted girls. Among the deponents against Giles were Elizabeth Woodwell and Mary Walcot, who claimed they both saw the specter of Giles Corey "at meeting at Salem on lecture-day" after he had been confined to prison, and that "his apparition came in and sat in the middlemost seats of the men's seats" (Deposition of Elizabeth Woodwell v. Giles Corey). Clearly, this testimony was not directed against the act of attending a church meeting, but rather that Corey's spiritual likeness—intimating a contractual relationship with Satan—was capable of wandering beyond the confines of Salem jail. More directly, Mary Warren testified that Corey's specter had afflicted her "because she caused her master (John Proctor) to ask more for a piece of meadow than he (Corey) was willing to give" (Deposition of Mary Warren v. Giles Corey). When the Court of Oyer and Terminer decided to charge Corey with the crime of witchcraft and set a date for his trial, he refused to enter a plea, standing mute before his accusers. This stratagem was an ultimately successful attempt to avoid a trial where he might be found guilty of the capital crime of witchcraft, and besides losing his life, also lose his personal estate to Massachusetts Colony, which would have the right to confiscate the property of a convicted felon.

In order to prevent this confiscation, "he accordingly made up his mind not to be tried." And "when called into court to answer to the indictment found by the Grand Jury, he did not plead guilty or not guilty but rather 'stood mute' before the Court." What Giles Corey resorted to on this occasion was a time-honored tradition in English Common Law whereby an accused person, usually a person charged with a capital offense, could avoid a trial, and thereby a verdict, by not cooperating in any way with a court. Without responding to the charge leveled against him, no trial could take place. In choosing this course, however, Corey left himself open to a method of judicial coercion traditionally used in England in such cases called *peine forte et dure,* essentially translated as "punishment strong and hard" more colloquially known as pressing.

Pressing was a means of court-authorized torture whereby the accused would be staked out upon the bare ground with weights placed upon his chest, then asked to enter a plea to the criminal charges against him. Death was not the theoretical objective of this process; rather the prisoner's cooperation with the court's proceedings was what was sought. If court officers met with continued refusal on the part of the accused, the amount of weight was gradually increased, until the victim either entered a plea, or died. While in England under English Common Law, predetermined weights of cast iron were most often used, in this, the only known American case, weights of stone were employed. Remarkably, the 81-year-old yeoman farmer lasted for two days under these conditions until finally his chest was crushed. He thus became yet another victim of the Salem witch trials, but one whose guilt or innocence was never officially determined by the Court of Oyer and Terminer.

A morbidly interesting anecdote from Robert Calef's *More Wonders of the Invisible World* concerning Giles Corey's death involves the infamous Sheriff George Corwin who presided at the scene of Corey's pressing. Calef's eyewitness account records that at the time of the venerable farmer's death, Corwin was somewhat less than sympathetic "when his (Corey's) tongue was pressed out of his mouth, the Sheriff with his cane, forced it in again" (Robert Calef, *More Wonders of the Invisible World,* p. 218).

It should be noted here that the long-held explanation that Corey chose *peine fort et dure* to save his property for his family has been challenged by several recent scholars who suggest that his action was taken simply because of his obdurate nature, and that he actually did plead *innocent,* but simply did not wish to "put himself upon trial by a Jury." This he accomplished by refusing to answer the second essential question as to whether he would allow his case to be tried by a jury of his peers. These scholars contend that once the ordeal was underway, it became essentially, an alternative, yet legitimate form of execution reserved for stubborn, uncooperative capital offenders, who simply refused to submit to the process of trial-by-jury.

If this is the case, it is very fortuitous that Corey had, during his period of imprisonment at the jail in Ipswich, taken legal steps to guarantee that, upon his death, his entire estate would be passed safely into the possession of his family. With remarkable forethought, he prepared a will stating that "I, Giles Corey, lying under great trouble and affliction, . . . knowing how soon I may depart this life; and for the fatherly love and affection which I have and do bear unto my beloved son-in-law, William Cleves of the town of Beverly and to my son-in-law, John Moulton, of the town of Salem, give and grant lands, meadow, housing, cattle, stock, movables and immovable, money apparel . . . and all other the aforesaid premises . . . to the said Cleves and Moulton, their heirs, executors, administrators and assigns freely and quietly, forever" (Will of the Estate of Giles Corey, August, 1692).

Giles Corey's wife, Martha Cory would be hanged on September 22 along with the final group of witch trial victims including: Mary Easty, Alice Parker, Mary Parker, Ann Pudeater, Margaret Scott, Wilmot Reed, and Samuel Wardwell. Martha had been a member in good standing of Reverend Samuel Parris's congregation. After her conviction by the Court of Oyer and Terminer in September, Parris brought her name to the attention of the Salem Village congregation which, "by general consent, voted (her) to be excommunicated out of the church." Parris, together with a delegation consisting of Lieutenant Nathaniel Putnam and two deacons, visited Martha Corey in prison to deliver the news of her exclusion and banishment from Christian fellowship.

Concerning this incident, Parris recorded in his church record book:

11 September, Lord's Day. Sister Martha Corey—taken into the church 27 April, 1690—was, after examination upon suspicion of witchcraft, 27 March, 1692, committed to prison for that fact, and was condemned to the gallows for the same yesterday (10 September, 1692) and was this day, in public, by a general consent, voted to

be excommunicated out of the church, and Lieutenant Nathaniel Putnam, and the two deacons chosen to signify to her, with the pastor, the mind of the church herein.

Apparently, although suspected of witchcraft as early as March, and imprisoned for over five months, Martha's Salem Village Church membership had remained in effect up to the time of her final condemnation by the court.

It is hardly surprising to discover, in Parris's commentary, that Martha was less than receptive to the announcement that her fellow church-members joined the court in their belief that she was guilty of practicing witchcraft and being in league with the Devil.

Parris concludes: "Accordingly, this 14 September, 1692, the three aforesaid brethren went with the pastor to her (Martha Corey) in the Salem Prison; who we found very obdurate (stubborn), justifying herself and condemning all that had done anything to her just discovery or condemnation. Whereupon, after a little discourse (for her imperiousness [arrogance] would not suffer much), and after prayer, which she was willing to decline, the dreadful sentence of excommunication was pronounced against her."

On September 18, 1692, just four days later, her husband Giles Corey was also excommunicated. This seems odd insofar as neither his guilt nor innocence of the charge of witchcraft was ever determined. Regardless, Reverend Parris justifies the punishment by pointing out that "September 18 . . . G. Corey was excommunicated: the cause of it was, that he being accused and indicted for the sin of witchcraft, *he refused to plead (italics mine)*, and so incurred the sentence and penalty of *pain fort dure* [sic]; being undoubtedly guilty of the sin of witchcraft, or of throwing himself upon sudden and certain death, if he were otherwise innocent" (Reverend Samuel Parris, *Salem Village Church Records*, September 1692). It was assumed that either he would enter a plea and be tried for witchcraft, or else, he would end his life voluntarily as a *suicide*. The crime of self-murder, the same as witchcraft, in Parris's view, was enough to warrant excommunication.

For Martha Corey, however, her passing was similar to that of Reverend Burroughs, or as Robert Calef observed: "Martha Corey, protesting her innocency, concluded her life with an eminent prayer upon the ladder" (Robert Calef, *More Wonders of the Invisible World*, p. 218).

It was an altogether appropriate end to the life of one who, despite the injustice of her sentence, set an example of near Christ-like long-suffering and forbearance toward her persecutors.

Another fellow-sufferer on September 22 was Mary Easty, a resident of nearby Topsfield, sister to Sarah Cloyce and the already executed Rebecca Nurse. Her initial examination took place on April 22, 1692, when Mercy Lewis claimed that she was unable to unclasp her hands until Easty unclasped hers. Mercy also claimed that Mary's specter had afflicted her at her home in her bed. And collectively, the afflicted girls mimicked the bodily movements of Easty when they confronted her in court, claiming they were forced to do so by her specter.

In spite of this, Easty retained her composure and was asked how far had she complied with the Devil? Her response to Justice John Hathorne was simply that she had "prayed against him (Satan) all my dayes" and that "I am clear of this sin." She, like her sister Rebecca Nurse, enjoyed a momentary reprieve when Mary Easty was released from custody on May 18 and returned to her home. The outcry of the afflicted was such that she was re-arrested and returned to prison, largely on the spectral evidence presented against her by Mercy Lewis.

Mary Easty's case is quite remarkable insofar as she was able to plead her case primarily in two well-written, legal documents, or petitions, the first presented to the court prior to her trial, and the latter after she was condemned and sentenced by the court. In the case of the former document, she speaks on behalf of herself and her one surviving sister:

> Whereas we two sisters, Mary Easty and Sarah Cloyse, stand now before the honored Court charged with suspicion of witchcraft, our humble request is,—First, that seeing we are neither able to plead our own cause, nor is counsel allowed to those in our condition, that you, who are our judges would please to be of counsel to us, to direct us wherein we may stand in need.—Secondly, that whereas we are not conscious to ourselves of any guilt in the least degree of that crime whereof we are now accused (in the presence of the Living God we speak it, before whose awful tribunal we know we shall ere long appear), nor of any other scandalous evil or miscarriage inconsistent with Christianity,—(that) those who have had the longest and best knowledge of us, being persons of good report, may be suffered to testify upon oath what they know concerning each of us. ("*The Humble Petition of Mary Easty . . .*")

Here is clearly laid out two of the strongest arguments presented against the court that none of the victims were given legal counsel and that the court seemed to pay little attention to testimony presented on behalf of the accused, giving greater weight to spectral evidence of the so-called afflicted than was warranted.

In Mary Easty's concluding remarks, she underscores the tendency of the court to condemn those accused with spectral evidence presented by individuals who either claim to have been former witches or else were still being oppressed by satanic power. In effect, the testimony of those persons whose truthfulness should be most suspect is being given greater credibility than the evidence of those whose deportment and life have been above reproach. This prejudicial tendency, she says, needs to be acknowledged and addressed in her imminent trial: "Thirdly, that the testimony of witches, or such as are afflicted as is supposed by witches, may not be improved to condemn us *without other legal evidence concurring. WE hope the honored Court and jury will be so tender (sympathetic) of the lives of such as we are,* who have for many years lived under the unblemished reputation of Christianity, as not to condemn them without a fair and equal hearing of what may be said *for us as well as against us*" ("The Humble Petition of Mary Easty"). Despite this reasonable request that the testimony of the friends and neighbors of the accused should be given equal credence with the spectral testimony of the afflicted, the court tried the case of Mary Easty separate from that of her sister, and Mary was condemned to hang on September 22, 1692. Sister Sarah's case would be dealt with at a later time, and as Charles Upham observed, "Circumstances to which we have no clue rescued her from the fate of her sisters."

Perhaps for this very reason, Mary Easty produced one last document on behalf of all future alleged witches, begging the court to exercise greater care and discernment in all pending proceedings. Doubtless, Mary suspected that her sister Sarah would soon be standing before the court, and she wanted her to receive justice even if she did not. Mary Easty's final petition stands out as one of the most sensitive, poignant, and remarkable of all documents resulting from the trials:

> The Humble Petition of Mary Easty unto his Excellency Sir William Phips, and to the Honored Judges and Bench now sitting in Judicature in Salem, and the Reverend Ministers, . . . whereas your poor and humble petitioner, being condemned to die, do humbly beg of you to take it into your judicious and pious consideration, that your poor and humble petitioner, knowing my own innocency [sic], blessed be the Lord for it! And seeing plainly the wiles and subtilty [sic] of my accusers by myself, cannot but judge charitably of others that are going the same way of myself, if the Lord not steps mightily in. I petition to Your Honors not for my own life, for I know I must die, and my appointed time is set; but the Lord he knows it is that, if it be possible, no more innocent blood may be shed, which undoubtedly cannot be avoided in the way and course you go in. ("The Humble Petition of Mary Easty to Gov. Sir William Phips, et als")

This not so subtle criticism must have caused all members of the court to reflect upon their actions up to this point, planting small seeds of self-doubt in the minds of many that would within a month's time begin to take root. This would most certainly be the case with Governor Sir William Phips, who by September was already receiving criticism from other sources than the victims themselves, and would on October 29 close the Salem court down. But Mary was not finished in gently heaping coals of fire upon the minds and consciences of the members of the court:

> By my own innocency [sic], I know you are in the wrong way. The Lord in his infinite mercy direct you in this great work, if it be his blessed will that no more innocent blood shall be shed! I would humbly beg of you, that Your Honors would be pleased to examine these afflicted persons strictly, and keep them apart some time, and likewise try some of these confessing witches; I being confident there is [sic] several of them has belied themselves and others, as will appear, if not in this world, I am sure in the world to come, whither I am now agoing [sic]. ("The Humble Petition of Mary Easty to Governor Sir William Phips, et als.")

Mary Easty had witnessed the court proceedings, and as a victim of the afflicted girls and their spectral evidence, she points directly to the primary failing of the court, that is its unwillingness to physically isolate *the afflicted* so they might not be able to take visual and audible cues from each other. Her second suggestion was much in the same line of reason, to carefully question the accuracy and consistency of their testimony under private circumstances. To add further common sense to her argument, Mary Easty was by this time well aware of Margaret Corey's retraction of her confession and was certain that other self-confessed witches might respond to their pangs of conscience in much the same way if placed on trial.

This would greatly undermine the public's general belief in a widespread out-break by literally reducing the number of confessed witches who, like young Margaret Jacobs, were only seeking to save their lives by perjuring themselves and accusing others. Mary's powerful conclusion dramatically underscores the pervasive belief system that, in spite of the court's failings and judicial errors, she was a firm believer in the reality of a spiritual, unseen world that posed a real satanic threat to the godly community. Though innocent herself, she wished the court success in its future efforts to find and eliminate the true spiritual dangers to the colony and God's church:

> I question not but you will see an alteration of these things. They (the afflicted) say myself and others, having made a league with the Devil, we cannot confess. I know, and the Lord knows, as will appear, *they (the afflicted) belie me,* and so I question not but they do others. The Lord above, who is the searcher of all hearts, knows as I shall answer it at the tribunal seat, that I know not the least thing of witchcraft; there-fore I cannot, I dare not, belie my own soul. I beg Your Honors not to deny this, my humble petition from a poor, dying, innocent person. And I question not, but the Lord will give a blessing to your endeavors. ("The Humble Petition of Mary Easty to Governor Sir William Phips, et als.")

The only possible motive for such a concluding statement, especially in the light of Mary Easty's looming execution, would be her sincere hope that future cases—like that of her sister Sarah Cloyce—might be tried with greater objectivity and discernment, resulting in more equitable justice. The statement must be seen as a genuine commentary motivated by a sincere desire to understand why the trials were happening, and how some of the serious injustices might be addressed. As one historian noted concerning her petition, "it would be hard to find, in all the records of human suffering and of Christian deportment under them, a more affecting production. It is a most beautiful specimen of strong good sense, pious fortitude and faith, genuine dignity of soul, noble benevolence and true eloquence of a pure heart." (Charles Upham, *Witchcraft at Salem Village,* Vol., 3, p. 327).

The Decline of the Trials from October to May 1693

After the executions of September 22, the firestorm of witchcraft began to slowly subside. Out of a total 150 formal charges, a grand total of 28 trials took place in 1692, from which there emerged 28 convictions. Yet, after September's hangings, a total of 19 persons had been executed, while nine convicted witches remained in custody, but none of these would be executed. In addition to the remaining convicted witches, some 53 persons had confessed to the crime of witchcraft, yet none of these would be executed. Altogether 19 hanging deaths would take place and one death by pressing, not forgetting an additional five prison-related deaths—Sarah Osborne, Roger Toothaker, Ann Foster, Lydia Dustin, and Sarah Good's infant for a total of 25 victims. Nonetheless, after September 1692, the firestorm began to subside and slowly die through the long winter, until by May 1693, the last of those still held in jail, including Tituba, Reverend Parris's West Indian slave, were released.

What combinations of factors led to the demise of the Court of Oyer and Terminer and the removal of its trial activities from Salem? The essential facts were that the accusations had gotten out of control both numerically and geographically; and the accusations were spreading far beyond the societal boundaries of those people who, given their elite stations in colonial Massachusetts, should have been virtually untouchable. Finally, and most significantly, there arose an intellectual skepticism and resistance from contemporary observers, such as Thomas Brattle of Boston, challenging the royal governor, as well as Court of Oyer and Terminer's methods and results, circulating critical letters among the most influential persons in government, and swaying public opinion against the trials. This growing public and political hostility in the form of written criticism intimidated the newly appointed royal governor, Sir William Phips, prompting him to ask his pastor and adviser, Reverend Cotton Mather, to fight back with an explanatory account. The resulting *Wonders of the Invisible World: Observations Historical as Well as Theological, upon the Nature, the Number and the Operations of the Devils* (1693) was clearly an attempt to deflect blame way from Phips, and perhaps Mather as well, while attempting to rationally analyze the witchcraft outbreak, justify the court's proceedings, and explain to all interested parties why the witch episode engulfed nearly the entire eastern half of Massachusetts Colony, in the face of a major colonial military conflict with the French and their Native allies.

As to the growing numbers of accusations, by the conclusion of the episode in spring 1693, a documented, grand total of 172 Massachusetts residents were formally accused, cried-out against, or unofficially denounced as suspected witches. A goodly number were never formally charged (Baker, *A Storm of Witchcraft*, p. 126). Since many of the court records, and consequently names, have been lost, quantifiably, we may never know the full extent of these accusations. Yet, it is not unrealistic to estimate that the number may have reached as high as 200 suspected witches. Beyond the sheer numbers of those accused, the breadth and full extent of the episode was logistically remarkable, since the accusations also travelled significantly beyond the geographical boundaries of Salem Village. Individuals were accused in Andover, Amesbury, Boston, Ipswich, Lynn, Marblehead, Newbury, Salem, Topsfield, Wenham, Wells, Maine, and throughout the colony. Social boundaries were crossed as well. By late summer of 1692, accusations of the afflicted were beginning to touch upon the lives and reputations of the social elite, which, in a hierarchical society like colonial Massachusetts, was severely discouraged. This would bring further societal and political pressure to bear, compelling the royal governor Sir William Phips, whose own wife was cried out against, to bring the episode to a speedy—and if possible, quiet end.

Phips was genuinely concerned that, if accusations and convictions continued to expand and generally go awry, news of his mishandling of the trials might well reach the ears of royal authorities in England. He rightly feared that such tidings could result in his dismissal as royal governor, and a public inquiry resulting in public humiliation and disgrace, or even worse, the revocation of the new 1691 Massachusetts charter and the installation of an unsympathetic, non-Puritan royal governor as a Phips's replacement.

All this was unacceptable not only to Phips but also the Mathers—both father and son—who had struggled so hard after Andros's removal to reestablish a puritan commonwealth with a locally born governor and a reasonable charter. To minimize the chance of negative reports slipping out of Boston and back to England, Phips instituted an immediate publication ban on any and all writers wishing to produce a printed commentary on the subject of the Salem trials. All were prohibited to write such accounts, except Reverend Cotton Mather, whom Phips authorized to write the only published assessment of the Salem event, the previously mentioned *Wonders of the Invisible World* (1693).

Both Reverend Increase and Reverend Cotton Mather did their best to minimize the damage done to the colony's reputation by "praising the wisdom of the judges" of the special witch trial court and wrongfully claiming that "spectral evidence had not been a deciding factor in any of the court's cases" (Baker, *A Storm of Witchcraft*, pp. 204–205).

Interestingly, the mishandling of the witch trials and the governor's efforts to censor the truth ultimately resulted in the demise of the careers of both Reverend Increase Mather and Reverend Cotton Mather as influential power brokers in the post–witch trial Massachusetts Colony. It also left the door open for Phips's political enemies to contact English officials responsible for colonial policy, and have him removed from office. And of this opportunity they took full advantage.

The spring elections in 1693 resulted in a general house cleaning of many of those who had supported Phips and the witch trials. As a result, new political figures, less radical and more skeptical, now controlled the Great and General Court and the Governor's Council. Within a year following the last executions, "distrust and antagonism between governor and legislature would become the face of things to come" and the angry and embarrassed legislature would be tardy and reluctant to pay Phips his salary. Ultimately, critical voices against Phips were heard in England, and by 1694, King William and Queen Mary would remove him from office and demand his return to England to face a public inquiry. "He would die in London in February, 1695, while awaiting the chance to refute the long list of complaints against him."

Chronology

1647	Alice Young, a resident of Windsor, Connecticut, becomes the first person to be hanged in New England for the crime of witchcraft.
1648	Boston resident, Margaret Jones, is the first individual to be hanged for witchcraft in Massachusetts Bay Colony.
1662	The Half-Way Covenant, sponsored by more liberal Puritan churches, is adopted in New England to encourage increased church membership. Conservative Puritans see this as a spiritual compromise by lowering the expectations and standards of what is required to become an accepted church member.
1675–1676	King Philip's War breaks out across New England driving English colonists back from their frontier settlements and causing them to question God's covenant to protect them.
1686–1688	Sir Edmund Andros is appointed Royal Governor of the Dominion of New England by England's King James II, revoking long-held, Puritan charters and property rights. It becomes a political crisis until the Glorious Revolution results in Andros's removal from office.
1688	The Goodwin Family of Charlestown, Massachusetts, claim to be attacked by a local Irish laundress, Goody Glover. The spectral evidence and behavior exhibited by the Goodwin children is very similar to what will happen in Salem Village with the afflicted children. Reverend Cotton Mather tells the Goodwin story in his 1689 book, *Memorable Providences*, which becomes a best-selling publication.
1689	Reverend Samuel Parris accepts the offer of the Salem Village Church to serve as its minister. He subsequently takes up residence in the Salem Village parsonage with his wife, Elizabeth, his niece, Abigail Williams, his daughter Betty Parris and two West Indian slaves, John Indian and his wife, Tituba.
February 1692	During the winter, Abigail Williams and Betty Parris begin to act strangely in the home of Reverend Samuel Parris, and the local physician Dr. William Griggs is called in to examine them. He declares them to be under the power of the evil hand of witchcraft. In response, local ministers

are brought into the Parris Parsonage to pray for the two distraught girls, but with no positive result or relief from their torment.

February 29, 1692	Three suspected witches, Sarah Good, Sarah Osborne, and Tituba Indian, are arrested and brought to Ingersoll's Tavern in Salem Village to undergo questioning by local magistrates, John Hathorne and Jonathan Corwin.
March 19, 1692	Pretrial examinations are fully underway at the Meeting House of Salem Village. Reverend Deodat Lawson, a former pastor of Salem Village Church, returns to observe the proceedings and witnesses the displays of the spectral evidence presented by the afflicted children.
March 24, 1692	Rebecca Nurse is arrested and brought into the court for questioning.
April 18, 1692	Mary English, wife of Salem's wealthiest merchant, Philip English, is arrested by Sheriff George Corwin. Later, her husband would also be accused. They would both escape jail in Boston and sail to New York, where they would live in exile for nearly a year before returning to Salem.
May 10, 1692	Sarah Osborne, one of the first three persons accused of witchcraft, dies in prison. On this date, George Jacobs, a prosperous local farmer is arrested for suspicion of witchcraft. Four days later, his pretrial examination would take place.
May 14, 1692	Newly appointed Royal Governor Sir William Phips and Boston minister Reverend Increase Mather arrive in Boston bearing the new royal Massachusetts charter, and immediately discover the colony's growing witchcraft crisis.
May 25, 1692	Governor Phips creates a special Court of Oyer and Terminer to hear the growing number of witchcraft cases and dispense justice upon those found guilty.
May 27, 1692	Governor Phips appoints seven judges to serve on the special court's bench, and names Deputy Governor William Stoughton as its chief justice.
May 31, 1692	Captain John Alden, son of the famous Pilgrim father, is arrested for suspicion of witchcraft. He is imprisoned in Boston, and escapes to New York in late July.
June 10, 1692	Bridget Bishop is hanged for witchcraft, and becomes the first victim to be executed.
June 15, 1692	A report entitled "The Return of Several Ministers" is delivered to Chief Justice William Stoughton and the Court of Oyer and Terminer, containing recommendations emphasizing that spectral evidence should not be used.
June 29, 1692	Rebecca Nurse is initially found innocent of witchcraft, but the verdict is reversed.

July 19, 1629	Execution day in Salem. The first group of victims is executed, including Sarah Good, Rebecca Nurse, Susannah Martin, Elizabeth Howe, and Sarah Wildes.
August 5, 1692	George Jacobs Sr. is brought from the Boston jail to stand trial in Salem. Among those who testify against him is his granddaughter, Margaret, a confessed witch, who later withdraws both her confession and her testimony against her grandfather.
August 19, 1692	Execution day in Salem. The second group of victims is executed including John Proctor, John Willard Martha Carrier, and Reverend George Burroughs. On this occasion, Burroughs startles the crowd of onlookers by reciting *The Lord's Prayer* perfectly before he is hanged, causing many to question the actions of the court and his guilt as a witch.
September 9–17, 1692	Mary Easty writes and submits to the court her famous petition that "no more innocent blood may be shed," and suggests that the court keep the afflicted persons apart and try some of the confessing witches whom she believes to be innocent of witchcraft, but guilty of perjury.
September 19, 1692	Giles Corey is charged with witchcraft, along with his wife, Martha, and brought to stand trial. When asked if he would be willing to be tried "by God and by country," meaning trial by jury, he refused to respond, but rather remained "mute before his accusers." As a result, he is subjected to the torture of *peine forte et dure,* more popularly known as pressing, and dies after being placed for two days beneath a large pile of stones, all the while steadfastly refusing to cooperate with the court by responding to a single question.
September 22, 1692	Execution day in Salem. The third and final group of victims is executed including Martha Corey, Mary Easty, Alice Parker, Ann Pudeater, Margaret Scott, Wilmot Redd, Samuel Wardwell, and Mary Parker.
October 3, 1692	Prominent Boston minister, Reverend Increase Mather, points out the court's procedural errors in his new book, *Cases of Conscience.* In it he states that "it were better that ten suspected witches should escape than that one innocent person should be condemned."
October 8, 1692	Boston merchant and intellectual, Thomas Brattle, issues his challenge to the court in "A Letter to a Reverend Gentleman." In it he questions the wisdom of accepting the testimony of afflicted girls as trustworthy.
October 29, 1692	Governor Sir William Phips bows to public pressure and criticism and closes the Court of Oyer and Terminer in Salem.
November 5, 1692	New witchcraft accusations are made against three women from Gloucester, Massachusetts. The public responds

differently to these charges and, according to witch trial critic Robert Calef, "they found not the encouragement they had done elsewhere, and soon withdrew."

December 14, 1692

The Great and General Court of Massachusetts passes several new ordinances in light of the recent witch trial episode, whereby a widow of a condemned witch may keep her dowry and inheritance; and a condemned witch may be given a Christian burial.

January 3, 1693

A new Superior Court, presided over by Chief Justice William Stoughton, meets in Salem. Governor Phips forbids the use of spectral evidence, nullifying all the testimony of the afflicted witnesses.

January—February 1693

Deputy Governor Stoughton does not bow to public pressure. He persists in trying and condemning accused witches, bringing in three more guilty verdicts to be added to the five other condemned witches already awaiting execution. Governor Phips grants a *stay of execution* for all eight condemned prisoners.

May 9, 1693

The Court of Assizes of Ipswich, MA, issues an indictment against Tituba Indian for the crime of witchcraft, claiming that by "covenanting with the Devil she, the said Tituba, is become a detestable witch." The court's Grand Jury rejected this indictment, and Tituba was allowed to be set free once her jailer's bill was paid.

May 1693

Governor Phips received word from England that he should discontinue the trials and put an end to all witch trial–related proceedings. Phips immediately issues a proclamation stopping all court activities, and pardons all those who remained in jail.

1694

Governor William Phips is recalled to England to answer charges for misappropriation of government funds. He dies in 1695 while awaiting trial.

December 17, 1696

Acting Governor William Stoughton issues a proclamation declaring a colony-wide day of prayer and fasting "so that God's people may offer up fervent supplications (prayers) that all iniquity may be put away which hath stirred God's Holy jealousy against this land. . . . referring to the late tragedy raised among us by Satan . . . through the awful judgment of God."

1696

During the colony-wide Fast-Day Service at Third Church in Boston, Judge Samuel Sewell stands before the congregation while his pastor Reverend Samuel Willard read his apology for his role during the Salem witch trials where "he desires to take the blame and shame of it, asking pardon of men. . . ."

1697	Boston merchant Robert Calef writes and publishes *More Wonders of the Invisible World,* a scathing analysis of the Salem witch trials targeting both the actions of the court and especially Reverend Cotton Mather.
1702	Reverend John Hale (1636–1700) was an active participant and supporter of the Salem witch episode from its beginnings until his wife, Sarah Noyes Hale, was cried out against by Mary Herrick on November 14, 1692. Reacting to the mistakes made by the court, he had published posthumously in 1702, *A Modest Inquiry into the Nature of Witchcraft,* where he acknowledges that the court mishandled the process of the trials and consequently executed innocent persons. He never questions the reality of witchcraft or the necessity of discovering and eliminating witches.
1706	Ann Putnam Jr. presents herself to the Salem Village Congregation, standing before them while their pastor, Reverend Joseph Green reads her apology and confession for the role she played in the Salem trials, especially for her testimony that ultimately resulted in the deaths of Rebecca Nurse and several others.
December 17, 1711	The Great and General Court of Massachusetts approved "payment of £578 pounds of the £796 claimed. Damages were awarded only to families of executed witches and to those who had been convicted" (Baker, *Storm of Witchcraft,* p. 250).
1764	Royal Governor Thomas Hutchinson writes the first volume of his three-volume *The History of the Colony of Massachusetts Bay,* where he discusses the Salem witch trial episode from the perspective of an educated and enlightened gentleman, two generations removed from the event. He concludes that, the afflicted children of 1692 Salem Village were consciously and dramatically performing affliction in a manner remarkably similar to the afflicted Goodwin children described by Reverend Cotton Mather's in his best-selling book, *Memorable Providences Relating to Witchcrafts and Possessions* (1689). He credits them as being extremely talented actors in a play with life-and-death consequences.

Chapter 1

February to May 1692

The documents dating from February through May 1692 are essential in understanding the genesis of the Salem episode in that: (1) they communicate the prevailing attitude of the accusers; (2) they identify the type of admissible evidence against the accused; and (3) they generally set the virulent tone for the entire event. Most of these documents were prepared as a direct result of the preliminary hearings conducted by Justice John Hathorne and Justice Jonathan Corwin before the arrival of Royal Governor William Phips in May 1692. Some were the scribal work of Ezekiel Cheever, the court clerk, while others were chronicled by Reverend Samuel Parris himself. To the scribes of the court we are most deeply indebted, since not only do they provide a verbatim narrative of exchanges between the accusers and accused, but at specific intervals, they have done us the added service of adding personal notes of observation describing facial expressions, bodily movements, gestures, spontaneous exclamations, and other spontaneous trial behavior, which greatly facilitate our understanding of the activities and attitudes demonstrated during the examinations. These non-narrative descriptions need to be read as well the verbal exchanges between judge and witness. In addition, in this chapter we have included a large number of depositions identifying the accusers and the accused. In many cases, although the accused may vary, the accusers tend to consist of a rather narrow group, at least in the very start of the trials. Familiarity with their names and the nature of their complaints against the victims helps the student to understand how it was possible for a relatively small circle of "afflicted children"—with assistance from adult allies—to initiate, sustain, and expand an entire community's anxiety and sense of satanic paranoia. Finally, it is in these first documents that the reader comes to the gradual realization of two major exceptions to all previous trials in New England: (1) the willingness of the justices to allow the exclusive use of spectral evidence to stand as sole proof of witchcraft; (2) the willingness of the justices to reverse all prior legal precedence by not condemning and executing confessed witches, such as Tituba; and (3) the willingness of the justices to execute only those convicted by the jury, who steadfastly proclaimed their innocence in the face of only spectral and circumstantial evidence.

A third exception is also worth noting, that the Salem justices were willing to allow any number of depositions against any number of accused without requiring the usual mandatory bond of money to be posted by the deponent. This legal practice was traditionally calculated to help minimize frivolous cases of libel. Court bonds of money, posted by deponents, would be taken by the court if the deposition proved groundless or simply false. The "afflicted children" would have to possessed substantial sums in the court had held them to this customary requirement.

Document 1

GOVERNOR WILLIAM PHIPS, "LETTER TWO OF GOVERNOR WILLIAM PHIPS," FEBRUARY 21, 1692/1693

The following document represents Governor Sir William Phips's second attempt to convey to his superiors [Rt. Hon. The Earl of Nottingham] in England that he had followed what he felt were appropriate steps in creating a Court of Oyer and Terminer and appointing the Lieutenant Governor [Stoughton] to act as Chief Justice. He underscores the genuine level of the crisis, and his efforts to put the best men in charge of resolving it. Phips then places the blame for the extreme measures resulting in 20 deaths squarely upon Chief Justice Stoughton, characterizing him as a man "enraged and filled with passionate anger." Beyond this, Phips accuses Stoughton of theft in that "from the beginning [he] hath hurried on these matters with great precipitancy and by his warrant, he hath caused the estates, goods and chattles [sic] of the executed to be seized and disposed of without my knowledge or consent."

Boston in New England, February 21st, 1692/93
    May it please your Lordship.
    By the Captain of the Samuel and Henry I gave an account that my arrival here I found the prisons full of people committed upon suspicion of witchcraft and that continual complaints were made to me that many persons were grievously tormented by witches and that they cried out upon several persons by name, as the cause of their torments. The number of these complaints increasing every day, by advice of the Lieut. Governor and the [Governor's] Council, I gave a Commission of Oyer and Terminer to try the suspected witches and at that time the generality of the people represented to me as real witchcraft and gave very strange instances of the same. The first in commission was the Lieut. Governor and the rest persons of the best prudence and figure that could be pitched upon and I depend upon the Court for a right method of proceeding in cases of witchcraft. At that time I went to command the Army at the Eastern part of the Province, for the French and Indians had made an attack upon some of our frontier towns. I continued there for some time, but when I returned I found people much dissatisfied with the proceedings of the Court, for about twenty persons were condemned and executed of which number, some were thought by many persons to be innocent. The Court still proceeded in the same method of trying them, which was by the evidence of the afflicted persons who, when they were brought into the Court, as soon as the suspected withes looked upon them, instantly fell to the ground in strange agonies and grievous torments, but when touched by them upon the arm, or some other part of their flesh, they immediately revived and came to themselves, upon which they made oath that the Prisoner at the Bar, did afflict them and that they saw their shape or spectre come from their bodies, which put them to such pains and torments. When I enquired into the matter I was informed by the judges that

they began with this, but had humane testimony against such as were condemned and undoubted proof of their being witches, but at length I found that the Devil did take upon him the shape of innocent persons and some were accused whose innocency [sic] I was well assured and many considerable persons of unblameable [sic] life and conversation were cried out upon as witches and wizards. The Deputy Governor notwithstanding, persisted vigorously in the same method, to the great dissatisfaction and disturbance of the people, until I put an end to the Court and stopped the proceedings, which I did because I saw many innocent persons might otherwise perish and at that time I thought it my duty to give an account thereof that their Majesties's pleasure might be signified, hoping that for the better ordering thereof, the Judges learned in the Law of England, might give such rules and directions as have been practized in England for proceedings in so difficult and so nice a point. When I put an end to the Court there were at least fifty persons in prison in great misery by reason of the extreme cold and their poverty, most of them having only spectre evidence against them, and their mittimusses being defective, I caused some of them to be let out upon bayle and put the Judges upon considering a way to relieve others and prevent them from perishing in prison, upon which some of them were convinced and acknowledged that their former proceedings were too violent and not grounded upon a right foundation, but that if they might sit again, they would proceed after another method, and whereas Mr. Increase Mather and several other Divines did give it as their judgement that the Devil might afflict in the shape of an innocent person, and that the look and touch of the suspected persons was not sufficient proof against them, these things had not the same stress laid upon them as before, and upon this consideration, I permitted a special Superior Court to be held at Salem in the County of Essex on the third day of January, the Lieutenant Governor being Chief Judge. Their method of proceeding being altered, all that were brought to trial to the number of fifty-two, were cleared, saving three. And I was informed by the King's Attorney General that some of the cleared and the condemned were under the same circumstances or that there was the same reason to clear the three condemned as the rest, according to his judgement. The Deputy Governor signed a warrant for their speedy execution and also of five others who were also condemned at the former Court of Oyer and Terminer, but considering how the matter had been managed, I sent a reprieve whereby the execution was stopped until their Majesties' pleasure be signified and declared. The Lieutenant Governor upon this occasion was enraged and filled with passionate anger, and refused to sit upon the Bench in a Superior Court then held at Charles Towne, and indeed hath, from the beginning hurried on these matters with great precipitancy and by his warrant, hath caused the estates, goods, and chattles of the executed to be seized and disposed of without my knowledge or consent. The stop put the first method of proceedings hath dissipated the black cloud that threatened this Province with destruction. For whereas delusion of the Devil did spread and its dismal effects touched the lives and estates of many of their Majesties' subjects and the reputation of some of the principal persons here, and indeed unhappily clogged and interrupted their Majesties' affaires which hath been a great vexation to me, I have no new complaints but people minds before divided and distracted by offering differing opinions concerning this matter are now well composed.

I am Your Lordships' most faithful humble Servant,
William Phips
To the Right Honourable The Earl of Nottingham at Whitehall, London
May 24, '93 About Witches

Source: George Lincoln Burr, ed. *Narratives of the Witchcraft Cases, 1648–1706.* New York: Charles Scribner's Sons, 1914, 198–202.

Document 2

UNKNOWN, "DEPOSITION OF ELIZABETH HUBBARD V. TITUBA," FEBRUARY 25, 1691/1692

The first trial document reflects the interrogation of Tituba, the slave of Reverend Samuel Parris. It is with Tituba that the crisis begins, since her name is the first to be given by the "afflicted" girls. Tituba, the wife of John Indian, was a West Indian slave brought by Reverend Samuel Parris from Barbados. In all probability, she was a Native American, not of African descent. It has long been assumed that Parris acquired her from the Island of Barbados, while he was still a sugar plantation owner and merchant there.

She is one of the first three individuals cried out against by Betty Parris and Abigail Williams, and the first of over 50 persons to confess to having been a witch. Like all confessed witches in the Salem episode, she was imprisoned and gave evidence against others. Interestingly, she, as with all confessed witches, was never executed. Ultimately, she was released in May 1693 after her jailer's bill was paid, and removed from Salem and disappeared from the historical record.

The deponent, Elizabeth (aka Betty) Hubbard, was an orphan and household servant who had only recently [late February] begun to exhibit evidence of malefic affliction and testify as one of the "afflicted children."

The Deposition of Elizabeth Hubbard aged about 17 years who testifies that on the 25th February 1691/92 I saw the apparition of Tituba Indian which did immediately most grievously torment me by pricking, pinching, and almost choking me and so continued hurting me most grievously by times til the day of her examination being the first of March and then also at the beginning of her examination but as soon as she began to confess she left off hurting me and has hurt me but little since.

Elizabeth Hubbard contra Tituba.

Source: Essex County Court Archives, vol. 1, no. 32, Massachusetts Supreme Judicial Court, Judicial Archives, on deposit James Duncan Phillips Library, Peabody Essex Museum, Salem, MA.

Document 3

UNKNOWN, "DEPOSITION OF ANN PUTNAM, JR. V. TITUBA," FEBRUARY 25, 1691/1692

Twelve-year-old Ann Putnam Jr. was the daughter of Salem Village farmer Thomas Putnam and his wife, Ann Carr Putnam Sr. They were supporters of the ministry of Reverend Samuel Parris. Both Ann Jr. and Ann Sr. would become involved in providing extensive spectral evidence during the trials against many suspects and would be instrumental in the condemnation of both Rebecca Nurse and Sarah Good.

The deposition of Ann Putnam who testifies and says that on the 25'th of February 1691/92 It was the apparition of Tituba, Mr. Parris's Indian woman which did torture me most grievously by pricking and pinching me most dreadfully till the first day of March being the day of her examination and then also most grievously also at the beginning of her examination but since she confessed she has hurt me but little.

Ann Putnam against Tituba Indian.

Source: Essex County Court Archives, vol. 1, no. 35, Massachusetts Supreme Judicial Court, Judicial Archives, on deposit James Duncan Phillips Library, Peabody Essex Museum, Salem, MA.

Document 4

EZEKIEL CHEEVER, "THE EXAMINATION OF TITUBA," MARCH 1, 1691/1692

What is especially interesting in the following examination of Tituba is the method of interrogation used by the court. Questions are phrased in a manner to lead the witness to admit guilt, and guilt is clearly presumed by the court. No attempt is made to defend the accused nor is the alleged witch provided with any legal counsel.

Question: Tituba what evil spirit have you familiarity with?

Tituba: None.

Question: Why do you hurt these children?

Tituba: I do not hurt them.

Question: Who is it then?

Tituba: The Devil for ought I know.

Question: Did you never see the Devil?

Tituba: The Devil came to me and bid me serve him.

Question: Who have you seen?

Tituba: Four women sometimes hurt the children.

Question: Who were they?

Tituba: Goody Osburne and Sarah Good and I do not know who the other were. Sarah Good and Osburne would have me hurt the children but I would not she further said there was a tale man of Boston that she did see.

Question: When did you see them?

Tituba: Last night at Boston.

Question: What did they say to you?

Tituba: They said hurt the children.

Question: And did you hurt them?

Tituba: No there is four women and one man they hurt the children and then lay all upon me and they tell me if I will not hurt the children they will hurt me.

Question: But did you not hurt them?

Tituba: Yes, but I will hurt them no more.

Question: Are you not sorry you did hurt them?

Tituba: Yes.

Question: And why then do you hurt them?

Tituba: They say hurt children or we will do worse to you.

Question: What have you seen?

Tituba: A man come to me and say serve me.

Question: What service?

Tituba: Hurt the children and last night there was an appearance that said kill the children and if I would not go on hurting the children they would do worse to me.

Question: What is this appearance you see?

Tituba: Sometimes it is like a hog and sometimes like a great dog this appearance she said she did see four times.

Question: What did it say to you?

Tituba: The black dog said serve me but I said I am afraid he said if I did not he would do worse to me.

Question: What did you say to it?

Tituba: I will serve you no longer then he said he would hurt me and then he looks like a man and threatens to hurt me she said that this man had a yellow bird that kept with him and he told me he had more pretty things that he would give me if I would serve him.

Question: What were these pretty things?

Tituba: He did not show me them.

Question:	What else have you seen?
Tituba:	Two rats, a red rat, and a black rat.
Question:	What did they say to you?
Tituba:	They said serve me.
Question:	When did you see them?
Tituba:	Last night and they said serve me but she said I would not.
Question:	What service?
Tituba:	She said hurt the children.
Question:	Did you not pinch Elizabeth Hubbard this morning?
Tituba:	The man brought her to me and made me pinch her.
Question:	Why did you go to Thomas Putnam's last night and hurt this child?
Tituba:	They pull and haul me and make go.
Question:	And what would have you do?
Tituba:	Kill her with a knife left fuller and others said at this time when the child saw these persons and was tormented by them that she did complain of a knife that they would have her cut her head off with a knife.
Question:	How did you go?
Tituba:	We ride upon sticks and are there presently.
Question:	Do you go through the trees or over them?
Tituba:	We see nothing but are there presently.
Question:	Why did you not tell your master?
Tituba:	I was afraid they said they would cut off my head if I told.
Question:	Would not you have hurt others if you could?
Tituba:	They said they would hurt others but they could not.
Question:	What attendants hath Sarah Good?
Tituba:	A yellow bird and she would have given me one.
Question:	What meat did she give it?
Tituba:	It did suck her between her fingers.
Question:	Did not you hurt Mr. Curren's child?
Tituba:	Goody Good and Goody Osburne told that they did hurt Mr. Curren's child and would have had me hurt him too but I did not.
Question:	What had Sarah Osburne?
Tituba:	Yesterday she had a thing with a head like a woman with two legs and wings Abigail Williams that lives with her uncle Mr. Parris said that she did see this same creature and it turned into the shape of Goody Osburne.

Question:	What else have you seen with Goody Osburne?
Tituba:	Another thing hairy it goes upright like a man it hath only two legs.
Question:	Did you not see Sarah Good upon Elizabeth Hubbard last Saturday?
Tituba:	I did see her set a wolf upon her to afflict her the persons with this maid did say that she did complain of a wolf. She further said that she saw a cat with Good at another time.
Question:	What clothes doth the man go in?
Tituba:	He goes in black clothes a tall man with white hair I think.
Question:	How do the woman go?
Tituba:	In a white hood and a black hood with a top knot.
Question:	Do you see who it is that torments these children now?
Tituba:	Yes it is Goody Good she hurts them in her own shape.
Question:	And who is it that hurts them now?
Tituba:	I am blind no I cannot see.

Salem Village, March the 1st 1691/2
Written by *Ezekiel Cheever*

Source: Essex County Court Archives, vol. 1, no. 11–12, Massachusetts Supreme Judicial Court, Judicial Archives, on deposit James Duncan Phillips Library, Peabody Essex Museum, Salem, MA.

Document 5

SAMUEL PARRIS, "DEPOSITION OF SAMUEL PARRIS V. TITUBA," MARCH 1, 1691/1692

As the examinations and testimonies escalate, Reverend Samuel Parris grows increasingly disaffected in his relationship with his long-time, trusted servant, Tituba. He provides support for the case that she was guilty of witchcraft and, at the conclusion of the Salem episode, refuses to pay the jailer's bill for Tituba and take her back into his household.

The Deposition of Samuel Parris aged about thirty and nine years testifies and says that Elizabeth Hubbard was most grievously and several times tortured during the examination of Sarah Good, Sarah Osburne, and Tituba Indian before the Magistrates at Salem Village 1st March 1691/2. And the said Tituba being the last of the abovesaid that was examined they the abovesaid afflicted persons were grievously distressed until the said Indian began to confess and then they were immediately all quiet the rest of the said Indian woman's examination.

Source: Essex County Court Archives, vol. 1, no. 34, Massachusetts Supreme Judicial Court, Judicial Archives, on deposit James Duncan Phillips Library, Peabody Essex Museum, Salem, MA.

Document 6

DEODAT LAWSON, "A BRIEF AND TRUE NARRATIVE OF SOME REMARKABLE PASSAGES RELATING TO SUNDRY PERSONS AFFLICTED BY WITCHCRAFT, SALEM VILLAGE," MARCH TO APRIL 5, 1692

Reverend Deodat Lawson, the author of the following narrative, from 1684 to 1687/1688, had served as the pastor of the Salem Village congregation. Like his successor, Reverend Samuel Parris, he encountered factionalism and conflict on the part of his parishioners. There finally was a dispute concerning having Lawson formally ordained minister of a recognized, independent church separated from Salem Town. Arbitrators asked to help resolve this disagreement "sided with the opponents of ordination" forcing Lawson to withdraw from Salem Village and relocate elsewhere. He was the third minister to serve the contentious Salem Village congregation in less than 16 years. Reverend Parris would become the fourth asked to serve in 1689, and he would be confronted with an equally divided and hostile community. Salem Village was, for the time and place, unusually fractious and unfriendly to its ministers.

Reverend Lawson was invited to return to Salem Village as a guest preacher for the Sabbath service on March 20, 1691/1692, and was interrupted during his sermon whereby some of the afflicted girls in attendance "had several sore fits, in the time of public worship" going so far as to interrupt him during his public prayer for the congregation. Some went so far as to boldly instruct the young minister as to how he should conduct the worship service. This behavior, unseemly for Puritan children, prompted Lawson to delve more deeply into the events at Salem Village and produce what was to become the first eyewitness chronicle of the Salem witch episode. The following is the result of his observations.

On the Nineteenth day of March last I went to Salem Village, and lodged at Nathaniel Ingersols near to the Minister Mr. P s. house, and presently after, I came into my Lodging Capt. Walents Daughter Mary came to Lieut. Ingersols and spake to me, but, suddenly after as she stood by the door, was bitten, so that she cried out of her Wrist and looking on it with a Candle, we saw apparently the marks of Teeth both upper and lower set, on each side of her wrist.

In the beginning of the Evening, I went to give Mr. P. a visit When I was there, his Kins-woman, Abigail Williams, (about 12 years of age,) had a grievous fit; she was at first hurryed with Violence to and fro in the room; (though Mrs. Ingersol, endeavoured to Hold her,) sometimes makeing as if she would fly, stretching up her arms as high as she could, and crying Whish, Whish, Whish! several times; Presently after she said there was Goodw N. and said, Do you not see her? Why there she stands! And she said Goodw N. offered her THE BOOK, but she was resolved she would not take it, saying Often, I wont, I wont, I wont, take it, I do not know what Book it is: I am sure it is none of Gods Book, it is the Divels Book, for ought I know. After that, she run to the Fire, and begun to throw Fire Briands, about the house; and run against the Back, as if she would run up Chimney, and, as they said, she had attempted to go into the Fire in other Fits.

On Lords Day, the Twentieth of March, there were sundry of the afflicted Persons at Meeting, as, Mrs. Pope, and Goodwife Bishop Abigail Williams, Mary Walcut, Mary Lewes, and Docter Grigg's Maid. There was also at Meeting, Goodwife C. (who was afterward Examined on suspicion of being a Witch:) They had several Sore Fits, in the time of Publick Worship, which did something interrupt me in my First Prayer; being so unusual After Psalm was Sung, Abigail Williams said to me, Now stand up, and Name your Text. And after it was read, she said, It is a long Text. In the beginning of Sermon, Mrs. Pope, a Woman afflicted said to me, Now there is enough of that. And in the Afternoon, Abigail Williams, upon my referring to my Doctrine said to me, I know no Doctrine you had, If you did name one, I have forgot it.

In Sermon time when Goodw C was present in the Meeting house Ab. W. called out, Look where Goodw. C sits on the Beam suckling her Yellow bird betwixt her fingers! Anne Putman another Girle afflicted said there was a Yellow-bird sat on my hat as it hang on the Pin the Pulpit! but those that were by, restrained her from asking about it.

On Monday the 21st. of March, The Magistrates of Salem appointed to come to Examination of Goodw C. And about twelve of the Clock, they went into the Meeting-House, which was Thronged with Spectators: Mr. Noyes began with a very and pathetical Prayer; and Goodwise C. being called to answer to what was Alledged against her, she desired to go to Prayer, which was, much wondred at, in the presence of so many hundred, people. The Magistrates told her, they would not admit by they came not there to hear her Pray, but to Examine her, in was Alledged against her. The Worshipful Mr. Hathorne, asked her, why she Afflicted those Children? she said, she did not Afflict them. He asked her, who did then? she said, I do not know; How should I know? The Number of the Afflicted Persons were about that time Ten, viz. Four Married Women, Mrs. Pope, Mrs. Putman, Goodw. Bibber, and an Ancient Woman, named Goodall, three Maids, Mary Walcut, Mercy Lewes, at Thomas Putman's, and a Maid at Dr. Griggs's, there were three Girls from 9 to 12 Years of Age, each of them, or thereabouts, viz. Elizabeth Parris, Abigail William and Ann Putman; these were most of them at Examination, and did vehemently accuse her in the Assembly of afflicting them, by Biting, Pinching, Strangling, &c. And that they did in their Fit, her Likeness coming to them, and bringing a to them, she said, she had no Book; they affirmed, she had a Yellow-Bird, that used to suck betwixt her Fingers, and being asked about it, if she had any Familiar Spirit, that attended her, she said, She had no Familiarity with any such thing. She was a Gospel Woman which Title she called herself by; and the Afflicted Persons told her, ah! She was, A Gospel Witch. Ann Putman did there affirm, that one day when Lieutenant Fuller was at Prayer at her Fathers House, she saw the shape of Goodw. C. and she thought Goodw. N. Praying at the same time to the Devil, she was not sure it was Goodw. N. she thought it was; but very sure she saw the Shape of G. C. The said C. said, they were poor, distracted, Children, and no heed to be given to what they said. Mr. Hathorne and Mr. Corwen it was the judgment of all that were present, they were Bewitched, and only she the Accused Person said, they were Distracted. It was observed several times, that if she did but bite her Under lip in time of Examination the persons afflicted were bitten on their armes and wrists and produced the Marks before the Magistrates, Ministers and others. And being watched for that, if she did but Pinch her Fingers, or Graspe one Hand, hard in another, they were Pinched and produced the Marks before the Magistrates, and Spectators. After that, it was observed, that if she did but lean her Breast, against the Seat, in the Meeting House, (being the Barr at which she stood,) they were afflicted. Particularly Mrs. Rope complained of grievous torment in her Bowels as if they were torn out. She vehemently accused said C. as the instrument, and first threw her Muff at her; but that flying not home, she got off her Shoe. and hit Goodwife C. on the head with it. After these postures were watched, if said C. did but stir her feet, they were afflicted in their Feet, and stamped fearfully. The afflicted persons asked her why she did not go to the company of Witches which were before the Meeting house mustering? Did she not hear the Drum beat. They accused her of having Familiarity with the Devil, in the time of Examination, in the shape of a Black man whispering in her ear; they affirmed, that her Yellow-Bird, sucked betwixt her Fingers in the Assembly; and order being given to see if there were any sign, the Girl that saw it, said, it was too late now; she had removed a Pin, and put it on her head; which was found there sticking upright.

They told her, she had Covenanted with the Devil for ten years, six of them were gone, and four more to come. She was required by the Magistrates to answer that Question in the Catechism, How many persons, be there in the God-Head? she answered it but oddly, yet was there no great thing to be gathered from it; she denied all that was charged upon her, and said, They could not prove a Witch; she was that Afternoon Committed to Salem-Prison; and after she was in Custody, she did not so appear to them, and afflict them as before.

On Wednesday the 23 of March, I went to Thomas Putmans, on purpose to see his Wife: I found her lying on the Bed, having had a sore fit a little before she spake to me, and said, she was glad to see me; her Husband and she, both desired me to pray with her, while she was sensible; which I did, though the Apparition said, I should not go to Prayer. At the first beginning she attended; but after a little time, was taken with a fit: yet continued silent, and seemed to be Asleep: when Prayer was done, her Husband going to her, found her Fit; he took her off the Bed, to set her on his Knees; but at first she was so stiff, she could not be bended; but she afterwards set down; but quickly began to strive violently with her Arms and Leggs; she then began to Complain of, and as it were to Converse personally with, Goodw. N. saying, Goodw. N. Be gone! Be gone! Be gone! are you not ashamed, a Woman of your Profession, to afflict a poor Creature so? what hurt did I ever do you in my life! you have but two years to live, and then the Devil will torment your Soul, for this your Name is blotted out of Gods Book, and it shall never be put in Gods Book again, be gone for shame, are you not afraid of that which is coming upon you? I Know, I know, what will make you afraid; the wrath of an Angry God, I am sure that will make you afraid; be gone, do not torment me, I know what you would have (we judged she meant, her Soul) but it is out of your reach; it is Clothed with the white Robes of Christs Righteousness. After this, she seemed to dispute with the Apparition about a particular Text of Scripture. The Apparition seemed to deny it; (the Womans eyes being fast closed all this time) she said, She was sure there was such a Text; and she would tell it; and then the Shape would be gone, for said she, I am sure you cannot stand before that Text! then she was sorely Afflicted; her mouth drawn on one side, and her body strained for about a minute, and then said, I will tell, I will tell; it is, it is, it is! three or four times, and then was afflicted to hinder her from telling, at last she broke forth and said, It is the third Chapter of the Revelations. I did something scruple the reading it, and did let my scruple appear, lest Satan should make any, Superstitious lie to improve the Word of the Eternal God. However, tho' not versed in these things, I judged I might do it this once for an Experiment. I began to read, and before I had near read through the first verse, she opened her eyes, and was well; this fit continued near half an hour. Her Husband and the Spectators told me, she had often been so relieved by reading Texts that she named, something pertinent to her Case; as Isa. 40. 1. Isa. 49. 1. Isa. 50. 1. and several others.

On Thursday the Twenty fourth of march, (being in course the Lecture Day, at the Village,) Goodwife N. was brought before the Magistrates Mr. Hathorne and Mr. Corwin, about Ten of Clock, in the Fore Noon, to be Examined in the Meeting House, the Reverend Mr. Hale, begun with Prayer, and the Warrant being read, she was required to give answer, Why she aflicted those persons? she pleaded her owne innocency with earnestness. Thomas Putman's Wife, Abigail Williams and Thomas Putmans daughter accused her that she appeared to them, and afflicted them in their fitts: but some of the other said, that they had seen her, but knew not that ever she had hurt them; amongst which was Mary Walcut who was presently after she had so declared bitten, and cryed out of her in the meeting-house; producing the Marks of teeth on her wrist. It was so disposed that I had not leisure to attend the whole time of Examination but both Magistrates, and Ministers, told me, that the things alledged, by the afflicted, and defences made by her, were much after the same manner, as the former was. And her motions, did produce like effects as to, Biteing, Pinching, Bruising Tormenting, at their Breasts, by her Leaning, and when, bended Back, were as if their Backs was broken. The afflicted persons said, the Black Man, whispered to her in the Assembly, and therefore she could not hear what the Magistrates said unto her. They said also that she did then ride by the Meeting-house, behind the Black Man. Thomas Putman's wife, had a grievous Fit, in the time of Examination, to the very great Impairing of her strength, and wasting of her spirits, insomuch as she could hardly, move hand, or foot, when she was carried out. Others also were there grievously afflicted, so that there was once such an hideous scrietch and noise, (which I heard as I walked, at a little distance from the Meeting house,) as did amaze me, and some that were within, told me the whole assembly was struck with consternation, and they were afraid, that those that sate next to them, were under the influence of Witchcraft. This woman also was that day committed to Salem Prison. The Magistrates and Ministers also did informe me, that they apprehended a child of Sarah. G and Examined it, being between 4 and 5 years of Age. And as to matter of Fact, they did Unanimously affirm, that when this Child, "would" but "fix her" eye upon the afflicted persons, they were "afflicted," and they held her Head, and yet so many as her eye could fix upon were afflicted. Which they did several times make careful observation of: the afflicted complained, they had often been Bitten by this child, and produced the marks of a small set of teeth, accordingly, this was also committed to Salem-Prison, the child looked hail, and well as other Children. I saw it at Lievt. Ingersols After the commitment of Goodw. N. Tho: Putmans Wife was much better, and had no violent fits at all from that 24th of March, to the 5th of April. Some others also said they had not seen her so frequently appear to them, to hurt them.

On the 25th of March, (as Capt. Stephen Sewal, of Salem, did afterwards inform me) Eliza. Paris, had sore Fits, at his house, which much troubled himself, and his wife, so as he told me they were almost discouraged. She related, that the great Black Men came to her, and told her, if she would be ruled by him, she should have, whatsoever she desired, and go to a Golden City. She relating this to Mrs. Sewall, she told the child, is was the Divel, and he was a Lyar from the Beginning, and bid her tell him so, if he came again: which she did accordingly, at the next coming to her, in her fits.

On the 26th of March, Mr. Hathorne, Mr. Corwin, and Mr. Higison, were at the Prison-Keepers House, to Examine the Child, and it told them there, it had a little Snake. that used to Suck on the lowest Joynt of it Fore-Finger; and when they inquired where, pointing to other places, it told them, not there, but there, pointing on the Lowest point of the Fore-Finger; where they Observed, a deep Red Spot, about the Bigness of a Flea-bite, they asked who gave it that Snake? whether the great Black man, it said no, its Mother gave it.

The 31 of March there was a Publick Fast kept at Salem on account of these Afflicted Persons. And Abigal Williams said, that the Witches had a Sacrament that day at an house in the Village, and that they had Red Bread and Red Drink. The first of April, Mercy Lewis, Thomas Putman's Maid, in her fitt, said, they did eat Red Bread like Mans Flesh, and would have had her eat some: but she would not; but turned away her head, and Spit at them, and said I will not Eat, I will not Drink, it is Blood &c. She said, That is not the Bread of Life, that is not the Water of Life; Christ gives the Bread of Life, I will have none of it! This first of April also Mercy Lewis aforesaid saw in her fitt a White man and was with him in a Glorious Place, which had no Candles nor Sun, yet was full of Light and Brightness; where was a great Multitude in White glittering Robes, and they Sung the Song in the fifth of Reverlation the Ninth verse, and the 110 Psalm, and the 149 Psalm; and said with herself. How long shall I stay here! let me be along with you: She was loth to leave this place, and grieved that she could tarry no longer. This Whiteman hath appeared several times to some of them, and given them notice how long it should be before they had another Fit, which was sometimes a day, or day and half, or more or less: it hath fallen out accordingly.

The third of April, the Lords-Day, being Sacrament-day, at the Village, Goodw C. upon Mr. Parris's naming his Text, John 6, 70. One of them is a Devil, the said Goodw. C. went immediately out of the Meeting-House, and flung the door after her violently, to the amazement of the Congregation: She was afterward seen by some in their Fits, who said, O Goodw. C. I did not think to see you here! (and being at their Red bread and drink) said to her, Is this a time to receive the Sacrament, you ran away on the Lords-Day, & scorned to receive it in the Meeting-House, and, Is this a time to receive it? I wonder at you! This is the summ of what I either saw myself, or did receive Information from persons of undoubted Reputation and Credit.

Remarks of things more than ordinary about the Afflicted Persons.

1. They are in their Fits tempted to be Witches, are shewed the List of the Names of others, and are tortured, because they will not yield to Subscribe, or meddle with, or touch the BOOK, and are promised to have present Relief if they would do it.

2. They did in the Assembly mutually Cure each other, even with a Touch of their Hand, when Strangled, and otherwise Tortured, & would endeavour to get to their Afflicted, to Relieve them.

3. They did also foretel when another Fit was a-coming, and would say, Look to her! she will have a Fit presently, which fell out accordingly, as many can bear witness, that heard and saw it.

4. That at the same time, when the Accused Person was present, the Afflicted Persons saw her Likeness in other places of the Meeting-House, suckling her Familiar, sometimes in one place and posture, and sometimes in another.

5. That their Motions in their Fits are Preternatural, both as to the manner, which is so strange as a well person could not Screw their Body into; & as to the violence also it is preternatural being much beyond the Ordinary force of the same person when they are in their right mind.

6. The eyes of some of them in their fits are exceeding fast closed, and if you ask a question they can give no answer, and I do believe they cannot hear at that time, yet do they plainly converse with the Appearances, as if they did discourse with real persons.

7. They are utterly pressed against any persons Praying, with them, and told by the appearances, they shall not go to Prayer, so Tho. Putmans wife was told, I should not Pray; but she said, I should: and after I had done, reasoned with the Appearance, Did not I say he should go to Prayer!

8. The forementioned Mary W. being a little better at ease, the Afflicted persons said, she had signed the book; and that was the reason she was better. Told me by Edward Putman.

Remarks concerning the Accused

1. For introduction to the discovery of those that afflicted them, It is reported Mr. Parris's Indian Man, and Woman, made a Cake of Rye Meal, and the Childrens water, baked it in the Ashes, and gave it to a Dogge, since which they have discovered, and seen particular persons hurting of them.

2. In Time of Examination, they seemed little affected, though all the Spectators were much grieved to see it.

3. Natural Actions in them produced Preternatural actions in the Afflicted, so that they are their own Image without any Poppits of Wax or otherwise.

4. That they are accused to have a Company about 23 or 24 and they did Muster in Armes, as it seemed to the Afflicted Persons.

5. Since they were confined, the Persons have not been so much Afflicted with their appearing to them, Biteing or Pinching of them &c.

6. They are reported by the Afflicted Persons to keep dayes of Fast and dayes of Thansgiving, and Sacraments; Satan endeavour to Transforme himself to an Angel of Light, and to make his Kingdom and Administrations to resemble those of our Lord Jesus Christ.

7. Satan Rages Principally amongst the Visible Subjects of Christ's Kingdom and makes use (at least in appearance) of some of them to Afflict others; that Christ's Kingdom may be divided against it self, and so be weakened.

8. Several things used in England at Tryal of Witches, to the Number of 14 or 15 which are wont to pass instead of, or in Concurrence with Witnesses, at least 6 or 7 of them are found in these accused: see Keebles Statutes.

9. Some of the most solid Afflicted Persons do affirme the same things concerning seeing the accused out of their Fitts as well as in them.

10. The Witches had a Fast, and told one of the Afflicted Girles, she must not Eat, because it was Fast Day, she said, she would: they told her they would Choake her then; which when she did eat, was endeavoured.

FINIS.

Source: Deodat Lawson. *A Brief and True Narrative of Some Remarkable Passages Relating to Sundry Persons Afflicted by Witchcraft, at Salem Village Which Happened from the Nineteenth of March to the Fifth of April, 1692.* Boston: Printed for Benjamin Harris, 1692.

Document 7

UNKNOWN, "EXAMINATION OF SARAH OSBORNE," MARCH 1, 1691/1692

Sarah Osborne was one of the first three individuals accused of witchcraft by the "afflicted children." At the time of her accusation, she was in ill health and had not been participating in regular church attendance. Now, a widow, her reputation had been forever damaged when she scandalously married a man, Alexander Osborne, who had been her indentured servant. Like Sarah Good, she was an easy target for the early accusations with virtually no one to defend her when she underwent her pretrial examination under the critical interrogation of the Honorable John Hathorne.

Sarah Osburn her examination

(H)   what evil spirit have you familiarity with

(O)   none.

(H)   have you made no contract with the devill

(O)   no I never saw the devill in my life

(H)   why doe you hurt these children

(O)   I doe not hurt them

(H)   who do you imploy then to hurt them

(O)   I imploy no body

(H)   what familiarity have you with Sarah Good

(O)   none I have not seen her these 2 years.

(H)   where did you see her then

(O)   one day agoing to Town

(H)   what communications had you with her,

(O)   I had none, only how doe you doe or so, I did not know her by name

(H)   what did you call her then Osburn made a stand at that at last said, shee called her Sarah

(H)   Sarah good saith that it was you that hurt the children

(O)   I doe not know that the devil goes about in my likeness to doe any hurt

Mr. Harthorn desired all the children to stand up and look upon her and see if they did know her which they all did and every one of them said that this was one of the woman that did afflict them and that they had constantly seen her in the very habit that shee was now in, thiere evidence do stand that shee said this morning that shee was more like to be bewitched than that she was a witch Mr. Harthorn asked her what made her say so shee answered that shee was frighted one time in her sleep and either saw or dreamed that shee saw a thing like an indian all black which did pinch her in her neck and pulled her by the back part of her head to the dore of the house

(H)   did you never see anything else

(O)   no.

    it was said by some in the meeting house that shee had said that shee would never be teid to that lying spirit any more.

(H)   what lying spirit is this hath the devil ever deceived you and been false to you.

(O)   I doe not know the devil I never did see him

(H)   what lying spirit was it then.

(O)   it was a voice that I thought I heard

(H)   what did it porpound to you.

(O)   that I should goe no more to meeting but I said I would and did goe the next Sabbath day

(H)   were you never tempted furder

(O)   no

(H)   why did you yield thus far to the devil as never to goe to meeting since.

(O)   alas. I have been sike and not able to goe her housband and others said that shee had not been at Meeting this yeare and two months.

Source: William E. Woodward. Records of Salem witchcraft, copied from the original documents, vol. 2. Roxbury, MA: Priv. print. for W. E. Woodward, 35–36.

Document 8

EZEKIEL CHEEVER, "EXAMINATION OF SARAH GOOD," MARCH 1, 1691/1692

Sarah Good, like Sarah Osborne, was a likely target for early accusations of witchcraft. She was impoverished and known to live an independent, wandering, and shiftless life often separated from her husband, William Good. She was generally known to be unfriendly and resentful, suffering from a decidedly negative personal reputation among the people of Salem Village.

The examination of Sarah Good before the worshipful Assistants John Hathorne and Jonathan Curwen

(H.)   Sarah Good what evil spirit have you familiarity with

(S G)   none

(H)   have you made no contract with the devil,

(g)   good answered no

(H)   why doe you hurt these children

(g)   I doe not hurt them. I scorn it.

(H)   who doe you imploy then to doe it

(g)   I imploy no body,

(H)   what creature do you imploy then,

(g)   no creature but I am falsely accused

(H)   why did you go away muttering from mr Parris his house

(g)   I did not mutter but I thanked him for what he gave my child

(H)   have you made no contract with the devil

(g)   no

(H)   desired the children all of them to look upon her, and see, if this were the person that had hurt them and so they all did looke upon her and said this was one of the persons that did torment them—presently they were all tormented.

(H)   Sarah good doe you not see now what you have done why doe you not tell us the truth, why doe you thus torment these poor children

(g) I doe not torment them,

(H) who do you imploy then

(g) I imploy nobody I scorn it

(H) how came they thus tormented,

(g) what doe I know you bring others here and now you charge me with it

(H) why who was it.

(g) I doe not know but it was some you brought into the meeting house with you

(H) wee brought you into the meeting house

(g) but you brought in two more

(H) Who was it then that tormented the children

(g) it was osburn

(H) what is it that you say when you goe muttering away from persons houses

(g) if I must tell I will tell

(H) doe tell us then

(g) if I must tell I will tell, it is the commandments I may say my commandments I hope

(H) what commandment is it

(g) if I must tell you I will tell, it is a psalm

(H) what psalm

(g) after a long time shee muttered over some part of a psalm

(H) who doe you serve

(g) I serve god

(H) what god doe you serve

(g) the god that made heaven and earth though shee was not willing to mention the word God her answers were in a very wicked, spitfull manner reflecting and retorting aganst the authority with base and abusive words and many lies shee was taken in.it was here said that her housband had said that he was afraid that shee either was a witch or would be one very quickly the worsh mr Harthon asked him his reason why he said so of her whether he had ever seen any thing by her he answered no not in this nature but it was her bad carriage to him and indeed said he I may say with tears that shee is an enimy to all good.

(Salem Village March the 1st 1691/92)
Written by Ezekiel Cheever

Source: Essex County Court Archives, vol. 1, nos. 11 & 12, Massachusetts Supreme Judicial Court, Judicial Archives, on deposit James Duncan Phillips Library, Peabody Essex Museum, Salem, MA.

Document 9

EZEKIEL CHEEVER, "EXAMINATION OF TITUBA— A SECOND VERSION," MARCH 1, 1691/1692

In order to ascertain the accuracy of her earlier testimony, Tituba was subjected to a second examination where the same information was covered. The court was satisfied that the information contained in her second account was close enough to the first that her confession and testimony was reliable and trustworthy. The importance in this was that it established beyond doubt that there was indeed a Satanic conspiracy involving many local persons and Tituba, the first confessed witch, was the key to discovering the identity of the conspirators.

Tituba the Indian woman's examination March 1, 1691/2

Question: Why do you hurt these poor children? What harm have they done unto you?

Answer: They do no harm to me I no hurt them at all.

Question: Why have you done it?

Answer: I have done nothing. I can't tell when the Devil works.

Question: What did the Devil tell you that he hurts them?

Answer: No he tells me nothing.

Question: Do you never see something appear in some shape?

Answer: No never see anything.

Question: What familiarity have you with the Devil, or what is it if you converse with all? Tell the truth who it is that hurts them.

Answer: The Devil for ought I know.

Question: What appearance or how did he appear when he hurts them, with what shape or what is he like that hurts them?

Answer: Like a man I think yesterday I being in the Lentoe Chamber I saw a thing like a man, that told me serve him and I told him no I would not do such thing. She charges Goody Osburne and Sarah Good as those that hurt the children, and would have had her done it, she said she seen four two of which she knew not she saw them last night as she was washing the room, they told me hurt the children and would have had me gone to Boston, there was five of them with the man, they told me if I would not go and hurt them they would do so to me at first I did agree with them but afterward I told them I do so no more.

Question: Would they have had you hurt the children the last night?

Answer: Yes, but I was sorry and I said, I would do so no more, but told I would fear God.

Question: But why did not you do so before?

Answer: Why they tell me I had done so before and therefore I must go on, these were the four women and the man, but she knew none but Osburne and Good only, the others were of Boston.

Question: At first beginning with them, what then appeared to you what was it like that got you to do it?

Answer: One like a man just as I was going to sleep came to me this was when the children was first hurt he said he would kill the children and she would never be well, and he said if I would not serve him he would do so to me.

Question: Is that the same man that appeared before to you that appeared the last night I told you this?

Answer: Yes.

Question: What other likenesses besides a man have appeared to you?

Answer: Sometimes like a hog. Sometimes like a great black dog, four times.

Question: But what did they say unto you?

Answer: They told me serve him and that was a good way; that was the black dog I told him I was afraid, he told me he would be worse than to me.

Question: What did you say to him after that?

Answer: I answer I will serve you no longer he told me he would do me hurt then.

Question: What other creatures have you seen?

Answer: A bird.

Question: What bird?

Answer: A little yellow bird.

Question: Where does it keep?

Answer: With the man who hath pretty things there besides.

Question: What other pretty things?

Answer: He has not showed them [yet] unto me, but he said he would show them me tomorrow, and he told me if I would serve him I should have the bird.

Question: What other creatures did you see?

Answer: I saw two cats, one red, another black as big as a little dog.

Question: What did these cats do?

Answer: I don't know; I have seen them two times.

Question: What did they say?

Answer: They say serve them.

Question: When did you see them?

Answer: I saw them last night.

Question: Did they do any hurt to you or threaten you?

Answer: They did scratch me.

Question:	When?
Answer:	After prayer; and scratched me, because I would not serve them and when they went away I could not see but they stood before the fire.
Question:	What service do they expect from you?
Answer:	They say more hurt to the children.
Question:	How did you pinch them when you hurt them?
Answer:	The other pull me and haul me to the pinch the children, and I am very sorry for it.
Question:	What made you hold your arm when you were searched? What had you there?
Answer:	I had nothing.
Question:	Do not those cats suck you?
Answer:	No never yet I would not let them but they had almost thrust me into the fire.
Question:	How do you hurt those that you pinch? Do you get those cats or other thing to do it for you? Tell us, how is it done?
Answer:	The man sends the cats to me and bids me pinch them, and I think I went over to Mr. Grigg's and have pinched her this day in the morning. The man brought Mr. Grigg's maid to me and made me pinch her.
Question:	Did you ever go with these women?
Answer:	They are very strong and pull me and make me go with them.
Question:	Where did you go?
Answer:	Up to Mr. Putnam's and make me hurt the child.
Question:	Who did make you go?
Answer:	A man that is very strong and these two women, Good and Osburne but I am sorry.
Question:	How did you go? What do you ride upon?
Answer:	I rid upon a stick or pole and Good and Osburne behind me we ride taking hold of one another don't know how we go for I saw no trees nor path, but was presently there. When we were up.
Question:	How long since you began to pinch Mr. Parris' children?
Answer:	I did not pinch them at the first, but he make me afterward.
Question:	Have you seen Good and Osburne ride upon a pole?
Answer:	Yes and have held fast by me. I was not at Mr. Grigg's but once, but it may be send something like me, with or would I have gone, but that they tell me, they will hurt me; last night they tell me I must kill somebody with the knife.
Question:	Who were they that told you so?
Answer:	Sarah Good and Osburne and they would have had me killed Thomas Putnam's child.

Also affirmed that at the same time they would have had her cut [her own throat] off her own head for if she would not then told her Tituba would cut it off and then she complained at the same time of a knife cutting of her when her master hath asked her about these things she said they will not let her tell, but tell her if she tells her head shall be cut off.

Question: Who tells you so?

Answer: The man, Good and Osburne's wife. Goody Good came to her last night when her master was at prayer and would not let her hear and she could not hear a good while. Good had one of these birds the yellow bird and would have given me it, but I would not have it and prayer time she stopped my ears and would not let me hear.

Question: What should you have done with it?

Answer: Give it to the children. Which yellow bird has been several times seen by the children I saw Sarah Good have it on her hand when she came to her when Mr. Parris was at prayer I saw the bird suck Good between the fore finger and long finger upon the right hand.

Question: Did you never practices witchcraft in your own country?

Answer: No never before now.

Question: Did you [ever] see them do it now?

Answer: Yes. Today, but that was in the morning.

Question: But did you see them do it now while you are examining?

Answer: No I did not see them but I saw them hurt at other times. I saw Good have a cat beside the yellow bird which was with her.

Question: What has Osburne got to go with her?

Answer: Something I don't know what it is. I can't name it, I don't know how it looks she has two of them one of them has wings and two legs and a head like a woman the children saw the same but yesterday which afterward turned into a woman.

Question: What is the other thing that Goody Osburne have?

Answer: A thing all over hairy, all the face hairy and a long nose and I don't know how to tell how the face looks with two legs, it goes upright and is about two or three-foot-high and goes upright lie a man and last night it stood before the fire In Mr. Parris's hall.

Question: Who was that appeared like a wolf to Hubbard as she was going from Proctor's?

Answer: It was Sarah Good and I saw her send the wolf to her.

Question: What clothes did the man appear unto you in?

Answer: Black clothes sometimes. Sometimes serge coat or other color, a tall man with white hair, I think.

Question: What apparel do the women wear?

Answer: I don't know what color.

Question: What kind of clothes has she?

Answer: I don't know what color.

Question: What kind of clothes hath she?

Answer: A black silk hood with a white silk hood under it, with top knots, which woman I know not but have seen her in Boston when I lived there.

Question: What clothes the little woman?

Answer: A serge coat with a white cap as I think.

(The children having fits at this very time she was asked who hurt them, she answered Goody Good and the children affirmed the same but Hubbard being taken in an extreme fit after she was asked who hurt her and she said she could not tell, but said they blinded her, and would not let her see and after that was once or twice taken dumb herself.)

Source: Essex County Court Archives, vol. 1, nos. 11 & 12, Massachusetts Supreme Judicial Court, Judicial Archives, on deposit James Duncan Phillips Library, Peabody Essex Museum, Salem, MA.

Document 10

JONATHAN CORWIN, "SUMMARY OF EXAMINATIONS OF TITUBA," MARCH 1, 1691/1692

The important question has often been asked as to why Tituba, unlike all other previous confessed witches in New England, was never executed. The answer is unknowable, except to point out that she proved to be a valuable and highly cooperative witness capable of providing incredible detail on the activities of many suspected witches. Besides names, she described their meetings, their comings and goings, their conversations, and their motives for their actions. To eliminate, by hanging, such a rich source information so essential to the court would have been antithetical to the ultimate goal of the trials themselves, that is, the discovery and elimination of every individual witch.

What may be said is that by not executing Tituba, the Salem court set a very unusual legal precedent, a virtual reversal of what might have been expected. Contrary to all other prior legal cases involving self-confessed witches, all previous courts considered a confession the best proof of guilt. The death penalty for confessed witches was, historically, the only acceptable recourse. This well-established judicial viewpoint was confirmed and supported by all contemporary legal authorities. One only need look back to the 1688–1689 case of Goody Glover, who was hanged in Boston after having confessed to witchcraft. Further, this complete reversal of standard legal policy concerning treatment of Tituba and other self-confessed witches seems to account for the large numbers of confessions—over 50—during the Salem episode.

The following summary touches upon all the key points of Tituba's unusual and precedent-setting case and, incidentally, confirms her identity as a Native American, not an African American, as she has so often been portrayed.

Salem Village March 1st 1691

Tituba, an Indian woman, brought before us by Constable Joseph Herrick of Salem upon suspicion of witchcraft by her committed according to the complaint of Joseph Hutcheson and Thomas Putnam and of Salem Village as appears a warrant granted Salem 29 February 1691/2 Tituba upon examination and after some denial acknowledged the matter of fact according to her examination given in more fully will appear and who also charged Sarah Good and Sarah Osburne with the same Salem Village March the 1st 1691/2.

Sarah Good, Sarah Osburne, and Tituba, an Indian woman, all of Salem Village being this day brought before us upon suspicion of witchcraft and by them and every one of them committed. Tituba an Indian woman acknowledging the matter of fact and Sarah Osburne and Sarah Good denying the same before us but there appearing in all their examinations sufficient ground to secure them all. And in order to further examination they were all mittimus sent to the jails in the County of Essex.

Salem March 2nd Sarah Osburne again examined and also Tituba as will appear in their examinations given in.

Tituba again acknowledged the fact and also accuse the other two. Salem March 3rd Sarah Osburne and Tituba Indian again examined the examination now given in Tituba again said the same.

Salem March 5th Sarah Good and Tituba again examined and in their examination Tituba acknowledged the same she did formerly and accused the other two-abovesaid—Tituba again said the same.

p. us. *John Hathorne [unclear] Assis'ts
*Jonathan Corwin

Source: Essex County Court Archives, vol. 1, Massachusetts Supreme Judicial Court, Judicial Archives, on deposit James Duncan Phillips Library, Peabody Essex Museum, Salem, MA.

Document 11

CONSTABLE GEORGE LOCKER, "OFFICER'S RETURN," MARCH 1, 1691/1692

An "officer's return" is the official report of the court-appointed officer given the often difficult task to find, arrest, and transport individuals named in the court's warrant. In these brief documents, the court officer, often a sheriff or marshal, would simply acknowledge that they had fulfilled their assignment and delivered the person, or persons named in the warrant to the jail for safe keeping until the time of the first examination by the court. The following is a report on the arrest of Sarah Good, one of the first three persons accused of witchcraft during the Salem episode.

I brought the person of Sarah Good the wife of William Good according to the tenor of the within warrant as is Attest by me 1 March, 1691/2

  *George Locker, Constable

Source: Essex County Court Archives, vol. 1, Massachusetts Supreme Judicial Court, Judicial Archives, on deposit James Duncan Phillips Library, Peabody Essex Museum, Salem, MA.

Document 12

UNKNOWN, "TITUBA'S SECOND EXAMINATION," MARCH 2, 1691/1692

Tituba was essentially a limitless source of detail concerning the extent of the conspiracy and the activities of the coven of witches operating in the greater Salem area. From her vivid testimony came vast amounts of data concerning the who, what, and where of the Satanic activities of the witches being sought by the court.

Question: What Covenant did you make with that man that came to you? What did he tell you?

Answer: He tell me God, and I must believe him and serve him six years and he would give me many fine things.

Question: How long a gone was this?

Answer: About six weeks and a little more Friday night before Abigail was ill.

Question: What did he say you must do more? Did he say you must write anything? Did he offer you any paper?

Answer: Yes, the next time he come to me and showed me some fine things, something like creatures, a little bird something like green and white.

Question: Did you promise him then when he spoke to you then what did you answer him?

Answer: I then said this I told him I could not believe him God, I told him I ask my master and would have gone up but he stopped me and would not let me.

Question: What did you promise him?

Answer: The first time I believe him God and then he was glad.

Question: What did he say to you then? What did he say you must do?

Answer: Then he tell me they must meet together.

Question: When did he say you must meet together?

Answer: He tell me Wednesday next at my master's house, and then they all meet together and that night I saw them all stand in the corner, all four of them, and the man stand behind me and take hold of me to make me stand still in the hall.

Question: Where was your master then?

Answer: In the other room.

Question: What time of night?

Answer: A little before prayer time.

Question: What did this man say to you when he took hold of you?

Answer: He say go and do hurt to them and pinch them and then I went in, and would not hurt them.

Question: Did they pinch?

Answer: No, but they all looked on and see me pinch them.

Question: Did you go into that room in your own person and all the rest?

Answer: Yes, and my master did not see us, for they would not let my master see.

Question: Did you go with the company?

Answer: No I stayed and the man stayed with me.

Question: What did he then do to you?

Answer: He tell me my master go to prayer and he read in book and he ask me what I remember, but don't you remember anything.

Question: Did he ask you no more but the first time to serve him or the second time?

Answer: Yes, he ask me again, and that I serve him six years and he come the next time and show me a book.

Question: And when would he come then?

Answer: The next Friday and showed me a book in the day time betimes in the morning.

Question: And what book did he bring a great or little book?

Answer: He did not show it me, nor would not, but had it in his pocket.

Question: Did not he make you write your name?

Answer: No not yet for mistress called me into the other room.

Question: What did he say you must do in that book?

Answer: He said write and set my name to it.

Question: Did you write?

Answer: Yes once I make a mark in the book and made it with red blood.

Question: Did he get it out of your body?

Answer: He said he must get it out the next time he come again, he gave me a pin tied in a stick to do it with, but he no let me blood with it as yet but intended another time when he come again.

Question: Did you see any other marks in his book?

Answer: Yes a great many come marks red, some yellow, he opened his book a great many marks in it.

Question: Did he tell you the names of them?

Answer: They made marks Goody Good said she made her mark, but Goody Osburne would not tell she was cross to me.

Question: When did Good tell you, she set her hand to the book?

Answer: The same day I came hither to prison.

Question: Did you see the man that morning?

Answer: Yes a little in the morning and he tell me the Magistrates come up to examine me.

Question: What did he say you must say?

Answer: He tell me, tell nothing, if I did he would cut my head off.

Question: Tell us [true] how many women do use to come when you ride abroad?

Answer: Four of them these two Osburne and Good and those two strangers.

Question: You say that there was nine did he tell you who they were?

Answer: No he no let me see but he tell me I should see them the next time.

Question: What sights did you see?

Answer: I see a man, a dog, a hog, and two cats a black and red and the strange monster was Osburne that I mentioned before this was the hairy Imp. The man would give it to me, but I would not have it.

Question: Did he show you in the book which was Osburne and which was Good's mark?

Answer: Yes I see there marks.

Question: But did he tell the names of the other?

Answer: No sir.

Question: And what did he say to you when you made your mark?

Answer: He said serve me and always serve me the man with the two women came from Boston.

Question: How many times did you go to Boston?

Answer: I was going and then came back again I was never at Boston.

Question: Who came back with you again?

Answer: The man came back with me and the women go away, I was not willing to go.

Question: Did he tell you where the nine lived?

Answer: Yes, some in Boston and some herein this town, but he would not tell me where they were.

Source: Examination of Tituba (Mass.-Essex Co. Box); Manuscripts and Archives Division; The New York Public Library; Astor, Lenox, and Tilden Foundations, on deposit James Duncan Phillips Library, Peabody Essex Museum, Salem, MA.

Document 13

UNKNOWN, "MARY WALCOTT V. DOROTHY GOOD," MARCH 21, 1691/1692

Mary Walcott was, through her father's second marriage, directly connected to the family of Thomas Putnam and particularly his daughter Ann Putnam Jr. This family connection places Mary at the very center of the group of "afflicted girls" responsible for generating the greatest part of the spectral evidence responsible for convicting most of the victims during the trials. In this document, she is accusing Dorothy, the four-year-old daughter of Sarah Good of afflicting her with witchcraft and tempting her to join the followers of Satan by writing in the "Devil's Book."

The deposition of Mary Walcott aged about 17 years who testifeth that about the 21: march 1691/92 I saw the Apparition of Dorothy good. Sarah Goods daughter come to me and bit me and pinch me and so she continued afflicting me by times tell 24 march being the day of her examination and then she did torment and afflict me most grievously during the time of her examination and also several times since the Apparition of Dorothy good has afflicted me by biting pinching and almost choking me urging me to write in her book.

(Reverse) Mary Walcott against Dorothy Good—Dorothy good

Source: Essex County Court Archives, vol. 1, no. 64, Massachusetts Supreme Judicial Court, Judicial Archives, on deposit James Duncan Phillips Library, Peabody Essex Museum, Salem, MA.

Document 14

JOHN HATHORNE AND JONATHAN CORWIN, "WARRANT V. DOROTHY GOOD," MARCH 23, 1691/1692

The following warrant is the result of several depositions submitted to the court by the "afflicted girls" against four-year-old, Dorothy Good, daughter of Sarah Good, who was also arrested under suspicion of witchcraft. Dorothy Good would remain under arrest until December 1692, a period of over 10 months.

To The Marshall of Essex or his Dep't.
    You are in their Majests names hereby required to bring before us Dorcas Good the Daugter of W'm Good of Salem Village tomorrow morning upon suspicion of acts of Witchcraft by her committed according to Complaints made against her by Edw'd Putnam & Jonat putnam of Salem Village and hereof faile not
    Dated Salem. March 23d 1681/2
    P us
    *John Hathorne Assists.

*Jonathan Corwin Assists.

March 23d. 1791/2. I doe apoint mr Sam'll Bradbrook to bee my lawffull Deputy, to serve this summons and to make A true Returne

p'r *George Herrick Marshall of Essex.

Source: Essex County Court Archives, vol. 1, no. 61, Massachusetts Supreme Judicial Court, Judicial Archives, on deposit James Duncan Phillips Library, Peabody Essex Museum, Salem, MA.

Document 15

SAMUEL BRAYBROOK, "OFFICER'S RETURN," MARCH 24, 1691/1692

Samuel Braybrook, deputy marshal of Essex County, Massachusetts, was assigned the task of finding and arresting, Dorothy Good, the four-year-old daughter of Sarah Good, who was under suspicion of having committed acts of witchcraft against several of the "afflicted girls" who gave spectral evidence against her. Perhaps out of kindness or convenience, rather than delivering her immediately to the Salem jail, he left her in the temporary care of local militia Lieutenant Nathaniel Ingersoll, the proprietor of Ingersoll's Tavern in Salem Village. This is Braybrook's official report to the court that the suspected witch had been successfully apprehended.

(Reverse)

March 24. 1691/2 I have taken the body of Dorothy Good and brought her to the house of lieut Nath: Ingersol and is in Costody

*Samuel Braybrook

Marshall's Deputy.

Source: Essex County Court Archives, vol. 1, no. 61, Massachusetts Supreme Judicial Court, Judicial Archives, on deposit James Duncan Phillips Library, Peabody Essex Museum, Salem, MA.

Document 16

UNKNOWN, "ANN PUTNAM, JR. V. DOROTHY GOOD," MARCH 24, 1691/1692

The following deposition was filed by Ann Putnam Jr. in an effort to bring about the arrest of four-year-old Dorothy Good, daughter of suspected witch, Sarah Good. It should be noted that, in past outbreaks of witchcraft in New England, it was not unusual for both a mother and daughter to be suspected and accused. Dorothy would not be tried or hanged, while her mother would be executed on July 19, 1692, leaving her young daughter still in prison.

The Deposition of Ann Putnam who testifieth and saith that on the 3th March 1691/92 I saw the Apparition of Dorothy Good, Sarah Good's daughter who did immediately almost choke me and tortured me most grievously: and so she hath several times since tortured me by biting and pinching and almost choking me tempting me also to writ in her book and also on the day of her examination being the 24 March 1691/92 the Apparition of Dorothy Good ly torture me during the time of her Examination and several times since.

(Reverse) Ann Putnam against Dorothy Good

Source: Essex County Court Archives, vol. 1, no. 63, Massachusetts Supreme Judicial Court, Judicial Archives, on deposit James Duncan Phillips Library, Peabody Essex Museum, Salem, MA.

Document 17

JOHN HATHORNE AND JONATHAN CORWIN, "EXAMINATION OF REBECCA NURSE," MARCH 24, 1691/1692

Ann Putnam Jr. was initially responsible for accusing and involving elderly Rebecca Towne Nurse, a person of high moral character, whose neighbors submitted a testimonial signed by 39 individuals. At her trial held on June 29, 1692, the jury found her innocent, but Chief Justice William Stoughton asked the jury to reconsider their verdict. The result was a reversal of their decision. Rebecca was hanged on July 19 along with four other female victims.

The examination of Rebecca Nurse at Salem Village 24th March 1691/2

Question:	What do you say (speaking to one afflicted) have you seen this woman hurt you?
Answer:	Yes, she beat me this morning
Question:	Abigail. Have you been hurt by this woman?
Answer:	Yes. Ann Putnam in a grievous fit cried out that she hurt her.
Question:	Goody Nurse, here are two Ann Putnam the child and Abigail Williams complains of your hurting them. What do you say to it?
Answer:	I can say before my eternal father I am innocent and God will clear my innocency.
Questioner:	Here is never a one in the Assembly but desires it, but if you be guilty pray God discover you. Then Hen. Kenny rose up to speak.
Question:	Goodman Kenny what do you say?

Then he entered his complaint and further said that since this Nurse came into the house he was seized twice with an amazed condition.

Questioner: Here are not only these but, here is the wife of Mr. Thomas Putnam who accused you by credible information and that both of tempting her to iniquity, and of greatly hurting her.

Answer: I am innocent and clear and have not been able to get out of doors these eight or nine days.

Questioner: Mr. Putnam, give in what you have to say
Then Mr. Edward Putnam gave in his relate.

Question: Is this true Goody Nurse?

Answer: I never afflicted no child never in my life.

Question: You see these accuse you, is it true?

Answer: No.
Here Thomas Putnam's wife cried out, Did you not bring the Black man with you, did you not bid me tempt God and die how oft have you eat and drunk your own demon? What do you say to them?

Answer: Oh Lord help me, and spread out her hands, and the afflicted were grievously vexed.

Question: Do you not see what a solemn condition these are in? When your hands are loose the persons are afflicted.
Then Mary Walcott (who often heretofore said she had seen her, but never could say or did say that she either bit or pinched her, or hurt her) and also Elizabeth Hubbard under the like circumstances both openly accused her or hurting them.

Question: Here are these two grown persons now accuse you, what say you? Do not you see these afflicted persons, and hear them accuse you?

Answer: The Lord knows I have not hurt them. I am an innocent person.

Question: It is very awful to all to see these agonies and you an old Professor thus charged with contracting with the Devil by the [a] effects of it and yet to see you stand with dry eyes when there are so many whet—

Answer: You do not know my heart.

Question: You would do well if you are guilty to confess and give glory to God.

Answer: I am as clear as the child unborn.

Question: What uncertainty there may be in apparitions I know not, yet this with me strikes hard upon you that you are at this very present charged with familiar spirits this is your bodily person they speak to they say now they see these familiar spirits com to your bodily [spirits com to your bodily] person, now what do you say to that?

Answer: I have none Sir.

Question: If you have, confess and give glory to God I pray God clear you if you be innocent, and if you are guilty discover you and therefore give me an upright answer. Have you any familiarity with these spirits?

Answer: No, I have none but with God alone.

Question: How came you [to be] sick for there is an odd discourse of that in the mouths of many—

Answer: I am sick at my stomach—

Question: Have you no wounds?

Answer: I have none but old age.

Question: You do Know whither you are guilty, and have familiarity with the Devil, and now when you are here present to see such a thing as these testify a black man whispering in your ear, and birds about you what do you say to it?

Answer: It is all false. I am clear.

Question: Possibly you may apprehend you are no witch, but have you not been led aside by temptations that way?

Answer: I have not.

Question: What a sad thing it is that a church member here and now another of Salem, should be thus accused and charged.

Mrs. Pope fell into a grievous fit, and cried out a sad thing sure enough. And then many more fell into lamentable fits.

Question: Tell us have not you had visible appearances more than what is common in nature?

Answer: I have no nor never had in my life.

Question: Do you think these suffer voluntary or involuntary?

Answer: I cannot tell.

Question: That is strange everyone can judge.

Answer: I must be silent.

Question: They accuse you of hurting them, and if you think it is not unwillingly but by design, you must look upon them as murderers?

Answer: I cannot tell what to think of it.

Afterwards when this was somewhat insisted on she said I do not think so. She did not understand aright what was said.

Question: Well then give an answer now, do you think these suffer against their wills or not?

Answer: I do not think these suffer against their wills.

Question: Why did you never visit these afflicted persons?

Answer: Because I was afraid I should have fits too.

> *Note:* Upon the motion of her body fits followed upon the complainants abundantly and very frequently.

Question: Is it not unaccountable case that when you are examined these persons are afflicted?

Answer: I have got nobody to look to but God.
Again upon stirring her hands the afflicted persons were seized with violent fits of torture?

Question: Do you believe these afflicted persons are bewitched?

Answer: I do think they are.
When this witchcraft came upon the stage there was no suspicion of Tituba (Mr. Parris's Indian woman) she professed much love to that child Betty Parris, but it was her apparition did the mischief, and why should not you also be guilty, for your apparition doth hurt also.

Answer: Would you have me belie myself—
She held her neck on one side, and accordingly so were the afflicted taken.
Then authority requiring it Samuel Parris read what he had in characters taken from Mr. Thomas Putnam's wife in her fits.

Question: What do you think of this?

Answer: I cannot help it, the Devil may appear in my shape.

This is a true account of the some of her examination but by reason of great noises by the afflicted and many speakers, many things are pretermitted.

Memorandum

Nurse held her neck on one side and Elizabeth Hubbard (one of the sufferers) had her neck set in that posture whereupon another patient Abigail Williams cried out set up Goody Nurse's head the maid's neck will be broke and when some set up Nurse's head Aaron Wey observed that Betty Hubbard's was immediately righted.

Salem Village March 24th 1691/2

The Reverend Mr. Samuel Parris being desired to take in writing the examination of Rebecca Nurse had returned it as aforesaid.

Upon hearing the aforesaid and seeing what we then did see together with the charge of the persons then present—we committed Rebecca Nurse the wife of Francis Nurse of Salem Village unto their Majesty's Jail in Salem as p a Mittimus then given out, in order to further examination.

*John Hathorne Assis'ts
*Jonathan Corwin

Source: Essex County Court Archives, vol. 1, no. 72, Massachusetts Supreme Judicial Court, Judicial Archives, on deposit James Duncan Phillips Library, Peabody Essex Museum, Salem, MA.

Document 18

UNKNOWN, "MERCY LEWIS V. DOROTHY GOOD," APRIL 3, 1692

Mercy Lewis was a 19-year-old domestic servant, whose parents had been killed in the Indian wars on the Maine frontier. She was given a position as a servant with the Putnam family, and as such she was very closely tied to Ann Putnam Jr. and became one of the primary "afflicted girls" in Ann Putnam's circle, accusing many of the same individuals targeted by Ann Putnam. In this deposition, she claims that a precocious, four-year-old Dorothy Good—daughter of suspected witch Sarah Good—brought the "Devil's Book" to her to sign, tempting her thereby to become a witch by agreeing to give her soul to Satan.

The Deposition of Mercy Lewis aged about 19 years who testifieth and saith that on the 3d April 1692 the Apparition of Dorothy Good Sarah Goods daughter came to me and did afflict me, urging me to writ in her book.
   (Reverse) Mercy Lewis against Dorothy Good

Source: Essex County Court Archives, vol. 1, no. 62, Massachusetts Supreme Judicial Court, Judicial Archives, on deposit James Duncan Phillips Library, Peabody Essex Museum, Salem, MA.

Document 19

JOHN HATHORNE AND JONATHAN CORWIN, "INDICTMENT NO. 1 V. SARAH CLOYCE, FOR AFFLICTING ABIGAIL WILLIAMS," APRIL 9, 1692

Abigail Williams, the author of this deposition, was the niece of Reverend Samuel Parris and resided in his home at the outbreak of the trials. At that time, she was 11 years of age. She is known, together with her cousin, Betty Parris, as the first to exhibit strange behavior during the winter of 1691/1692, which would be diagnosed by the local physician, Doctor Griggs, as attributed to "the evil hand" of witchcraft. Ultimately, she would accuse Tituba, Sarah Good, and Sarah Osborne of being responsible for her torment. As the trials progressed, she would accuse many more individuals, Sarah Cloyce among them.

Essex in the Province of the Massachusetts Bay in New England
Anno RR's & Reginae & Mariae Angliae &c Quarto Annoq'e Domini 1692.

The Jurors for our Soveraigne Lord & Lady the King and Queen
doe present That Sarah Cloyce Wife of Peter Cloyce of Salem—
in the County of Essex Husbandman upon or about the n'th Day of April—In the yeare aforesaid and divers other Days and times as
well before as after Certaine Detestable Arts called Witchcraft and
Sorceries Wickedly Mallitiously and felloniously hath used practised

and Exercised At and in the Towne of Salem in the Country of
Essex—aforesaid in upon and against one Abigail Williams of Salem—
aforesaid Single Woman—by which said Wicked Acts the said
Abigaill Williams the Day & Yeare—aforesaid and Divers other Days
and times both before and after was and is Tortured Aflicted Con-
sumed Wasted Pined and Tormented against the Peace of our Sov'r
Lord and Lady the King & Queen theire Crowne and Dignity and
The Law In that case made and Provided

(Reverse)
Ignoramus
Robert Payne
foreman

Source: Suffolk Court Files, docket no. 2677b, p. 8. James Duncan Phillips Library,
Peabody Essex Museum, Salem, MA.

Document 20

JOHN HATHORNE AND JONATHAN CORWIN, "INDICTMENT NO. 2 V. SARAH CLOYCE, FOR AFFLICTING MARY WALCOTT," APRIL 9, 1692

*The following indictment was prepared and submitted by the court under the jurisdiction
of the Honorable John Hathorne and Jonathan Corwin. It accuses Sarah Cloyce, sister
of Rebecca Nurse and Mary Easty, as being guilty of having committed acts of witchcraft against Mary Walcott. The accusation of Sarah Cloyce followed quickly after she
had attempted to defend her sister Rebecca from the charge of witchcraft. She would be
arrested as a result and made to spend the remainder of 1692 in jail until her release in
January 1692/1693.*

Essex in the Province of the Massachusetts Bay in New England
Anno RR's & Reginae Gulielmi & Mariae Angliae &c Quarto Annoq'e Domini, 1692
The Jurors for our Sovereign Lord and Lady the King and Queen do
present that Sarah Cloyce wife of Peter Cloyce of Salem—In the
County of Essex In or upon the Eleventh Day of April—In the year aforesaid
and Divers other Days and times as well before as
after Certain detestable arts called Withcrafts and Sorceries Wickedly Maliciously and feloniously hath used practised and Exercised At
and in the Towne of Salem—aforesaid in the County of Essex—
aforesaid in and upon & against one Mary Walcott of Salem—aforesaid Single Woman—by which said Wicked acts the said Mary Walcott—
the Day & year—aforesaid and divers other Days and times
both before and after was and is Tortured Afflicted Consumed Wasted
Pined and Tormented, and also for Sundry other Acts of Witchcraft
by the said Sarah Cloyce—Committed and done before and since that

time against the Peace of our Sovereign Lord and Lady the King and
Queen their Crown and Dignity and the form in the Statute
In that case made and Provided

(Reverse)
Ignoramus.
*Robert Payne
foreman

Source: Suffolk Court Files docket no. 2677a, p. 7. James Duncan Phillips Library, Peabody Essex Museum, Salem, MA.

Document 21

JOHN HATHORNE AND JONATHAN CORWIN, "WARRANT FOR THE ARREST OF GILES COREY, MARY WARREN, ABIGAIL HOBBS, AND BRIDGET BISHOP," APRIL 18, 1692

The following warrant document instructs George Herrick, Marshall of Essex County, to apprehend four individuals who have been cried out against by the afflicted girls. It is mid-April, and Governor Sir William Phips, bearing the new Massachusetts charter, has not yet arrived. What this document signifies is that the four individuals listed are to be arrested and brought before the local justices, John Hathorne and Jonathan Corwin, for a pretrial examination to determine if there is sufficient evidence to remand them to jail to be held for a trial. Of these four, only two would lose their lives; Bridget Bishop would be hanged and Giles Cory would be pressed to death.

Salem. April the 18th 1692
There being complaint this day made (before us) by Ezekiel Cheever and John Putnam Junior both of Salem Village yeomen in behalf of their Majesties, for themselves and also for their neighbors against Giles Corey, and Mary Warren both of Salem farms and Abigail Hobbs the daughter of William Hobbs of the Town of Topsfield and Bridget Bishop the wife of Edward Bishop of Salem Sawyer for high suspicion of sundry acts of witchcraft done of committed by them, upon the bodies of Ann Putnam, Mercy Lewis, and Abigail Williams, and Mary Walcott, and Elizabeth Hubbard—of Salem village—whereby great hurt and damage hath been done to the bodies of said persons above named. Therefore craved justice.

You are therefore in their Majesties names hereby required to apprehend and bring before us Giles Corey and Mary Warren of Salem farms, and Abigail Hobbs the daughter of William Hobbs of the Town of Topsfield and Bridget Bishop the wife of Edward Bishop of Salem tomorrow about eight of the clock in the forenoon, at the house of Lieutenant Nathaniel Ingersall's in Salem Village in order to their examination relating to the premises abovesaid and here of you are not to fail. Dated Salem April 18th 1692

To George Herrick Marshall of the County of Essex—
*John Hathorne
*Jonathan Corwin Assis'ts

Source: Essex County Court Archives, vol. 1, no. 112, Massachusetts Supreme Judicial Court, Judicial Archives, on deposit James Duncan Phillips Library, Peabody Essex Museum, Salem, MA.

Document 22

SAMUEL PARRIS, "EXAMINATION OF BRIDGET BISHOP, FIRST VERSION," APRIL 19, 1692

Bridget Bishop probably did not help her case when she decided to respond to the initial, pre-examination inquiries in a belligerent manner. Perhaps she was reacting to the obviously leading questions from a magistrate—Hon. John Hathorne—who seemed already convinced of her guilt. Her bold and remarkable observation that if she "were any such a person, you would certainly know it" was clearly a thinly veiled threat to the court, and unique in the annals of the Salem trials. On April 19, the court examined a total of only four possible suspects: Mary Warren, Abigail Hobbs, Giles Corey, and Bridget Bishop.

The Examination of Bridget Bishop at Salem Village 19th April 1692
    By John Hathorne and Jonathon Corwin Esquires
    As soon as she came near all fell into fits

Examiners:	Bridget Bishop, you are now brought before authority to give account of what witchcrafts you are conversant in.
Bridget:	I take all this people (turning her head and eyes about) to witness that I am clear.
Examiners:	Hath this woman hurt you? (Speaking to the afflicted.) Elizabeth Hubbard, Ann Putnam, Abigail Williams, and Mercy Lewis affirmed she had hurt them.
Examiners:	You are here accused by four or five for hurting them, what do you say to it?
Bridget:	I never saw these persons before, nor I never was in this place before. Mary Walcott said that her brother Jonathan stroke her appearance and she saw that he had tore her coat in striking, and she heard it tear. Upon some search in the court, a rent that seems to answer what was alleged was found.
Examiners:	They say you bewitch your first husband to death.
Bridget:	If it please your worship I know nothing of it. (She shakes her head and the afflicted were tortured.)

(The like again upon the motion of her head.)

Sam Braybrook affirmed that she told him to day that she had been accounted a witch these ten years, but she was no witch, the Devil cannot hurt her.

Bridget: I am no witch.

Examiners: Why if you have not wrote in the book, yet tell me how far you have gone? Have you not to do with familiar spirits?

Bridget: I have no familiarity with the Devil.

Examiners: How is it then, that your appearance doth hurt these?

Bridget: I am innocent.

Examiners: Why you seem to act witchcraft before us, by the motion of your body, which seems to have influence upon the afflicted.

Bridget: I know nothing of it. I am innocent to a witch. I know not what a witch is.

Examiners: How do you know, you are no Witch, and yet not know what a Witch is.

Bridget: I am clear if I were any such person you should know it.

Examiners: You may threaten, but you can do no more than you are permitted.

Bridget: I am innocent of a witch.

Examiners: What do you say of those murders you are charged with?

Bridget: I hope, I am not guilty of murder.

Then she turned her eyes, the eyes of the afflicted were turned up.

Examiners: It may be you do not know, that any have confessed to day, who have been examined before you, that they are witches.

Bridget: No. I know nothing of it.

John Hutchinson and John Lewis in open court affirmed that they had told her.

Examiners: Why look you, you are taken now in a flat lie.

Bridget: I did not hear them.

Note: Sam Gold said that after this examination he asked said Bridget Bishop if she were not troubled to see the afflicted persons so tormented, said Bishop answered no, she was not troubled for them. Then he asked her whither she thought they were bewitched, she said she could not tell what to think about them. Will Good, and John Buxton Jr. was by, and he supposed they heard her also.

Salem Village April the 19th 1692 Mr. Samuel Parris being desired to take into writing the examination of Bridget Bishop, had delivered it as aforesaid. And upon hearing the same, and seeing what we did then see, together with the charge of the afflicted persons then present. We committed said Bridget Olliver.

*John Hathorne

Source: Essex County Court Archives, vol. 1, Massachusetts Supreme Judicial Court, Judicial Archives, on deposit James Duncan Phillips Library, Peabody Essex Museum, Salem, MA.

Document 23

JOHN RUCKE, "INDICTMENT V. BRIDGET BISHOP, NO. 1," APRIL 19, 1692

The following document is an example of a formal indictment against the first person to be hanged during the Salem witch trial episode, Bridget Bishop. What is interesting is that despite all the extensive testimony and many depositions against Bishop, the indictment mentions only the name of one individual, 19-year-old Mercy Lewis, as the hurt and afflicted object of Bishop's alleged witchcraft. Mercy Lewis, like Susannah Sheldon and Ann Putman Jr., is one of the central members of the inner circle of afflicted girls. She is also a victim of the Maine Indian wars and a domestic servant of the Putnam family.

Anno Regni Regis et Reginae William et Mariae nunc Angliae and Quarto.

Essex Ss

The Jurors for our Sovereign Lord and Lady the King and Queen presents that Bridget Bishop als Olliver the wife of Edward Bishop of Salem in the County of Essex Sawyer the nineteenth day of April in the fourth year of the reign of our Sovereign Lord and Lady William and Mary by the Grace of God of England, Scotland, France, and Ireland King and Queen defenders of the faith and diverse other days and time as well before as after certain detestable arts called witchcraft and sorceries wickedly and feloniously hath used, practiced, and exercised, at and within the Township of Salem in the County of Essex aforesaid in upon and against one Mercy Lewis of Salem Village in the County aforesaid singlewoman by which said wicked arts the said Mercy Lewis—the said nineteenth day of April in the fourth year abovesaid and diverse other days and times as well before as after, was and is hurt, tortured, afflicted, pined, consumed, wasted, and tormented against the peace of our said Sovereign Lord and Lady the King and Queen and against the form of the statute in that case made and provided.

Witnesses
Mercy Lewis
Nathaniel Ingersoll
Mr. Samuel Parris
Thomas Putnam Junior
Mary Walcott
Ann Putnam Junior
Elizabeth Hubbard
Abigail Williams

*John Rucke foreman in the name of the rest of the Grand Jury.

Source: Essex County Court Archives, vol. 1, no. 121, Massachusetts Supreme Judicial Court, Judicial Archives, on deposit James Duncan Phillips Library, Peabody Essex Museum, Salem, MA.

Document 24

JOHN RUCKE, "INDICTMENT V. BRIDGET BISHOP, NO. 2," APRIL 19, 1692

The following second example of a formal indictment follows the precedent set by the first against Bridget Bishop in identifying only one victim, in this case, Abigail Williams, the 11-year-old niece of Reverend Samuel Parris. Since these two indictments essentially begin the process of the trials, it is important to note the names of those who, at this early date, are witnessing each document and helping to push the trials to the next level of intensity: Mercy Lewis, Ann Putnam Jr., Thomas Putnam, Reverend Samuel Parris, Mary Walcott, Elizabeth Hubbard, Nathaniel Ingersoll, John and Rebecca Bly, their son, William Bly, Samuel and Sarah Shattuck, and John Louder.

Anno Regni Regis et Reginae William et Mariae nunc Angliae and Quarto
  Essex Ss
The Jurors for our Sovereign Lord and Lady the King and Queen present that Bridget Bishop alias Olliver the wife of Edward Bishop of Salem in the County of Essex Sawyer—the nineteenth day of April in the fourth year of the reign of our Sovereign Lord and Lady William and Mary by the Grace of God of England, Scotland, France, and Ireland King and Queen defenders of the faith and diverse other days and times as well before as after, certain detestable arts called witchcrafts and sorceries wickedly and feloniously hath used, practiced, and exercised at and within the township of Salem in the County of Essex aforesaid in upon and against one Abigail Williams of Salem Village in the County of Essex aforesaid single-woman by which said wicked arts the said Abigail Williams the nineteenth day of April aforesaid in the fourth Year abovesaid and diverse other Days and times as well before as after, was, and is tortured, afflicted, pined, consumed, wasted, and tormented against the peace of our said Sovereign Lord and Lady the King and Queen and against the form of the statute in that case made and provided.

Witnesses
Abigail Williams
Mr. Samuel Parris sworn
Nathaniel Ingersoll sworn
Thomas Putnam sworn
Mercy Lewis
Ann Putnam Junior sworn
Mary Walcott sworn
Elizabeth Hubbard sworn
John Bly and Rebecca his wife sworn
Samuel Shattuck and Sarah his wife sworn
William Bly sworn
William Stacey sworn
John Louder sworn

*John Rucke foreman in the name of the rest.

Source: Essex County Court Archives, vol. 1, no. 122, Massachusetts Supreme Judicial Court, Judicial Archives, on deposit James Duncan Phillips Library, Peabody Essex Museum, Salem, MA.

Document 25

JOHN RUCKE, "INDICTMENT V. BRIDGET BISHOP, NO. 3," APRIL 19, 1692

In the following document, Elizabeth Hubbard, another orphan of the Maine Indian wars was, like Susannah Sheldon, one of the central members of the inner circle of afflicted children. She initially cried out against Sarah Good and Sarah Osborne, but quickly also developed symptoms of affliction from Bridget Bishop as well. She is supported in the indictment by essentially the same crowd of witnesses as seen in the two previous indictments.

Anno Regni Regis et Reginae Willima et Mariae nunc Angliae and Quarto
Essex Ss
The Jurors for our Sovereign Lord and Lady the King and Queen present that Bridget Bishop als Olliver the wife of Edward Bishop of Salem in the County of Essex Sawyer—the nineteenth day of April—in the fourth year of the reign of our Sovereign Lord and Lady William and Mary by the Grace of God of England, Scotland, France, and Ireland King and Queen defenders of the faith and diverse other days and times as well before as after, certain detestable arts, called witchcraft and sorceries, wickedly and feloniously hath used, practiced and exercised, at and within the Township of Salem in the County of Essex aforesaid in an upon and against one woman—by which said wicked arts the said Elizabeth Hubbard the said nineteenth day of April—in the fourth year abovesaid and diverse other days, and times as well before as after was and is hurt, tortured, afflicted, pined, consumed, wasted, and tormented against the peace of our said Sovereign Lord and Lady the King and Queen, and against the form of the statute in that case made and provided.

Witnesses
Elizabeth Hubbard
Mercy Lewis
Mr. Samuel Parris
Nathaniel Ingersoll
Thomas Putnam
Ann Putnam Junior
Mary Walcott
Abigail Williams

*John Rucke foreman in the name of the rest.

Source: Essex County Court Archives, vol. 1, no. 123, Massachusetts Supreme Judicial Court, Judicial Archives, on deposit James Duncan Phillips Library, Peabody Essex Museum, Salem, MA.

Document 26

JOHN RUCKE, "INDICTMENT V. BRIDGET BISHOP, NO. 4," APRIL 19, 1692

Twelve-year-old Ann Putnam Jr. is perhaps the most notorious of all the members of the inner circle of the afflicted children. Following Betty Parris's removal from Salem Village, Ann assumed the role of leader of the group. She was also a leading source of depositions, crying out against at least 62 persons throughout the course of the trials. Her father, Thomas Putnam, was also heavily involved in instigating legal procedures against many alleged witches. Despite her leading role in the accusations throughout the duration of the trials, Ann Jr. would seek forgiveness in 1706, when she would stand before the congregation of Salem Village Church while their new minister Reverend Joseph Green reads her personal apology for her actions during the episode.

Anno Regni Regis et Reginae Willim et Mariae nunc Angliae and Quarto
  Essex Ss
  The Jurors for our Sovereign Lord and Lady the King and Queen present that Bridget Bishop alias Olliver the wife of Edward Bishop of Salem in the County of Essex Sawyer the nineteenth day of April—in the fourth year of the reign of our Sovereign Lord and Lady William and Mary by the Grace of God of England, Scotland, France, and Ireland King and Queen defenders of the faith and diverse other days and times as well before as after certain detestable arts called witchcraft and sorceries, wickedly and feloniously have used, practiced, and exercised at and within the Township of Salem, aforesaid in upon against one Ann Putnam of Salem Village in the County aforesaid single-woman by which said wicked arts the Ann Putnam the said nineteenth day of April in the fourth year abovesaid and diverse other days and times as well before as after was and is hurt, tortured, afflicted, pined, consumed, wasted, and tormented against the peace of our said Sovereign Lord and Lady the King and Queen and against the form of the statute in that case made and provided.

Witnesses
Ann Putnam Junior
Mr. Samuel Parris
Nathaniel Ingersoll
Thomas Putnam
Mercy Lewis

Mary Walcott
Abigail Williams
Elizabeth Hubbard

*John Rucke foreman in the name of the rest
Bills against Bridget Bishop alias Olliver bound by the Grand Inquest Folio 966

Source: Essex County Court Archives, vol. 1, no. 124, Massachusetts Supreme Judicial Court, Judicial Archives, on deposit James Duncan Phillips Library, Peabody Essex Museum, Salem, MA.

Document 27

JOHN HATHORNE AND JONATHAN CORWIN, "EXAMINATION OF MARY WARREN," APRIL 19, 1692

Mary Warren was, at the time of the Salem episode, an orphaned maidservant serving in the household of John and Elizabeth Proctor, both of whom would later be convicted of witchcraft. During the initial stages of the trials, she was one of the inner circle of afflicted girls, but her master, John Proctor, displeased with her behavior brought her home and "kept her close to the spinning wheel & threatened to thrash her & she had no more fits until the next day. . . ." She became one of the first "confessed witches" after she was accused by the court, then turned state's evidence by providing the justices with testimony attacking those whom she claimed to be in league with: John and Elizabeth Proctor and Alice Parker. Both John Proctor and Alice Parker would be hanged. Elizabeth Proctor escaped execution by explaining to the court she was pregnant.

The Examination of Mary Warren at a court held at Salem Village
    by John Hathorne Esquires and Jonathan Corwin
    As soon as she was coming towards the bar the afflicted fell into fits.

Question: Mary Warren, you stand here charged with sundry acts of witchcraft, what do you say for yourself, are you guilty, or not?

Answer: I am innocent.

Question: Hath she hurt you (speaking to the sufferers—some were dumb).

    Betty Hubbard testified against her, then said Hubbard fell into a violent fit.

Question: You were a little while ago an afflicted person, now you are an afflicter. How comes this to pass?

Answer: I look up to God, and take it to be a great mercy of God.

Question: What do you take it to be a great mercy to afflict others?

Answer: Betty Hubbard testified that a little after this Mary was well, she the said Mary, said that the afflicted persons did but dissemble.

Now they were all but John Indian grievously afflicted, and Mrs. Pope also, who was not afflicted before hitherto this day and after a few moments John Indian fell into a violent fit also.

Well here was one just now that was a tormentor in her apparition and she owns that she had made a league with the Devil.

Now Mary Warren fell into a fit, and some of the afflicted cried out that she was going to confess, but Goody Corey, and Proctor, and his wife came in, in their apparition, and struck her down, and said she should tell nothing.

Mary Warren continued a good space in a fit that she did neither see, nor hear, nor speak.

Afterwards she started up, and said I will speak and cried out, Oh! I am sorry for it, I am sorry for it, and wringed her hands, and fell a little while into a fit again and then came to speak, but immediately her teeth were set, and then she fell into a violent fit, and cried out, Oh Lord help me, Oh good Lord save me!

And then afterwards cried again, I will tell, I will tell, and then fell into a dead fit again.

And afterwards cried, I will, they did, they did, they did, and then fell into a violent fit again.

After a little recovery she cried I will tell, I will tell, they brought me to it; and then fell into a fit again which fits continuing, she was ordered to be had out, and the next to be brought in, viz Bridget Bishop.

Sometime afterwards she was called in again, but immediately taken with fits, for a while.

Question: Have you signed the Devil's book?

Answer: No.

Question: Have you not touch it?

Answer: No.

Then she fell into fits again, and was sent forth for air.

After a considerable space of time she was brought in again, but could [not] give account of things, by reason of fits, and so sent forth.

Mary Warren called in, afterwards in private, before magistrates and ministers.

She said I shall not speak a word but I will speak Satan—She said she will kill me Oh! she said, she owes me a spite, and will claw me off—

Avoid Satan, for the name of God, avoid and then fell into fits again and cried will ye I will prevent ye in the name of God,—

Question: Tell us, how far have you yielded?

(A fit interrupts her again.)

Question: What did they say you should do, and you should be well?

(Then her lips were bit so that she could not speak. So she was sent away.)

Note: That not one of the sufferers was afflicted during her examination after once she began to confess, though they were tormented before.

Salem Village April 19th 1692.

Mr. Samuel Parris being desired to take in writing the examination of Mary Warren hath delivered it as aforesaid And upon hearing the same and seeing what we did then see; together with the charge of the afflicted persons then present. We committed said Mary Warren.

*John Hathorne Assis'ts

*Jonathan Corwin

The examination of Mary Warren 19th April 1692

Source: Essex County Court Archives, vol. 1, no. 111, Massachusetts Supreme Judicial Court, Judicial Archives, on deposit James Duncan Phillips Library, Peabody Essex Museum, Salem, MA.

Document 28

UNKNOWN, "EXAMINATION OF MARY WARREN IN PRISON," APRIL 20, 1692

The following document is an excellent example of the methods employed by the court to enlist the cooperation of a confessed witch to provide additional names and general information concerning the activities of local witches. In particular, Mary Warren reaches out of her prison cell to target her former master and mistress, John Proctor and his wife, Elizabeth, implicating him further into the role as a likely suspect for witchcraft and an enemy to Christian principles. Interestingly, she also identifies Giles Corey as one of the coven of Salem area witches.

Mary Warren's examination in Salem Prison

She testifies that her master Proctor was always very averse to the putting up bills for public prayer.

Question: Did you not know it was the Devils book when you signed?

Answer: No. But I thought it was no good book.

Question: After you had a mark in the book what did you think then?

Answer: Then I thought it was the Devil's book.

Question: How did you come to know your master and mistress were witches?

Answer: The Sabbath eve after I had put up my note for thanks in public, my mistress appeared to me, and pulled me out of the bed, and told me that she was a witch, and had put her hand to the book. She told me this in her bodily person, and that this examination might have known she was a witch, if she had but minded what books she read in.

Question: What did she say to you before you tormented the children?

Answer: The night after she told me she was a witch, she in son told me this examinant, that myself and her son John would quickly be brought out for witches.

This Examinant said that Giles Corey in apparition told her, the night before that the magistrates were going up to the farms, to bring down more witches to torment her. Moreover, being in a dreadful fit in the prison she charged it on Giles Corey, who was then in close prison, affirming that he came into the room where she was, and afflicting her, charged her not to come into the other room while he was examining, but being sent for and he commanded to look upon her, he no sooner turned his face to her but she fell into a dreadful fit again, and upon her recovery charged him to his face with being the procurer of it. Moreover the said Corey in prison formerly threatened her that he would fit her for it, because he told her she had caused her master to ask more for a piece of meadow than he was willing to give she likewise in her fit in the other room before she had seen Giles Corey in person, charging him with afflicting off her, described him in all his garments, both of hat, coat, and color of them, with a cord about his waist, and a white cap on his head and in chains, as several then in company can affirm.

Source: Essex County Court Archives, vol. 1, no. 115, Massachusetts Supreme Judicial Court, Judicial Archives, on deposit James Duncan Phillips Library, Peabody Essex Museum, Salem, MA.

Document 29

UNKNOWN, "EXAMINATION OF MARY WARREN," APRIL 21, 1692

The following examination of Mary Warren revolves directly around the question of how a person might make a pact or covenant with Satan, placing their body and soul into his care for whatever purposes he might desire. The inquisitor in this exchange is trying to establish if John and Elizabeth Proctor tempted their maidservant, Mary Warren, to become a witch by "signing the Devil's Book." This is a very common theme during the Salem witch trial episode and much testimony is provided by "afflicted children" concerning precisely who offered them "the book" to sign, and under what circumstances the offer to become a witch was made. The important point to understand is that among Puritans, becoming a witch was not being born with special, magical power. Becoming a witch was a voluntary act, not unlike the act of becoming a Christian—whereby a person deliberately chooses to turn their back upon Christ and his Church and instead offers body and soul to God's enemy, Satan. The question in this passage is: What constitutes a signature in the Devil's Book? For Mary, as well as her inquisitor, such an agreement might be accomplished with a simple touch of Mary's finger.

Mary Warrens examination of April 21, 1692

Being asked by the honored magistrates whether the Bible that then was showed her was the book that was brought to her to touch and that she saw the flourish in answered no she saw she was deceived.

Being asked whether she had not told Mercy Lewis that she had signed to a book answered no.

She was asked whether her Mistress had brought a book to her to sign answered her mistress brought none. But her master brought one being asked whether she signed to it answered not unless putting her finger to it was signing.

Being asked whether she did not see a spot where she had put her finger answered there was a spot.

She was asked what color the spot was answered black.

She was asked whether her master did not threaten her to run the hot tongs down her throat if she did not sign answered that her master threatened her to burn her out of her fit.

Being asked whether she had made a mark in the book answered she made no mark but with her top of her finger.

She was asked what she dipped her finger in when made the mark answered in nothing but her mouth.

She was asked whether her finger was wet when she touched the book with it answered she knew not that it was wet or whether it was wet with sweat or with cider that she had been drinking of she knew not but her finger did make a mark and the mark was black.

She was asked whether any but her master and mistress was with her when she was threatened with the hot tongs answered none but them.

She said her master put her hand to the book and her finger made a black spot which made her tremble. Then she said she was undone body and soul, and cried out grievously she was told that it was her own voluntary act she would have denied it but she was told the Devil could have done nothing if she had not yielded and that she for ease to her body not for any good of her soul had done it with this she much grieved and cried out. She said her master and mistress threatened to drown her and to make her run through the hedges.

She was asked whether she had not seen her master and mistress since she came to prison answered she thought she saw her master and dare say it was he she was asked what he said to her answered nothing.

After a fit she cried out I will tell I will tell though wicked creature it is you stopped my mouth but I will confess the little that I have to confess being asked who she would tell off whether Goodwife Proctor or no answered Betty Proctor it is she it is she I lived with last.

She then cried out it shall be known thou wretch; hast thou undone me body and soul she said also she wishes she had made me make a through league.

She was again asked what her finger was blacked with when she touched the book.

Answered she knew not that her finger was black till she see it black the book and after she had put her finger to the book she eat bread and butter and her finger blacked the bread and butter also.

Being asked what her mistress now said to her when she complained of her mistress she said her mistress bid her not tell that her mistress was a witch.

Coming out of another fit said she would tell she would tell she said her master now bid her not tell that he had some times gone to make away with himself for her master had told her that he had been about sometimes to make away with himself because of his wives quarrelling with him.

Being asked how she knew Goodwife Proctor was a witch she coming out of a fit said she would tell she would tell and she said her Mistress Proctor said she might know she was a witch if she harkened to what she used to read she said her Mistress had many books and her mistress carried one book with her riding when she went to see her sister.

Being asked whether she knew her mistress to be a witch before she touched the book, and how she knew it she said her mistress told her she had set her hand to the devils book that same night that I was thrown out of bed said she which was the same night after she had a note of thanksgiving put up at the meetinghouse.

She said her mistress came to her body not her shape as far as she knew she affirmed her mistress was a witch.

Being asked whether she had seen any of the witches since she came to prison said she had seen Goodman Corey and Sarah Good they brought the book to her to sign.

But she would not own that she knew her master to be a witch or wizard being asked whether she did not know her finger would make a mark if she touched the book with it she answered no but her master and mistress asked her to read and she said the first word she read was Moses the next word she could not tell what it was but her master and mistress bid her if she could not pronounce the word she should touch the book.

Being asked why she would not tell the whole truth she said had formerly not told all the truth. Because she was threatened to be torn in pieces if she did but now she would and had told the truth.

Being asked whether she did not suspect it was the Devil's book that she touched answered she was in her fit she should run into the fire or water if he would and destroy herself.

Being asked why she yielded to do as she did answer that her master said if she would not when she was in her fit she should run into the fire or water if he would and destroy herself.

Being asked whether she had not been instrumental to afflict the afflicted parsons answered no but when she heard they were afflicted in her shape she began to fear it was the devil [that hurt in her shape].

Being asked whether she had images to stick pins or thorns into to hurt people with answered no.

She was asked whether the Devil never asked her consent to hurt in her shape answered no she had heard her master and mistress tell of images and of sticking of thorns in them to hurt people with.

She was asked whether she knew of any images in the house said no.

Being asked if she knew of any ointment they had in the house she said her Masters annointed her once for some all she had but it was with ointment that came from Mrs. Bassit's of Lynn the color of it was greenish.

She was asked how it smelt said very ugly to her.

She said when she touched the book she went to put her finger to another line but still her finger went to the same place where her finger had blacked.

Mr. Noyes told her she had then touched the book twice and asked her whether she did not suspect it to be the Devil's book before she touched it the second time she said she feared it was no good book being asked what she meant by no good book she said a book to deceive.

Mary Warrens Examination

Source: Essex County Court Archives, vol. 1, nos. 113 and 114, Massachusetts Supreme Judicial Court, Judicial Archives, on deposit James Duncan Phillips Library, Peabody Essex Museum, Salem, MA.

Document 30

UNKNOWN, "DEPOSITION OF ANN PUTNAM, JR. V. GEORGE BURROUGHS, NO. 1," APRIL 21, 1692

Perhaps the most surprising of all cases to occur during the Salem episode is the accusation, trial, and execution of a minister, the Reverend George Burroughs. It is the first and only time a clergyman in American history is accused of witchcraft and represents a significant departure from the more typical accusations of disaffected and marginalized individuals. Interestingly, Ann Putnam Jr., who would have been only four years old at the time of Burroughs's departure from Salem Village, could not have known him personally. This has prompted some historians to question whether Ann Jr. was prompted by elder members of the Putnam family to seek revenge upon their former pastor in reaction to a long-standing economic dispute.

The Deposition of Ann Putnam who testifies and says that on 20'th of April 1692 at evening she saw the apparition of a minister at which she was grievously affrighted and cried out oh dreadful, dreadful here is a minister come. What are ministers witches to? Whence come you and what is your name? For I will complain of you though you be a minister if you be a wizard. And immediately I was tortured by him being racked and all most choked by him and he tempted me to write in his book which I refused with loud out cries and said I would not write in his book though he tore me all to pieces but told him that it was a dreadful thing that he which was a minister that should teach children to fear God should come to persuade poor creatures to give their souls to the Devil. Oh dreadful tell me your name that I may know who you are then again he tortured me and urged me to write in his book which I refused and then presently he told me that his name was George Burroughs and that he had had three wives and that he had bewitched the two first of them to death and that he killed Mistress Lawson because she was so unwilling to go from the village and also killed Mr. Lawson's child because he went to the eastward with Sir Edmon and preached so to the soldiers and that he had bewitched a great many soldiers to death at the eastward, when Sir Edmon was there. And that he had made Abigail Hobbs a witch and several witches more and he has continued ever since; by times tempting me to write in his book and grievously torturing me by beating, pinching, and almost choking me several times a day and he also told me that he was above which for he was a conjurer.

Jurat in Curia

Ann Putnam against Burroughs

Source: Essex County Court Archives, vol. 2, Massachusetts Supreme Judicial Court, Judicial Archives, on deposit James Duncan Phillips Library, Peabody Essex Museum, Salem, MA.

Document 31

JOHN HATHORNE AND JONATHAN CORWIN, "EXAMINATION OF MARY BLACK," APRIL 22, 1692

While it is commonly known that Reverend Samuel Parris's slave Tituba and her husband John Indian were both Native Americans, some African American slaves were also accused of witchcraft during the Salem episode. Among them was Candy, the domestic slave of Nathaniel Putnam of Salem Village. The following is a portion of her examination that resulted in a confession of witchcraft for which she remained in jail until she was released by Governor Phips's order in January 1692/1693.

The examination of Mary Black (a Negro) at a Court held at Salem Village
April 22, 1692
By the Magistrates of Salem

Mary, you are accused of sundry acts of witchcraft: Tell me be
you a Witch?
—Silent.
How long have you been a witch?
I cannot tell.
But have you been a witch?
I cannot tell you.
Why do you hurt these folks
I hurt no body
Who doth?
I do not know.
[Benj'a Putnam] Her Master saith a man sat down upon the farm with her about a twelve month agoe.
What did the man say to you?
He said nothing.
Doth this Negroe hurt you?
Severall of them said yes.
Why do you hurt them?

I did not hurt them.
Do you prick sticks?
No I pin my Neck cloth
Well take out a pin, and pin it again.
She did so, and several of the afflicted cried out they were pricked.

Mary Walcott was pricked in the arm till the blood came, Abigail Williams was pricked in the stomach and Mercy Lewis was pricked in the foot.

Mr. Samuel Parris, being desired to take in writing the Examination of Mary Black, a Negro Woman, delivered it as aforesaid and upon hearing the same and seeing what we did then see together with the charge of the afflicted persons then present we committed (to jail) said Mary Black.
[Pbar] us *John Hathorne
*Jonathan Corwin Assis'ts
(Reverse)
The Examination of Mary Black
April 22, 1692
Cleared by Governor's proclamation
January 11, 1692/93
Mr. Nathaniel Putnam of Salem Village
his negro

Source: Massachusetts State Archives Collection, vol. 135, no. 20.

Document 32

ELISHA HUTCHINSON, "WARRANT FOR ARREST OF GEORGE BURROUGHS," APRIL 30, 1692

Following the issuance of depositions against him and some significant in-court testimony of a spectral nature, Chief Justice Stoughton issued the following warrant for the arrest of Reverend Burroughs who at the time was residing in and pastoring a church in Wells, Maine. It should be noted that, despite the distance from Salem to Wells, Maine, it took the court officers only four days from the time of the issuance of the warrant to the time they delivered Reverend Burroughs to the court.

To John Partridge, Field Marshal
You are required in their Majesties names to apprehend the body of Mr. George Burroughs at present preacher at Wells in the province of Maine, and convey him with all speed to Salem before the Magistrates there, to be examined, he being suspected for a confederacy with the devil in oppressing of sundry about Salem as they relate. I having received particular order from the Governor and council of their Majesties colony of the Massachusetts, for the same, you may not fail herein.
Dated in Portsmouth in the Province of New Hampshire. April 30th 1692.
*Elisha Hutchinson Maj'r

By virtue of this warrant I apprehended said George Burroughs and have brought him to Salem and delivered him to the authority there this fourth day of May 1692.

*John Partridge field marshal of the Province of New Hampshire and Maine.

Source: Essex County Court Archives, vol. 1, Massachusetts Supreme Judicial Court, Judicial Archives, on deposit James Duncan Phillips Library, Peabody Essex Museum, Salem, MA.

Document 33

UNKNOWN, "DEPOSITION OF ANN PUTNAM, JR. V. GEORGE BURROUGHS, NO. 2," MAY 5, 1692

One of the great puzzles of the Salem witch trials is the execution of Reverend George Burroughs who had formerly served as minister of the Salem Village Church. The first accusations against this cleric were presented on April 23, 1692, before the return of Reverend Increase Mather and the arrival of Governor Sir William Phips on May 14, 1692. Burroughs had graduated from Harvard (class of 1670) and served as pastor in the frontier parish of Casco, Maine, until he was invited to fill the pulpit of Salem Village in 1680. Here he remained for the modest salary of £60 per year—only £20 cash—with the rest in the form of in-kind contributions. His two great achievements were to raise money for the construction of a new meeting house in Salem Village and petitioning the Massachusetts Great and General Court that Salem Village should be recognized as an independent community apart for Salem town. With the death of his wife in 1682, and his parishioners' unwillingness to pay the cash portion of his salary, he was forced to borrow money for funeral expenses, resign his position, and return to Maine. Here he remained for the next 10 years until the constable from Portsmouth, New Hampshire, arrived at his home in Wells with a warrant for arrest under suspicion of witchcraft. He was placed in jail in Boston, and brought to Salem on May 9, 1692, to be examined by Chief Justice Stoughton, Justice John Hathorne, Justice Samuel Sewell, and Justice Jonathan Corwin. The following deposition against Reverend Burroughs was drafted on or after May 9, 1692, and features testimony presented by 12-year-old Ann Putnam Jr.

The deposition of Ann Putnam who testifies and says that on the 5'th of May 1692 at evening I saw the apparition of Mr. George Burroughs who grievously tortured me and urged me to write in his book which I refused then he told me that his two first wives would appear to me presently and tell me a great many lies but I should not believe them. Then immediately appeared to me the form of two women in winding sheets and napkins about their heads, at which I was greatly affrighted, and they turned their faces towards Mr. Burroughs and looked very red and angry and told him that he had been a cruel man to them and that their blood did cry for vengeance against him, and also told him that they should be clothed with white robes in heaven, when he should be cast into Hell. And immediately he vanished away, and as soon as he was gone the two women turned their faces towards me and looked as pale as a white wall, and told me that they were Mr. Burroughs two first wives and that he had murdered them and one told me that she was his first wife and he stabbed her under the left arm and put a peace of sealing wax on the wound and she pulled aside the winding sheet and showed me the place and also told me that she was in the house Mr. Parris now lives when it was done. And the other told me that Mr. Burroughs and that wife which he has now killed her in the vessel as she was coming to see her friends because they would have one another and they both charged me that I should tell these things to the Magistrates before Mr. Burroughs' face and if he did not own them they did not know but that they should appear there. This morning also Mistress Lawson and her daughter Ann appeared to me whom I knew and told me that Mr. Burroughs murdered them. This morning also appeared to me another woman in a winding sheet and told me that she was Goodman Fullers first wife and Mr. Burroughs killed her because there was some difference between her husband and him. Also on the 9'th May during the time of his examination he did most grievously torment and afflict Mary Walcott, Mercy Lewis, Elizabeth Hubbard, and Abigail Williams by pinching, pricking, and choking them.

Jurat in Curia

Ann Putnam Contra George Burroughs Death of his wife and Lawson's Child

Source: Essex County Court Archives, vol. 2, no. 24, Massachusetts Supreme Judicial Court, Judicial Archives, on deposit James Duncan Phillips Library, Peabody Essex Museum, Salem, MA.

Document 34

UNKNOWN, "DEPOSITION OF DELIVERANCE HOBBS V. BRIDGET BISHOP ET AL.," MAY 3, 1692

Deliverance Hobbs and her daughter Abigail and her husband, William Hobbs, were refugees from the Indian war raging on the Maine frontier in the 1680s and 1690s. They had once been part of the congregation of Reverend George Burroughs in Casco, Maine, but were forced to flee when that community was attacked. She and her husband were arrested and jailed under suspicion of witchcraft on April 21, 1692. The following deposition was the result of an interview held in the Salem jail about two weeks following her arrest. It illustrates how court officers would use some of the imprisoned accused as sources of information to broaden their search for more suspects, or gather details against others already in custody.

Deliverance Hobbs. Examined May 3, 1692. Salem prison

Question: What have you done since whereby there is further trouble in your appearance?

Answer: Nothing at all.

Q: But have you not since been tempted?

A: Yes, Sir, but I have not done it, nor will not do it.

Q: Here is a great change since we last spoke to you, for now you afflict and torment again; now tell us the truth who tempted you to sign again?

A: It was Goody Olliver; she would have me to set my hand to the book, but I would not neither have I. Neither did consent to hurt them again.

Q: Was that true that Goody Wildes appeared to you and tempted you?

A: Yes, that was true.

Q: Have you been tempted since?

A: Yes, about Friday or Saturday night last.

Q: Did they bid you that you should not tell?

A: Yes, they told me so.

Q: But how far did they draw you or tempt you, and how far did you yield to the temptation? But do not you acknowledge that [that] was true that you told us formerly?

A: Yes.

Q: And you did sign then at the first, did you not?

A: Yes, I did it is true.

Q: Did you promise then to deny at last what you said before?

A: Yes, I did and it was Goody Oliver Alias Bishop that tempted me to deny all that I had confessed before.

Q: Do you not know the man with the wen? (A wen is a small, slow-growing cyst beneath the skin.)

A: No I do not know who it is; all that I confessed before is true.

Q: Who were they you named formerly?

A: Osburne, Good, Burroughs, Olliver, Wiles, Cory and his Wife, Nurse, Procter and his Wife.

Q: Who were with you in the chamber? (It being informed that some were talking with her there.)

A: Wildes and Bishop or Olliver, Good and Osburne, and they had a feast both of Roast and Boiled meat and did eat and drink and would have had me to have eat and drink with them but I would not; and they would have had me signed, but I would not then not when Goody Olliver came to me.

Q: Nor did not you con [torn] children in your likeness?

A: I do not know that I did.

Q: What is that you have to tell, which you cannot tell yet you say?

Source: Essex County Court Archives, vol. 1, no. 140, Massachusetts Supreme Judicial Court, Judicial Archives, on deposit James Duncan Phillips Library, Peabody Essex Museum, Salem, MA.

Document 35

UNKNOWN, "EXAMINATION OF REV. GEORGE BURROUGHS," MAY 9, 1692

In building a case against Reverend Burroughs, it was important that he first be discredited as a man-of-God by the clergy of the Salem-Boston area, since no true church leader could ever be considered a witch. This step was accomplished by Reverend Increase and Reverend Cotton Mather who spent some time in Boston interviewing Burroughs after his arrest, and reported that they were satisfied that he was guilty. Reverend Increase Mather would later make the observation about Burroughs: "If I were one of his judges, I could not have acquitted him." Once Burroughs was essentially "defrocked" by the puritan religious leadership, he was fair game for the court to ferret out his guilt in a pretrial examination in May. His trial would actually take place much later on August 5, 1692.

Being asked when he partook of the Lord's Supper, he being (as he said) in full communion at Roxbury, he answered it was so long since he could not tell, yet he owned he was at meeting one Sabbath at Boston part of the day, and the other at Charlestown part of a Sabbath when that sacrament happened to be at both, yet did not partake of either. He denied that his house at Casco was haunted, yet he owned there were toads. He denied that he made his wife swear that she should not write to her father Ruck without his approbation of her letter to her father. He owned that none of his children but the eldest was baptized. The above said was in private, none of the bewitched being present.

At his entry into the room, many if not all the bewitched were grievously tortured.

Susannah Sheldon testified that Burroughs' two wives appeared in their winding sheets and said that that man killed them. He was bid to look upon Susannah Sheldon. He looked back and knocked down all or most of the afflicted who stood behind him. Mercy Lewis's deposition going to be read, he looked upon her and she fell into a dreadful and tedious fit. Mary Walcott, Elizabeth Hubbard, Susannah Sheldon's testimony going to be read, they all fell into fits. Susannah Sheldon and Ann Putnam, Jr., affirmed each of them that he brought the book and would have them write.

Being asked what he thought of these things, he answered it was an amazing and humbling providence, but he understood nothing of it and he said, "Some of you may observe, that when they begin to name my name, they cannot name it."

Ann Putnam, Jr. and Susannah Sheldon testified that his two wives and two children did accuse him. The bewitched were so tortured that authority ordered them to be taken away, some of them. Sarah Bibber testified that he had hurt her, though she had not seen him personally before as she knew.

Source: William E. Woodward. *Records of Salem Witchcraft, Copied from the Original Documents*, vol. 2. Roxbury, MA: Priv. print. for W. E. Woodward, 109–111.

Document 36

UNKNOWN, "INDICTMENT V. GEORGE BURROUGHS, FOR AFFLICTING ELIZABETH HUBBARD," MAY 9, 1692

The following is one of four indictments leveled against Reverend George Burroughs by the "afflicted girls." This particular indictment was the result of a deposition submitted by Elizabeth Hubbard, one of several orphans who had lost her parents in attacks on the Maine frontier, but now worked as a servant in the home of her aunt and uncle, Dr. William Griggs and Rachel Griggs. In a sense it was her uncle, Dr. Griggs, who helped initiate the crisis by proclaiming the malady of Parris's daughter and niece to be the result of the "evil hand" of witchcraft.

Anno Regis et Reginae Willim et
Mariae nunc Angliae &c Quarto
Essex ss The Jurors for our Sovereigne Lord and Lady the King
and Queen pr'sents That George Burroughs late of Falmouth w'thin
the province of the Massachusetts Bay in New England Clerke—The
Ninth Day of May—in the fourth Year of the Reign of our Sovereigne
Lord and Lady William and Mary by the Grace of God of England
Scotland France and Ireland King and Queen Defenders of the
faith &c Diver other Days and times as well before as after, certain
Detestable Arts called witchcraft & Sorceries—wickedly and felon
iously hath used Practiced & Exercised at and within the Township
of Salem in the County of Essex & aforesaid, in Upon & against one
Elizabeth Hubbard of Salem in the County of Essex Single-woman—
by which said wicked Arts the said Elizabeth Hubbard the Ninth Day of May—
in the fourth Year aboves'd and Divers other Days
and Times as well before as after was and is Tortured afflicted Pined
Consumed wasted and Tormented also for Sundry other Acts of
witchcrafts by Said George Burroughs. Committed and done ag't
the Peace of our Sovereigne Lord & Lady the King & Queen their
Crowne and dignity and ag't the forme of the Statute in that case
made & Provided:

Witnesses.
Elizabeth Hubbard
Mary Wolcott
Ann Putman

Source: Essex County Court Archives, vol. 2, no. 30, Massachusetts Supreme Judicial Court, Judicial Archives, on deposit James Duncan Phillips Library, Peabody Essex Museum, Salem, MA.

Document 37

UNKNOWN, "INDICTMENT V. GEORGE BURROUGHS, FOR AFFLICTING MERCY LEWIS," MAY 9, 1692

Mercy Lewis was another servant girl who had lost her parents in attacks on the Maine frontier and was taken in by the family of Thomas Putnam as a refugee and household domestic servant. She was very close to Ann Putnam Jr. despite the disparity in age— Ann Jr. was 12 and Mercy was 19—and strongly supported the accusatory efforts of the afflicted girls throughout the Salem episode.

Anno Regis et Reginae Willim et
Mariae nunc: Angliae &c Quarto
Essex ss The Jurors for our Sovereigne Lord and Lady the King and
Queen pr'sents That George Burroughs late of falmouth in the province
of the Massachusets Bay in New England—Clarke—The ninth Day of May in the forth
Year of the Reigne of our Sovereigne
Lord and Lady William and Mary by the Grace of God of England
Scottland France and Ireland King and Queen Defenders of the faith
&c and Divers other Dayes and times, as well before as after certaine
Detestable Arts called Witchcrafts and Sorceries. Wickedly and
felloniously, hath used—Practised and Exercised at and within the
Towneship of Salem in the County of Essex afores'd in, upon.and ag't
one Mercy Lewis of Salem Villiage in the County of Essex in New
England—by which wicked Arts the said Mercy Lewis—the Ninth Day of May—in the
fourth Year afores'd and Divers other Dayes
and times as well before as after was and is Tortured afflicted Pine
Consumed Wasted and Tormented: ag't the Peace of our Sovereigne
Lord and Lady the King and Queen, and ag't the forme of the Statute
in that case made and Provided/.

Witnesses.
Mercy Lewis
Mary Walcott
El. Hubbard
Ann Putnam

Source: Essex County Court Archives, vol. 2, no. 25, Massachusetts Supreme Judicial Court, Judicial Archives, on deposit James Duncan Phillips Library, Peabody Essex Museum, Salem, MA.

Document 38

UNKNOWN, "INDICTMENT V. GEORGE BURROUGHS, FOR AFFLICTING ANN PUTNAM," MAY 9, 1692

By far the most influential of the "afflicted girls" and one who had a significant role in identifying those individuals to be accused was Ann Putnam Jr. The following indictment against former Salem Village pastor Reverend George Burroughs is a result of a deposition submitted against Reverend Burroughs by Ann who would have been only four years old at the time of his departure from Salem Village. Interestingly, Reverend Burroughs and Ann's father, Yeoman Thomas Putnam, had a long-standing dispute over a debt.

Anno Regis et Reginae Willm et
Mariae nunc: Anglia &c Quarto
Essex ss: The Jurors for our Sovereign Lord and Lady the King
& Queen presents That George Burroughs late of falmouth within
the Province of the Massachusetts Bay in New England Clarke the
Ninth Day of May in the fourth Year of the Reigne of our Soverigne Lord & Lady
William and Mary by the Grace of God of England
Scottland France and Ireland King and Queen Defenders of the faith
&c Diver other Dayes and times as well before as After certain Detestable
Artes called Witchcrafts & Sorceries: Wickedly and feloniously
hath used Practised & Exercised at and within the Towne of
Salem in the County afores'd in upon and ag't one: Ann Putman of
Salem Village Single Woman—by which said wicked arts the Said
Ann Putman the Ninth Day of May in the fourth year above said and
Divers other Dayes and times as well before as after was and is
Tortured Afflicted Pined Consumed Wasted and Tormented also
for sundry other Acts of Witchcrafts by said George Burroughs Committed
and Done ag't the Peace of our Sovereigne Lord and Lady
the King and Queen their Crowne & Dignity and ag't the form of
the Statute in tha[t] case made and Provided:

Witnesses Ann Putnam
Mary Wolcott
Elizabeth Hubbard
Mary Warren
(On reverse side of paper) Geo. Burroughs

Source: Essex County Court Archives, vol. 2, no. 26, Massachusetts Supreme Judicial Court, Judicial Archives, on deposit James Duncan Phillips Library, Peabody Essex Museum, Salem, MA.

Document 39

UNKNOWN, "INDICTMENT V. GEORGE BURROUGHS, FOR AFFLICTING MARY WALCOTT," MAY 9, 1692

This indictment is the result of a deposition submitted by 17-year-old Mary Walcott, a cousin by marriage to Ann Putnam Jr., since her father, Captain Jonathan Walcott, had married for his second wife, Deliverance Putnam, Thomas Putnam's sister. Mary proved to be a supporting member of the "afflicted girls" but not one of the most outspoken testifiers during the trials.

Anno Regis et Reginae Willim et
Mariae nunc Angliae &c Quarto
Essex ss The Jurors for our Sovereigne Lord and Lady the King
and Queen pr'sents That George Burroughs late of falmouth in the
province of the Massach'ts Bay in New England, Clerk—the Ninth Day of May in the
fourth Year of the Reigne of Our Sovereigne Lord
and Lady William and Mary by the Grace of God of England Scottland
France and Ireland King and Queen Defenders of the faith &c
and Divers other Days and times, as well before, as after, Certaine
Detestable Arts called Witchcrafts, and Sorceries, Wickedly, and
felloniously, hath used Practised.&.Exercised at and within.the
Towneship of Salem in the County of Essex aforesaid in upon and
ag't one Mary Walcott of Salem Villiage in the County of Essex
Singlewoman—by which said wicked Arts the said Mary Walcott
the Ninth Day of May in the forth Year aboves'd and Divers other
Days and times as well before as after was and is Tortured afflicted
Pined Consumed wasted and Tormented.ag't the Peace of our Sovereigne
Lord and Lady the King and Queen and ag't the forme of the
Statute in that case made and Provided:

Witnesses
Mary Walcott
Sarah Vibber Jurat
Mercy Lewis
Ann Putnam
Eliz. Hubbard

Source: William E. Woodward. Records of Salem Witchcraft, copied from the original documents, vol. 2. Roxbury, MA: Priv. print for W. E. Woodward, 109–111.

Document 40

UNKNOWN, "EXAMINATION OF MARY WARREN," MAY 12, 1692

As in previous examinations, the focus in this discussion revolves around the activities of John and Elizabeth Proctor. The range of subject touches upon the signing of The Devils' Book, spectral appearances of Goody Parker, Goody Corey, Bridget Bishop, and Ann Pudeater, and a new theme, the use of poppets to perform acts of malefic magic upon the bodies of distant victims. This theme was first brought to the attention of New England witch trial audiences in Memorable Providences *by Reverend Cotton Mather as he described Goody Glover's method of harming the Goodwin children. It was introduced to the Salem trials in the testimony of John Bly Sr. in his deposition against Bridget Bishop.*

Mary Warren's examination May 12th 1692

> **Question:** Whether you did not know that it was the Devil's book when you signed?
>
> **Answer:** I did not know it then but I know it now, to be sure it was the Devil's book, in the first place to be sure I did set my hand to the Devil's book; I have considered of it, since you were here last and it was the Devil's book that my Master Proctor brought to me, and he told me if I would set my hand to that book I should be well; and I did set my hand to it, but that which I did it was done with my finger, he brought the book and he told me if I would take the book and touch it that I should be well and I thought then that was the Devil's book.
>
> **Question:** Was there not your consent to hurt the children, when you were hurt?
>
> **Answered:** No sir, but when I was afflicted my Master Proctor was in the room and said if you are afflicted I wish you were more afflicted and you and all. I said Master, what make you say so? He answered because you go to bring out innocent persons. I told him that could not be and whether the Devil took advantage at that I know not to afflict them and one night talking about them I said I did not care though you were tormented if you charged me.
>
> **Question:** Did you ever see any poppets?
>
> **Answer:** Yes once I saw one made of cloth in Mistress Proctor's hand.
>
> **Question:** Who was it like or which of the children was it for?
>
> **Answer:** I cannot tell, whether for Ann Putnam or Abigail Williams, for one of them it was I am sure, it was in my mistress's hand.
>
> **Question:** What did you stick into the poppet?
>
> **Answer:** I did stick in a pin about the neck of it as it was in Proctor's hand.
>
> **Question:** How many more did you see afterwards?
>
> **Answer:** I do not remember that ever I saw any more. Yes I remember one and that Goody Parker brought a poppet unto me of Mercy Lewis and she gave me another and I stuck it somewhere about the waists; and she appeared

once more to me in the prison, and she said to me what are you got here? And she told me that she was coming here herself. I had another person that appeared to me, it was Goody Pudeator and said she was sorry to see me there, it was in apparition and she brought me a poppet, it was like to Mary Walcott and it was a piece of stick that she brought me to stick into it and somewhere about her arms I stuck it in.

Question: Where did she bring it to you?

Answer: Up at Proctors. Goody Parker told me she had been a witch these 12 years and more; and Pudeator told me that she had done damage, and told me that she had hurt James Cloyces' child taking it out of the mother's hand.

Question: Who brought the last to you?

Answer: My mistress and when she brought it, she brought it in her own person and her husband with his own hands brought me the book to sign, and he brought me an Image which looked yellow and I believe it was for Abigail Williams being like her and I put a thing like a thorn into it, this was done by his bodily person after I had signed. The night after I had signed the book while she was thus confessing Parker appeared and bit her extremely on her arms as she affirmed unto us.

Question: Who have you seen more?

Answer: Nurse and Cloyce and Good's child after I had signed.

Question: What said [they] to you?

Answer: They said that I should never tell of them nor anything about them, and I have seen Goody Good herself.

Question: Was that true of Giles Corey that you saw him and that he afflicted you the other day?

Answer: Yes I have seen him often and he hurts me very much and Goody Oliver had appeared to me and afflicted me and brought the book to tempt me, and I have seen Goody Corey the first night I was taken, I saw as I thought the apparition of Goody Corey and caught at it as I thought and caught my master in my lap though I did not see my master in that place at that time, upon which my master said it is nobody but I it is my shadow that you see, by my master was not before me as I could discern, but catching at the apparition that looked like Goody Corey I caught hold of my master and pulled him down into my lap; upon which he said I see there is no heed to any of your talkings, for you are all possessed with the Devil for it is nothing but my shape, I have seen Goody Corey at my masters house in person, and she told me that I should be condemned for a witch as well as she herself, it was at my master's house, and she said that the children would cry out and bring out all.

Question: Was this before you had signed?

Answer: Yes, before I had any fits.

Question: Now tell the truth about the Moutebank what writing was that?

Answer: I don't know. I asked her what it was about but she would not tell me saying she had promised not to let anybody see it.

Question: Well, but who did you see more?

Answer: I don't know any more.

Question: How long hath your Master and Mistress been witches?

Answer: I don't know, they never told me.

Question: What likeness of appearance have you had to bewitch you?

Answer: They never gave me anything.

While I was reading this over upon the coming in of Mr. Higginson and Mr. Hale as soon as I read the name Parker, she immediately fell into dreadful fits as she affirmed. After her fit was over by the appearance of Goody Parker, and Mr. Hathorne presently but naming Goody Pudeator she also appeared and tormented her very much and Goody Parker in the time of her examination in one of Warren's fits told this examinant that she had bewitched the examinants sister and was the cause of her dumbness as also that she had lately killed a man aboard a vessel and told me that his name was Michael Chapleman aboard the vessel in the harbor after they ware come to anchor and that he died with a pain in his side and that she had done it by striking something into his side and that she had struck this examinant's sister dumb that she should never speak more and Goody Pudeator at the same time appeared and told this examinant that she had thrown John Turner off of a cherry tree and almost killed him and Goody Parker said that she had cast away Captain Price's ketch Thomas Westgate master, and Venus Colefox in it and presently told her than John Lapshorne was lost in it and that they were found in the sea and she said that Goody Pudeator told her that she went up to Mr. Corwin's house to bewitch his mare that he should not go up to the farms to examine the witches, also Mr. Burroughs appearing at the same time and afflicting her told her that he went to tie Mr. Hathorne's horses legs when he went last to Boston and that he tried to bewitch him though he could not his horse. Goody Pudeator told her that she killed her husband by giving him something whereby he fell sick and died, it was she told her about seven or ten years since and Goody Parker told her that she was instrumental to drown Orne's son in the harbor also she said she did bewitch John Searles's boy to death as his master was carrying him out to sea so that he was forced to bring him back again, also Burroughs told her that he killed his wife off of Cape Ann. Parker told her also that Margaret Jacobs was a witness against her and did charge her yesterday upon her (that is Jacobs's) examination.

Source: Essex County Court Archives, vol. 1, no. 115, Massachusetts Supreme Judicial Court, Judicial Archives, on deposit James Duncan Phillips Library, Peabody Essex Museum, Salem, MA.

Document 41

JOHN HATHORNE AND JONATHAN CORWIN, "WARRANT V. ROGER TOOTHAKER," MAY 18, 1692

Roger Toothaker was both a farmer and a physician of northern Essex County, who was knowledgeable about herbal remedies and was what might be better known as a folk-healer. He was regarded as a medical competitor of Dr. William Griggs. It is interesting to note that one of the three afflicted girls responsible for accusing him of witchcraft was Elizabeth Hubbard, a niece and domestic servant of Dr. Griggs.

To: The Marshall of Essex or his dep't or Constables in Salem.

You are in theire Majest's names hereby required to apprehend forthwith and bring before us (Roger Toothaker of Bilrica who stands Charged with Sundry acts of Witchcraft by him Committed or done on the bodies of Eliz Hubbert, Ann Putnam, Mary Walcot &c of Salem Village in order to his Examination Relating to the premises fail not

Dated Salem May 18'th 1692

*John Hathorne [Assists]

*Jonathan Corwin [Assists]

[pbar] order of the Gover'r and Councill

the parson specified in this warrant was Apprehended this day and brought before the court According to the tenor of this warrant by me

*Joseph Neall

constable in Salem i: May 18'th: 1692:

(Reverse)

Ag'st Toothaker

Source: Essex County Court Archives, vol. 1, no. 273, Massachusetts Supreme Judicial Court, Judicial Archives, on deposit James Duncan Phillips Library, Peabody Essex Museum, Salem, MA.

Document 42

JOHN HALE, "DEPOSITION OF REV. JOHN HALE ET AL. V. SARAH BISHOP," MAY 20, 1692

The following deposition is exceedingly rare in that it was submitted by Reverend John Hale, the well-loved pastor of the First Church of Beverly, Massachusetts, against one of his own parishioners, Goodwife Sarah Bishop. Hale, as a fellow minister, was directly involved with Reverend Parris during the early days of the episode in Salem Village until his wife, Sarah, was cried out against by Mary Herrick in late 1692.

For many years this document was mistakenly identified with the case of Bridget Bishop, but recent scholarship has corrected the mistaken identity of Sarah Bishop, whose husband was also known as Edward Bishop. It was Sarah Bishop, not Bridget who operated an unlicensed public house in Beverly, and entertained people "in her house at unseasonable hours." Perhaps Reverend Hale's greatest fear was that "our young people were in danger to be corrupted" by this woman, and believed her capable of being involved in the untimely death of Goody Christian Trask "by the work of the Devil or witchcraft."

John Hale of Beverly aged about 56 years [torn] and says that about five or six years ago I, Christiana, the wife of John Trask (living in Salem bounds bordering on the abovesaid Beverly) being in full communion in our Church came to me to desire that Goodwife Bishop her neighbor [and] wife of Edward Bishop Jr. might not be permitted to receive the Lords Supper in our church till she had given her the said Trask satisfaction for some offenses that were against her viz. because the said Bishop did entertain people in her house at unseasonable hours in the night to keep drinking and playing at shovel-board whereby discord did arise in other families and young people were in danger to be corrupted and that the said Trask knew these things and had once gone into the house and finding some at shovel-board had taken the pieces they played with and thrown them into the fire and had reproved the said Bishop for promoting such disorders, but received no satisfaction from her about it.

I gave said Christian Trask direction how to proceed further in this matter if it were clearly proved and indeed by the information I have had otherwise I do fear that if a stop had not been put to those disorders said Edward Bishop's house would have been a house of great profaneness and iniquity.

But as to Christian Trask the next news I heard of her was that she was distracted and asking her husband Trask when she was so taken [he told] me she was taken distracted that night after she [came from] my house when she complained against Goody Bishop.

She continuing some time distracted we sought the Lord by fasting and prayer and the Lord was pleased to restore the said [Trask] to the use of her reason again. I was sitting with her often in [her] distraction (and took it then to be only distraction, yet fearing sometimes somewhat worse) but since I have seen the fits of those bewitched at Salem Village I call to mind some of hers to be much like some of theirs.

The said Trask when recovered as I understood it did manifest strong suspicion that she had been bewitched by the said Bishop's wife and showed so much averseness from having any conversation that I was then troubled at it hoping better of said Goody Bishop at that time for we have since [torn] at length said Christian Trask [was] again in a distracted fit on a Sabbath day in the forenoon at the public meeting to our public disturbance and so continued sometimes better sometimes worse unto her death, manifesting that she under temptation to kill herself or somebody else.

I enquired of Margaret King who kept at or nigh the house, what she had observed of said Trask before this last distraction she told [me] Goody Trask was much given to reading and search the prophecies of scripture.

The day before she made that disturbance in the meeting [house] she came home and said she had been with Goody Bishop and that they two were now friends or that effect.

I was oft praying with and counselling of Goody Trask before her death and not many days before her end being there she seemed more rational and earnestly desired Edward Bishop might be sent for that she might make friends with him, I asked her if she had wronged Edward Bishop she said not that she knew of unless it were in taking his shovel-board pieces when people were at play with them and throwing them into the fire and if she did evil in it she was very sorry for it and desired he would be friends with her or forgive her. This was the very day before she died, or a few days before.

Her distraction (or bewitching) continued about a month and in those intervals wherein she was better she earnestly desired prayers and the Sabbath before she died I received a note for prayers on her behalf which her husband said was written by herself and I judge was her own hand writing being well acquainted with her hand.

As to the wounds she died of I observed three deadly ones; apiece of her wind pipe cut out and another wound above that threw the windpipe and gullet and the vein they call jugular. So that I then judge and still do apprehend it impossible for her with so short a pair of scissors to mangle herself so without some extraordinary work of the devil or witchcraft.

Signed 20th May 1692 by *John Hale*

To several parts of this testimony can witness Maj'r Gedney, Mr. Parris, Joseph Herrick Jr. and his wife, Thomas Raiment and his wife, John Trask, Margaret King, Hannah wife of Cornell Baker, Miles and others.

As also about the said Goody Bishop, Captain William Raiment, his son William Raiment about creatures strangely dying. James Kettle, and the abovesaid Joseph Herrick and Thomas Raiment about sundry actions that [have] appearance of witchcraft.

Source: Essex County Court Archives, vol. 1, no. 142, Massachusetts Supreme Judicial Court, Judicial Archives, on deposit James Duncan Phillips Library, Peabody Essex Museum, Salem, MA.

Document 43

JOHN HATHORNE AND JONATHAN CORWIN, "DEPOSITION OF THOMAS PUTNAM AND EZEKIEL CHEEVER V. TITUBA," MAY 23, 1692

Thomas Putnam, a farmer and one of Reverend Samuel Parris's most loyal supporters, played a significant role in the trials, like his wife and daughter, in providing testimony calculated to identify suspected witches. Ezekiel Cheever, husband of Abigail Cheever, served the court as a recording secretary as well as a deponent.

Also Thomas Putnam aged about forty years and Ezekiel Cheever aged about thirty and six years testifies to the whole of the abovesaid and all three deponents aforesaid farther testify that after the said Indian began to confess she was herself very much afflicted and in the face of authority at the same time and openly charged the abovesaid Good and Osburne as the persons that afflicted her the aforesaid Indian.

   Sworn Salem May the 23rd 1692. Before us.
   *John Hathorne
   *Jonathan Corwin
   Pord'r of the Governor and Council
   Mr. Parris on his oath owned this to be the truth before the Jurors for inquest this 28th of June, 1692.
   Jurat in Curia
   The Deposition of Samuel Parris, Thomas Putnam, and Ezekiel Cheever against [unclear] Sarah Good, Sarah Osburne, Tituba Indian.

Source: Essex County Court Archives, vol. 1, no. 34, Massachusetts Supreme Judicial Court, Judicial Archives, on deposit James Duncan Phillips Library, Peabody Essex Museum, Salem, MA.

Document 44

UNKNOWN, "THOMAS GAGE AND PICKWORTH V. ROGER TOOTHAKER," MAY 23, 1692

This deposition offered by Thomas Gage implicates Dr. Roger Toothaker as a person who was conversant with "white magic" potent enough to kill a witch at a distance, and had passed this magical knowledge on to his daughter. This was a dangerous claim insofar that to claim to be able to kill by magic—even if your target was a witch was regarded as a form of malefic witchcraft. Toothaker was arrested under suspicion of witchcraft. He would be arrested and sent to the Boston jail in May 1692 and would die there of "natural causes" in June. He was 57 years of age, and should be considered a victim of the trials as well.

The Deposition of Thomas Gage Aged about six and thirty-six years of age
   This Deponent saith & doth testify that sometime this Last spring of the year, that Docter Toothaker was in his house in Beverly (upon some occasion) & we Discoursed about John Mastons Childe of salem that was then sick & having unwonted fitts: & Likewise another Childe of Phillip Whites of Beverly who was then strangly sick I persuaded said Toothaker to go & see said Children and said toothaker answered he had seen them both allready and that his opinion was they were under an Evill hand And farther said Toothaker sd that his Daughter had

killed a witch & I asked him how she Did it, & sd Toothaker answered readily that his Daughter had Learned something from him I asked by what means she Did it, & he sd that there was a [a] Certaine person bewitched & sd person Complained of being afflicted by another person that was suspected by the afflicted person: & farther sd Toothaker sd that his sd Daughter gott some of the afflicted persons urine & put it into an Earthen pott & stopt sd pott very Close & putt sd pott (up Close) [in] to a hott oven & stopt up sd oven & the next morning sd [witch] was Dead other things I have forgotten & farther saith not ias Pickworth Aged aboute thirty foure years testifieth to all that is above written.

(Reverse) Sworne by Thomas Gage Salem Village May. 23'd
before us
*John Hathorne, Assists
*Jonathan Corwin, Assists
Gouge Contra, Toothaker

Source: Essex County Court Archives, vol. 1, no. 275, Massachusetts Supreme Judicial Court, Judicial Archives, on deposit James Duncan Phillips Library, Peabody Essex Museum, Salem, MA.

Document 45

JOHN HATHORNE AND JONATHAN CORWIN, "WARRANT FOR APPREHENSION OF MARTHA CARRIER AND OFFICER'S RETURN," MAY 28, 1692

A housewife and mother of eight children, Martha Carrier, was a resident of Andover, Massachusetts. She was the first individual to be accused of witchcraft in Andover, but certainly not the last. Her first accuser was a neighbor, Benjamin Abbot, who blamed an illness upon her in retaliation, following a heated argument. Soon the team of "afflicted girls" were transported to Andover from Salem, and initiating an intensive witch hunt in Andover where the afflicted accused total strangers of witchcraft, as evidenced in the warrant below.

To the Marshall of Essex or his dept or to the Constables of Andover

You are in theire Majests names hereby required [to] apprehend
and forthwith secure, and bring before [us] martha Carrier the wife
of Thomas Currier of An[dover] on Tuesday next being the 31't
day of this Instant mo[nth] of May about ten of the clock in the
forenoon or as soon as may be afterwards at [the] house of L't
Nathaniell Ingersalls in Salem Village who stands charged with haveing
Committed Sundry [acts] of Witchcraft on the Bodys of Mary Walcot and abi[gail]
williams of Salem Village to theire great hurt
& [injury] in order to her Examination Relateing to the prem[ises]
abovesaid faile not

Dated Salem May 28'th 1692.
[pbar] us
*John Hathorne
*Jonathan Corwin
Assis'ts
(Reverse) I have apprehend the w'tin named parson and brought her
to the place appinted—
by me *John Ballard. const andover

Source: Essex County Court Archives, vol. 1, no. 310, Massachusetts Supreme Judicial Court, Judicial Archives, on deposit James Duncan Phillips Library, Peabody Essex Museum, Salem, MA.

Document 46

WILLIAM STACEY, "DEPOSITION OF WILLIAM STACY V. BRIDGET BISHOP," MAY 30, 1692

Probably no other deposition pulls together so many imaginative details of circumstantial evidence attributable to the malefic abilities of Bridget Bishop than this lengthy account submitted by William Stacy. As with the cases of John Louder and Richard Coman, Stacy strings together a narrative of incidents which, in his mind, could not have happened randomly or coincidentally, but must be attributable to Bridget Bishop's alleged malefic witchcraft.

William Stacy of the town of Salem aged thirty-six years or thereabouts deposeth and says,

That about fourteen years ago this deponent was visited with the small pox, then Bridget Bishop did give him a visit, and withal professed a great love for this deponent in his affliction. More than ordinary, at which this deponent admired, sometime after this deponent was well, the said Bishop got him to do some work for her. For which she gave him three pence, which seemed to the deponent as if it had been good money but he had not gone out above three or four rods before he looked in his pocket where he put it, for it, but could not find any. Sometime after this deponent met the said Bishop in the street a-going to mill; she asking this deponent whether his father would grind her grist? He put it to the said Bishop, why she asked? She answered because folks counted her a witch. This deponent made answer [that] he did not question but that his father would grind it, but being gone about six rod from her, the said Bishop; with a small load in his cart suddenly the off wheels slumped or sunk down into a hole upon plain ground. That this deponent was forced to get one to help him get the wheel out. Afterwards this deponent went back to look for said hole. Sometime after in the winter about midnight this deponent felt something between his lips pressing hard against his teeth and with all was very cold in so much that it did awake him so that he got up and sat upon his bed. He at the same time seeing the said Bridget Bishop sitting at the foot of his bed being, to his seeming, it was then as light as if it had been day, or one in the said Bishop's shape she having then a black cap and a black hat, and a red coat with two [Eakes] of two colors. Then she, the said Bishop or her shape, clapped her coat close to her legs and hopped upon the bed and about the room and then went out and then it was dark again. Sometime after the said Bishop went to this deponent and asked him whither that which he had reported was true. That he had told to several he answered that was true and that it was she, and bid her deny it, if she dare. The said Bishop did not deny it and went away very angry and said that this deponent did her more mischief than any other body. He asked why? She answered because folks would believe him before anybody else. Sometime after the said Bishop threatened this deponent and told him he was the occasion of bringing her out about the brass she stole. Sometime after, this deponent in a dark night was going to the barn, who was suddenly taken or hoisted from the ground and threw against a stone wall. After that [he was] taken up again a[nd] throwed down a bank at the end of his house. Sometime after, this deponent met the said Bishop by Isaac Sterne's brick kiln. After he had passed buy her, this deponent's horse stood still with a small load going up the hill so that the horse striving to draw all his gears and tacking flew in pieces and the cart fell down. Afterward, this deponent went to lift a bag of corn of about two bushels but could not budge it with all his might. This deponent hath met with several other of her pranks at several times which would take up a great time to tell of. This deponent doth verily believe that she [the] said Bridget Bishop was instrumental to his daughter Prisilla's death about two years ago, the child was a likely thriving child. And suddenly shreaked out and so continued in an unusual manner for about a fortnight and so died in that lamentable manner.

Sworn Salem May the 30th 1692 before us.

*John Hathorne Assis'ts

*Jonathan Corwin

Jurat in Curia June. 2'd 1692 (Written on side of paper) William Stacey

Source: Essex County Court Archives, vol. 1, nos. 138 and 139, Massachusetts Supreme Judicial Court, Judicial Archives, on deposit James Duncan Phillips Library, Peabody Essex Museum, Salem, MA.

Document 47

UNKNOWN, "EXAMINATION OF MARTHA CARRIER," MAY 31, 1692

In this intense examination of Martha Carrier, the entire array of key deponents is arrayed against the Andover matron: Abigail Williams, Elizabeth Hubbard, Mary Walcott, Susannah Sheldon, and, of course, Ann Putnam Jr. While the afflicted girls had never

previously known Martha Carrier, they were capable of testifying to encounters with her, including incidences when she performed acts of black magic and offered to tempt the girls to sign the "Devil's Book." When Martha would look upon the afflicted, they would fall, causing the justices to attribute the falling to Martha's evil eye. Martha firmly held to her plea of innocence and responded to the actions of the afflicted to observe that they were out of their wits.

Abigail Williams, who hurts you?
  Goody Carrier of Andover.
  Eliz: Hubbard who hurts you?
  Goody Carrier
  Susan: Sheldon, who hurts you?
  Goody Carrier, she bites me, pinches me, & tells me she would cut my throat, if I did not sign her book.
  Mary Walcot said she afflicted her & brought the book to her.
  What do you say to this you are charged with?
  I have not done it.
  Sus: Sheldon cried she looks upon the black man.
  Ann Putman complained of a pin stuck in her.
  What black man is that?
  I know none
  Ann Putman testifyed there was.
  Mary Warrin cryed out she was prickt.
  What black man did you see?
  I saw no black man but your own presence.
  Can you look upon these & not knock them down?
  They will dissemble if I look upon them.
  You see you look upon them & they fall down
  It is false the Devil is a liar.
  I lookt upon none since I came into the room but you
  Susan: Sheldon cryed out in a Trance I wonder what could you murder. 13. persons?
  Mary Walcot testifyed the same that there lay.13. Ghosts.
  All the afflicted fell into most intollerable out-cries & agonies.
  Eliz: Hubbard & Ann Putman testifyed the same that she had killed 13. at Andover.
  It is a shamefull thing that you should mind these folks that are out of their wits.
  Do not you see them?
  If I do speak you will not believe me?
  You do see them, said the accusers.
  You lye, I am wronged.
  There is the black man wispering in her ear said many of the afflicted.
  Mercy Lewes in a violent fit, was well upon the examinants grasping her arm.

The Tortures of the afflicted was so great that there was no enduring of it, so that she was ordered away & to be bound hand & foot with all expedition the afflicted in the mean while almost killed to the great trouble of all spectators Magistrates & others.

Note. As soon as she was well bound they all had strange & sodain ease.

Mary Walcott told the Magistrates that this woman told her she had been a witch this 40 years.

(Reverse) Martha Carriers Carrier Examination

Source: Essex County Court Archives, vol. 1, no. 311, Massachusetts Supreme Judicial Court, Judicial Archives, on deposit James Duncan Phillips Library, Peabody Essex Museum, Salem, MA.

Document 48

UNKNOWN, "INDICTMENT NO. 1 V. MARTHA CARRIER, FOR AFFLICTING MARY WALCOTT," MAY 31, 1692

This is a deposition submitted by Mary Walcott, one of the so-called afflicted girls against Andover housewife, Martha Carrier.

Anno Regis et Reginae Willm
et Mariae Nunc Angliae &c Quarto./

Essex ss The Jurors: for our Sovereign Lord & Lady the King and
Queen presents that [Bridgett] Martha Carrier wife of [Richard]
Thomas Carrier of Andover in the County of Essex husbandman the
thirty first Day of May—in the fourth Year of the Reign of our Sovereign Lord and Lady
William and Mary by the Grace of God of
England, Scotland, France and Ireland King, and Queen Defenders
of the faith &c and divers other Days and times as well before, as
after, certain Detestable Arts called Witchcrafts and Sorceries,
Wickedly and feloniously hath Used. Practiced. and Exercised, at
and within the Township of Salem in the County of Essex afores'd
in, Upon, and against, one Mary Walcott of Salem Village Single-
woman in the County of Essex aforesaid by which said wicked Arts
the said Mary Walcott the thirty first Day of May—in the fourth year above said and
divers other Dayes and times, as well before, as
after, was and is Tortured, Afflicted, Pined, Consumed wasted
& Tormented against the Peace of our Sovereign Lord and Lady the King
and Queen and against the form of the Statute in that case made and Provided.

Witnesses
J't
Mary Walcott

Ju't
Elizabeth Hubbard
Ann Putman

Source: Essex County Court Archives, vol. 1, no. 309, Massachusetts Supreme Judicial Court, Judicial Archives, on deposit James Duncan Phillips Library, Peabody Essex Museum, Salem, MA.

Document 49

UNKNOWN, "INDICTMENT NO. 2 V. MARTHA CARRIER, FOR AFFLICTING ELIZABETH HUBBARD," MAY 31, 1692

This second indictment by Elizabeth Hubbard reaffirms the accusation, this time by Elizabeth Hubbard, that Carrier was a witch. It would be later contended by the afflicted children that Carrier commanded an "army" of witches, and later, Reverend Cotton Mather referred to her as the "Queen of Hell." By the end of her examination, the outcry of the afflicted girls against her was so great that, according to Reverend Parris, "there was no enduring of it, so she [Carrier] was ordered away and to be bound hand and foot with all expedition."

Anno Regis et Reginae Willm et
Mariae nunc Angliae &c Quarto:

Essex ss The Jurors of our Sovereigne Lord and Lady the King
and Queen: pr'sents That Martha Carrier wife of [Richard] Thomas
Carier of Andover in the county of Essex husbandman the 31 Day of May in the fourth
year of the Reigne of our Sovereigne Lord and Lady
William and Mary by the Grace of God of England Scottland France
and Ireland King and Queen Defenders of the faith: &c And Divers
other Dayes and Times as well before as after, certaine Detestable
Arts called Witchcrafts: and Sorceries, Wickedly and felloniously
hath used Practised and Excercised at and within the Towneship
of Salem in the County of Essex afores'd in and upon and ag't
one Elizabeth Hubbard of Salem in the County of Essex afores'd
by which said Wicked Arts. the said Elizabeth Hubbard the thirty
first Day of May in the forth Year aboves'd and Divers other Dayes,
and times, as well before as after was and is Tortured Afflicted Pined
Consumed Wasted and Tormented ag't the Peace of our Sovereigne
Lord and Lady the King and Queen: and ag't the forme of the Stat—
ute in that case made and Provided

Witnesses
Elizabeth Hubbard Jurat.
Mary Walcutt Jurat.
Ann Putnam
Mary Warren Jurat.
(Reverse) bila vera No 2 Martha Carier

Source: Essex County Court Archives, vol. 1, no. 312, Massachusetts Supreme Judicial Court, Judicial Archives, on deposit James Duncan Phillips Library, Peabody Essex Museum, Salem, MA.

Document 50

JOHN HATHORNE AND JONATHAN COWRIN, "WARRANT FOR APPREHENSION OF WILMOTT REED," MAY 28, 1692

After the afflicted girls cried out against Wilmot "Mammy" Reed (or Redd), depositions followed from Mary Walcott, Mercy Lewis, and other members of the group of afflicted. Following these, Judges Hathorne and Corwin summoned Reed/Redd to appear in court to be examined. The following is the warrant for her arrest.

To the Constables of Marblehead
    You are in theire Majest's names hereby required to apprehend and bring before Us willmut Reed the wife of Samuell Reed of Marblehead, on Tuesday next being the 31 day of this Instant moneth of May aboute ten of the Clock in the forenoon at the house of L't Nathan'l Ingerslls in Salem Village; who Stands Charged with having Committed Sundry acts of Witchcraft on the bodys of Mary Walcot and Marcy Lewis and Others[?] of Salem Village to theire great hurt &c, in order to her Examination Relateing to the aboves'd premises and hereof you are not to faile
    Dated Salem May 28'th 1692
    P us *John Hathorne Assis'ts
    *Jonathan Corwin Assis'ts
    (Reverse) In answer to the withinmentioned warrant I have apprehended Willmot Reed Wife to Sam'll Reed of Marblehead & brought her to the house of L't Ingersals, *May the 31'th 92.*
    *James Smith Con'st for Marblehead

Source: Essex County Court Archives, vol. 2, no. 6, Massachusetts Supreme Judicial Court, Judicial Archives, on deposit James Duncan Phillips Library, Peabody Essex Museum, Salem, MA.

Document 51

UNKNOWN, "INDICTMENT V. WILMOTT REED, NO. 1," MAY 31, 1692

The following indictment for the crime of witchcraft names as its victim a lesser-known afflicted girl, 18-year-old Elizabeth Booth. As a member of the less prominent group of afflicted girls, she was not especially involved in the greater number of accusations, but contributed depositions against Wilmot "mammy" Reed/Redd, Giles Corey, John Proctor, and Elizabeth Proctor.

Essex in the Province of the Massachusetts Bay in New England Ss

Anno RR's & Reginae Gulielmi & Mariae Angliae &ca Annoq'e Domini 1692

The Juriors for our Sov'r Lord and Lady the King & Queen doe present That Willmott Redd Wife of Samuel Redd of Marblehead In the County of Essex fisherman upon the Thirty first day of May In the Yeare afores'd and divers other days and times as well before as after Certaine detestable Arts called Witchcraft and Sorceries Wickedly Mallitiously and felloniously hath used practised and exercised At and in the Towne of Salem in the County of Essex-Aforesaid in upon and against one Eliza' Booth of Salem Aforesaid Single Woman—by which said Wicked Acts the said Eliz'a Booth The day & yeare afore said and divers other days and times both before and after was and is Tortured Aflicted Consumed Pined Wasted and Tormented and also for Sundry other Acts of Witchcraft by the said Willmott Redd Comitted and done before and Since that time against the peace of our Sov'r Lord & Lady the King & Queen theire Crown and Dignity and the forme Of the Stattute in that case made and Provided.

(Reverse) Indictm't Vs Willmott Redd for bewitching Eliza' Booth Ignoramus

Source: Essex County Court Archives, vol. 2, no. 5, Massachusetts Supreme Judicial Court, Judicial Archives, on deposit James Duncan Phillips Library, Peabody Essex Museum, Salem, MA.

Document 52

UNKNOWN, "INDICTMENT V. WILMOTT REED, NO. 2," MAY 31, 1692

Elizabeth Hubbard's deposition resulted in this indictment against Wilmot "mammy" Reed/Redd of Marblehead, Massachusetts. Prior to her accusation of Wilmot Reed, it is doubtful that Elizabeth Hubbard had ever had an opportunity to see the suspected witch from Marblehead.

Hubbard was an orphan, having lost her parents in the Indian attacks of settlements on the Maine frontier. She had been adopted by the family of her mother's sister, Rachel Hubbard Griggs and her husband, Dr. William Griggs, the physician responsible for diagnosing Abigail Williams and Betty Parris as being under the "evil hand" of witchcraft prior to the outbreak of the witchcraft episode in Salem Village.

Essex in the province of the Massachusetts Bay in New England ss

Anno RR's & Reginae Gulielmi & Mariae Angliae, &c Quarto Annoq'e Domini 1692.

The Juriors for our Sov'r Lord and Lady the King & Queen doe present that Willmott Redd wife of Samuel Redd of Marblehead In the County of Essex fisherman upon the Thirty first day of May In the year aforesaid and divers other days and times as well before as after Certaine Detestable Arts. called Witchcraft and Sorceries Wickedly Mallitiously and felloniously hath used practised and

Exercised at and in the Towne of Salem in the County of Essex aforesaid in Upon and against one Eliz'a Hobert of Salem aforsaid in the County of Essex aforesaid Single Woman by which said wicked Acts the said Eliz'a Hobert the day & yeare aforesaid and Divers other dayes and times both before and after was and is Tortured aflicted Consumed Pined Wasted and Tormented and also for Sundry other Acts of Witchcraft by the said Willmot Redd Comitted and done before and Since that time against the peace of o'r Soveraigne Lord and Lady the King and Queen theire Crowne and Dignity And the forme Of the Stattute in that Case made and Provided.—

(Reverse) Indictm't agst Willmott Redd for bewitching Eliz'a Hobert Billa vera-Ponet se

Source: Essex County Court Archives, vol. 2, no. 9, Massachusetts Supreme Judicial Court, Judicial Archives, on deposit James Duncan Phillips Library, Peabody Essex Museum, Salem, MA.

Document 53

UNKNOWN, "EXAMINATION OF WILMOTT REED," MAY 31, 1692

In the text of this examination is a wonderful example of the "touch test" with Susan Sheldon, which suggested that if a person was seized by a spell-induced fit, spasm, or other affliction, his or her condition would be relieved if he or she touched the witch responsible for casting the malefic spell. By touching the witch, the evil humors or spirits causing the affliction would pass back into the being responsible for casting the spell. Such tests were considered inappropriate by some clergy, such as Increase Mather, using the Devil's tools to discover the Devil, and held that magic of any kind for any purpose was wrong and out-of-bounds for Christians. For others it was considered positive proof of a suspect's guilt.

The examination of Wilmot Redd. Wife of Samuell Redd of Marblehead, fisherman, May 31, 1692

When this Examinant was brought in Mercy Lewes Mary Walcot & Abigail Williams fell into fits

Mercy Lewes said this Woman hath Pinched me a great many times. Mary Walcot says, this Woman brought the Book to her.

Ann Putman jun'r saith she never hurt her, but (she hath seen) she hath seen her once upon Mercy Lewes & once upon Mary Walcot the last fast day.

ELIZ: Hubbard said this Examinant had brought the book to her, & told her she would knock her in the head, if she would not write.
Ann Putman said she brought the Book to her just now

ELIZ: Booth fell into a fit, & Mary Walcott & Ann Putman said it was this Woman afflicted her.

SUSAN: Sheldon was ordered to go to the Examinant but was knock down before she came to her, & being so, [was] carried to said Redd in a fit, was made well after said Redd had grasped her arm.

ELIZ: Hubbard dealt with after the same manner
This Examinant was bid by the Magistrates to Look upon Eliz: Hubbard, & upon the examinant's casting her eye upon said Hubbard, she the said Hubbard was knocked down.

ABIG: Williams & John Indian being carried to the Examinant in a grevious fit were made Well by her grasping their arms.

This examinant being often urged what she thought these Persons ailed; would reply, I cannot tell. Then being asked if she did not think they were Bewitched: she answered I cannot tell and being urged for her opinion in the case All she would say was: my opinion is they are in a sad condition.

(Reverse) Examination of Willmott Redd

Source: Essex County Court Archives, vol. 2, no. 8, Massachusetts Supreme Judicial Court, Judicial Archives, on deposit James Duncan Phillips Library, Peabody Essex Museum, Salem, MA.

Document 54

REVEREND COTTON MATHER, "REVEREND COTTON MATHER LETTER TO JOHN RICHARDS," MAY 31, 1692

The following letter was written by Reverend Cotton Mather to Justice John Richards of the governor's newly established Court of Oyer and Terminer. In it Mather seeks to provide spiritual advice and wise counsel as to how to view the witch trials then looming before the court. In it he strongly advises Richards to be careful not to "lay too much stress upon spectre testimony" since it is known that "the devils have sometimes represented the shapes of not only innocent persons, but also very virtuous." It is similar in some ways to the advice offered in "The Return of Several Ministers," presented to the court as a whole in June, after the execution of Bridget Bishop.

May 31, 1692

Honorable Sir,

I could not have asked you as I now do to excuse me from waiting upon you, with the utmost of my little skill and care to assist the noble service whereto you are called of God this week, the service of encountering the wicked spirits in the high places of our air, and of detecting and confounding of their confederates, were it not that I am languishing under such an overthrow of my health as makes it very dubious that my company may prove more troublesome than serviceable; the least excess of travel, or diet, or anything that may discompose me, would at this time threaten perhaps my life itself, as my friends advise me; and yet I hope before you can get far into that mysterious affair which is now before you, I may with God's blessing recover so far as to attend your desires, which to me always are commands. In the meantime, least I should be guilty of any sinful omission in declining what no good man amongst us can decline, even to do the best I can for the strengthening of your honorable hands in that work of God, whereto (I thank Him) He hath so well fitted you, as well as called you, I thought it my duty briefly to offer you my poor thoughts on this astonishing occasion.

I. I am not without very lively hopes that our good God will prosper you in that undertaking which He hath put you now upon. His people have been fasting and praying before Him for your direction; and yourselves are persons whose exemplary devotion disposeth you to such a dependence on the wonderful Counselor, for His counsel in an affair thus full of wonder, as He doth usually answer with the most favorable assistances. You will easily pardon me that I do not back my thoughts with confirming histories; it is not a sudden letter that will admit them, and it would be too like ostentation to produce them; nevertheless, I cannot for once forbear minding of the famous accidents at Mohra in Swedeland, where a fast was kept among the people of God because of a stupendous witchcraft, much like ours, making havoc of the kingdom, was immediately [followed] with a remarkable smile of God upon the endeavors of the judges to discover and extirpate the authors of that execrable witchcraft. Wherefore be encouraged.

II. And yet I must humbly beg you that in the management of the affair in your most worthy hands, you do not lay more stress upon pure specter testimony than it will bear. When you are satisfied or have good, plain, legal evidence that the demons which molest our poor neighbors do indeed represent such and such people to the sufferers, tho this be a presumption, yet I suppose you will not reckon it a conviction that the people so represented are witches to be immediately exterminated. It is very certain that the devils have sometimes represented the shapes of persons not only innocent, but also very virtuous, tho I believe that the just God then ordinarily provides a way for the speedy vindication of the persons thus abused. Moreover, I do suspect that persons who have too much indulged themselves in malignant, envious, malicious ebullitions of their souls, may unhappily expose themselves to the judgment of being represented by devils, of whom they never had any vision, and with whom they have much less written any covenant. I would say this: if upon the bare supposal of a poor creature being represented by a specter, too great a progress be made by the authority in ruining a poor neighbor so represented, it may be that a door may be thereby opened for the devils to obtain from the courts in the invisible world a license to proceed unto most hideous desolations upon the repute and repose of such as have yet been kept from the great transgression. If mankind have thus far once consented unto the credit of diabolical representations, the door is opened! Perhaps there are wise and good men that may be ready to style him that shall advance this caution, a witch advocate; but in the winding up, this caution will certainly be wished for.

III. Tho tis probable that the devils may (tho not often, yet sometimes) make most bloody invasions upon our exterior concerns, without any witchcrafts of our fellow creatures to empower them, and I do expect that as when our Lord was coming in His human nature among us, there was a more sensible annoyance of the destroyer upon our human nature than at other times, thus it will be just before our Lord's coming again in His human nature, when He will also dispossess the devils of their aerial region to make a New Heaven for His raised there. Nevertheless there is cause enough to think that it is a horrible witchcraft which hath given rise to the troubles wherewith Salem Village is at this day harassed; and the indefatigable pains that are used for the tracing this witchcraft are to be thankfully accepted, and applauded among all this people of God.

IV. Albeit the business of this witchcraft be very much transacted upon the stage of imagination, yet we know that, as in treason there is an imagining which is a capital crime, and here also the business thus managed in imagination yet may not be called imaginary. The effects are dreadfully real. Our dear neighbors are most really tormented, really murdered, and really acquainted with hidden things. Which are afterwards proved plainly to have been realities. I say, then, as that man is justly executed for an assassinate, who in the sight of men shall with a sword in his hand stab his neighbor into the heart, so suppose a long train laid unto a barrel of gunpowder under the floor where a neighbor is, and suppose a man with a match perhaps in his mouth, out of sight, set fire unto the further end of the train, tho never so far off. This man also is to be treated as equally a malefactor. Our neighbors at Salem Village are blown up, after a sort, with an infernal gunpowder; the train is laid in the laws of the kingdom of darkness limited by God himself. Now the question is, who gives fire to this train? and by what acts is the match applied? Find out the persons that have done this thing, and be their acts in doing it either mental, or oral, or manual, or what the devil will, I say abeant quo digni sunt.

V. To determine a matter so much in the dark as to know the guilty employers of the devils in this work of darkness, this is a work, this is a labor. Now first a credible confession of the guilty wretches is one of the most hopeful ways of coming at them, and I say a credible confession because even confession itself sometimes is not credible. But a person of a sagacity many times thirty furlongs less than yours, will easily perceive what confession may be credible, and what may be the result of only a delirious brain, or a discontented heart. All the difficulty is how to obtain this confession. For this I am far from urging the un-English method of torture, but instead thereof I propound these three things: first, who can tell but when the witches come upon their trials, they may be so forsaken, as to confess all. The Almighty God having heard the appeals of our cries to Heaven, may so thunder-strike their souls, as to make them show their deeds. Moreover, the devils themselves who aim at the entrapping of their own miserable clients, may treacherously depart from them in their examinations, which throws them into such toiling vexations that they'll discover all. Besides, when you come solemnly in God's name to exhibit yourselves as His viceregents, and when you come to form a most awful type of the Last Judgment, whereat the devils of all things tremble most, even they also may be smitten with such terrors as may contribute a little to their departure from the miscreants whom they have entangled. An unexpected confession, is that whereunto witches are very often driven. Secondly, I am ready to think that there is usually some expression or behavior whereto the devils do constantly oblige the witches, as a kind of sacrament, upon their least failure wherein the witches presently lose the thus forfeited assistances of the devils, and all comes out. Please then to observe, if you can find any one constant scheme of discourse or action, whereto the suspected seem religiously devoted, and (which may easily be done by the common policies of conversation) cause them to transgress that, a confession will probably then come on apace. Thirdly, whatever hath a tendency to put the witches into confusion is likely to bring them unto confession too. Here cross and swift questions have their use, but besides them for my part, I should not be unwilling that an experiment be made whether accused parties can repeat the Lord's Prayer, or those other systems of Christianity which, it seems, the devils often make the witches unable to repeat without ridiculous depravations or amputations. The danger of this experiment will be taken away if you make no evidence of it, but only put it to the use I mention, which is that of confounding the lisping witches to give a reason why they cannot, even with prompting, repeat those heavenly composures. The like I would say of some other experiments, only we may venture too far before we are aware.

VI. But what if no confession can be obtained; I say yet the case is far from desperate. For if there have been those words uttered by the witches, either by way of threatening, or of asking, or of bragging, which rationally demonstrate such a knowledge of the woeful circumstances attending the afflicted people, as could not be had without some diabolical communion, the proof of such is enough to fix the guilt. Moreover, I look upon wounds that have been given unto specters, and received by witches as intimations broad enough, in concurrence with other things, to bring out the guilty. Tho I am not fond of assaying to give such wounds, yet the proof such when given carries with it what is very palpable.

Once more, can there be no puppets found out? and here I would say thus much, I am thinking that some witches make their own bodies to be their puppets. If therefore you can find that when the witches do anything easy, that is not needful (and it is needful that I put in that clause not needful because it is possible that a prestigious demon may imitate what we do, tho we are none of his) I say if you find the same thing, presently, and hurtfully, and more violently done by any unseen hand unto the bodies of the sufferers, hold them, for you have catched a witch. I add, why should not witch-marks be searched for? The properties, the qualities of those marks are described by diverse weighty writers. I never saw any of those marks, but it is doubtless not impossible for a chirurgeon, when he sees them, to say what are magical, and if these become once apparent, it is apparent that these witches have gone so far in their wickedness as to admit most cursed succages, whereby the devils have not only fetched out of them, it may be the spirits of which they make vehicles, wherein they visit the afflicted, but also they have infused a venom into them which exalts the malignity of their spirits as well as of their bodies; and it is likely that by means of this ferment they would be found buoyant (if the water-ordeal were made upon them).

VII. I begin to fear that the devils do more easily proselyte poor mortals into witchcraft than is commonly conceived. When a sinful child of man distempers himself with some exorbitant motions in his mind (and it is to be feared the murmuring frenzies of late prevailing in the country have this way exposed many to sore temptations) a devil then soon presents himself unto him, and he demands, Are you willing that I should go do this or that for you? If the man once comply, the devil hath him now in a most horrid snare, and by a permission from the just vengeance of God he visits the man with buffetings as well as allurements, till the forlorn man at first only for the sake of quietness, but at length out of improved wickedness, will commission the devil to do mischief as often as he requires it. And for this cause tis worth considering, whether there be a necessity always by extirpations by halter or fagot every wretched creature that shall be hooked into some degrees of witchcraft. What if some of the lesser criminals be only scourged with lesser punishments, and also put upon some solemn, open, public, and explicit renunciation of the devil? I am apt to think that the devils would then cease afflicting the neighborhood whom these wretches have stood them upon, and perhaps they themselves would now suffer some impressions from the devils, which if they do, they must be willing to bear till the God that hears prayer deliver them. Or what if the death of some of the offenders were either diverted or inflicted, according to the success of such their renunciation.

But I find my free thoughts thus freely laid before Your Honor, begin to have too much freedom in them. I shall now therefore add no more but my humble and most fervent prayers to the God who gives wisdom liberally, that you and your honorable brethren may be furnished from on high, with all that wisdom, as well as justice, which is requisite in the thorny affair before you. God will be with you. I am persuaded He will; and with that persuasion I subscribe myself,

Sir, Your very devoted servant.

Source: Collections of the Massachusetts Historical Society, 7th series, vols. VII and VIII. Boston: Massachusetts Historical Society, 1911–1912.

Further Reading

Baker, Emerson W. *A Storm of Witchcraft: The Salem Trials and the American Experience.* Oxford, UK: Oxford University Press, 2015.

Boyer, Paul, and Stephen Nissenbaum. *Salem Possessed: The Social Origins of Witchcraft.* Cambridge, MA: Harvard University Press, 1974.

Godbeer, Richard. *The Salem Witch Hunt: A Brief History with Documents.* Boston and New York: Bedford/St. Martin's, 2011.

Hoffer, Peter Charles. *The Salem Witchcraft Trials: A Legal History.* Lawrence: University Press of Kansas, 1997.

Levin, David. *What Happened in Salem?* New York: Harcourt, Brace and Company, 1960.

Norton, Mary Beth. *In the Devil's Snare: The Salem Witchcraft Crisis of 1692.* New York: Random House, 2003.

Reis, Elizabeth. *Damned Women: Sinners and Witches in Puritan New England.* Ithaca, NY: Cornell University Press, 1997.

Upham, Charles. *The History of Witchcraft and Salem Village, Vols. 1 and 2.* Boston: Wiggin and Lunt, 1867.

Weisman, Richard. *Witchcraft, Magic and Religion in 17th Century Massachusetts.* Amherst: University of Massachusetts Press, 1984.

Chapter 2

June to July 1692

The period from June through July 1692 is perhaps the most important period in terms of actual events. By this time, the afflicted children are a clearly defined group with a longstanding practice of providing magistrates, juries, and observers with dramatic demonstrations of spectral evidence. As of June, Reverend Increase Mather has returned from England, bringing with him his choice for royal governor, newly knighted and appointed Sir William Phips bearing a new royal colonial charter making Massachusetts a royal crown colony and uniting it with old Plymouth Colony. By June, the governor's Court of Oyer and Terminer with Deputy Governor, Chief Justice William Stoughton is now well in place, hearing cases. By this period, the jails of eastern Massachusetts, especially Salem, Boston, and Ipswich were full of persons awaiting trial for witchcraft, largely as a result of the earlier efforts of the Honorable John Hathorne and Honorable Jonathan Corwin.

Most importantly, people begin to hang for witchcraft at this stage. Bridget Bishop is tried and by June 12, 1692, will be executed, causing all of the trial participants to pause briefly to reflect upon where the entire episode was headed. As a direct result, the ministers of Boston produce, with the help of Reverend Cotton Mather, "The Return of Several Ministers," a philosophical narrative to help the court in its deliberations moving forward, and especially to give them guidance of the use and dangers of spectral evidence now quickly becoming the only type of evidence employed by the court in condemning the accused.

Finally, on July 22, 1692, the largest group of condemned witches would be hanged. This becomes the point-of-no-return of the trials, since this July groups of five condemned alleged witches represented the largest number of individuals ever executed on a single date in colonial history up to that point.

Document 55

ELIZABETH HUBBARD, "DEPOSITION OF ELIZABETH HUBBARD V. BRIDGET BISHOP AND MARY WARREN," JUNE 1, 1692

In the following brief deposition, servant and afflicted child Betty Hubbard strives to strike a blow against a former afflicted child, Mary Warren, by linking her with the most notorious of all witchcraft suspects up to that time, Bridget Bishop (aka Bridget Oliver). This strategy is commonly identified as "guilt by association." The problem, as always, is that it is spectral evidence and cannot be confirmed visually by anyone except by the deponent.

Now whilst I was writing these lines there came in Mary Warren and another woman with her which woman Mary Warren said was Goody Oliver and that woman came in her shift.

Elizabeth Hubbard against Mary Warren.

Source: Essex County Court Archives, vol. 1, no. 152, Massachusetts Supreme Judicial Court, Judicial Archives, on deposit James Duncan Phillips Library, Peabody Essex Museum, Salem, MA.

Document 56

THOMAS NEWTON, "CONFESSION OF SARAH CHURCHILL," JUNE 1, 1692

Sarah Churchill, often referred to as Sarah Churchwell, was an orphaned maidservant of George Jacobs Sr. Jacobs was a harsh master who apparently earned Sarah's contempt as a result of ill treatment and physical beatings. Consequently, when presented with the opportunity, Sarah clearly implicates not only herself by confessing witchcraft, but Bridget Bishop, Ann Pudeater, and George Jacobs Jr., as well. In later testimony, she claims that he forced her to sign the Devil's Book. The ironic difference is that while Sarah saved her life by confessing, Bishop, Pudeater, and Jacobs—who all claimed innocence— were all hanged for witchcraft.

Sarah Churchill confesses that Goody Pudeator brought the book to this examinant and she signed it, but did not know her at that time but when she saw her she knew her to be the same and that Goody Bishop alias Olliver appeared to this examinant and told her she had killed John Trask's Child, (whose Child died about that time) and said Bishop alias Olliver afflicted her as also did old George Jacobs, and before that time this examinant being afflicted could not do her service as formerly and her said Master Jacobs called her bitch, witch, and ill names and then afflicted her as [before] above and that Pudeator brought three images like Mercy Lewis, Ann Putnam, Elizabeth Hubbard and they brought her thorns and she stuck them in the Images and told her the persons whose likeness they were, would be afflicted and the other day saw Goody Olliver [sit] sat upon her knee.

Jurat in Curia by *Sarah Churchill*

This confession was taken before John Hathorne and Jonathan Corwin Esquires l'o June 1692, as attests

*Thomas Newton

Source: Essex County Court Archives, vol. 1, no. 262, Massachusetts Supreme Judicial Court, Judicial Archives, on deposit James Duncan Phillips Library, Peabody Essex Museum, Salem, MA.

Document 57

JOHN HATHORNE AND JONATHAN COWRIN, "DEPOSITION OF MARY WARREN V. BRIDGET BISHOP AND NATHANIEL CARY," JUNE 1, 1692

After Bridget Bishop's arrest and imprisonment, depositions continued to be presented against her. The following testimony submitted to the court by Mary Warren underscores the widely accepted belief that a witch's spirit might leave the jail to visually afflict others, but if her body was restrained by iron chains she was incapable of doing any physical harm to her victims.

Mary Warren aged 20 years of thereabouts testifies and says that several times after the nineteenth day of April last when Bridget Bishop alias Olliver who was in the jail at Salem she did appear to this deponent tempting her to sign the book and oft times during her being there as aforesaid the said Bridget did torture and afflict this deponent and being in chains said though she could not do it, she would bring one that should do it which now she knows to be Mr. Cary that then came and afflicted her.

    Sworn before us the 1st day of June 1692
    *John Hathorne
    *Jonathan Corwin Assists

Source: Essex County Court Archives, vol. 1, nos. 117, Massachusetts Supreme Judicial Court, Judicial Archives, on deposit James Duncan Phillips Library, Peabody Essex Museum, Salem, MA.

Document 58

SUSANNAH SHELDON, "DEPOSITION OF SUSANNAH SHELDON V. BRIDGET BISHOP, MARY ENGLISH, PHILLIP ENGLISH, GILES COREY, AND MARTHA COREY," DATE UNKNOWN

Susannah Sheldon was one of the principal members of the group of afflicted girls responsible for the greater weight of spectral evidence presented during the Salem episode, filing at least 24 depositions. She was another young refugee from Maine province, having fled the destruction of the Indian wars on the frontier. She was 18 years old when she first joined the group of young female deponents in giving testimony against the accused. Her first deposition was entered during the last week of April 1692. Interestingly, she was personally responsible for bringing accusations against Salem's most wealthy and prominent couple, Philip and Mary English.

On the fourth day at night came Goody Olliver and Mrs. English and Goodman Corey and a black man with a high crowned hat with books in their hands Goody

Olliver had me touch her book. I would not. I did not know her name she told me her name was Goody Olliver and bid me touch her book now I bid her tell me how long she had been a witch she told me she had been a witch above twenty years. Then there came a streaked snake creeping over her shoulder and crept into her bosom. Mrs. English had a yellow bird in her bosom and Goodman Corey had two tercels hang to his coat and he opened his bosom and put his tercels to his breast and gave them suck then Goodman Corey and Goody Oliver kneeled down before the black man and went to prayer and then the black man told me Goody Olliver had been a witch twenty years and a half. Then they all set to biting me and so went away the next day came Goodman Corey and Mrs. English in the morning and told me I should not eat not vitals. I took a spoon and put on spoonful in my mouth and Goodman Corey gave me a blow on the ear and all most choked me then he laughed at me and told me I would eat when he told me I should not then he clenched my hands that they could not be opened for more than a quarter of an our then came Phillip English and told me if I would touch his book he would not hit me but I refused then he did bite me and went away.

The sixth day at night came Goody Olliver and Mrs. English and Goodman Corey and his wife Goody Corey she proffered me a book I refused it and asked her where she lived she told me she lived in Boston prison then she pulled out her breast and the black man gave her a thing like a black pig it had no hair on it and she put it to her breast and gave it suck and when it had sucked on breast she put it the other and gave it suck there then she gave it to the black man. Then went to prayer to the black man then Goody Olliver told me that she had killed four women two of them were the Foster's wives and John Trask's wife and did not name the other then they did all bite me and went away then the next day came Goody Corey choked me and told me I would not eat when my dame bid me but now I should eat none.

Susannah Sheldon against Oliver, English, and his wife, Corey and his wife, Goody Bucklie and her daughter and Boston woman.

Source: Essex County Court Archives, vol. 1, nos. 153, 154, and 168, Massachusetts Supreme Judicial Court, Judicial Archives, on deposit James Duncan Phillips Library, Peabody Essex Museum, Salem, MA.

Document 59

J. BARTON ET AL., "PHYSICAL EXAMINATION OF BRIDGET BISHOP, REBECCA NURSE, ELIZABETH PROCTOR, ALICE PARKER, SUSANNAH MARTIN, AND SARAH GOOD, NO. 1," JUNE 2, 1692

The traditional belief that Satan gave to his witches a demonic creature, called a familiar, was widespread during the 17th century. Familiars were supernatural beings that did the witch's bidding and served as an intermediary between themselves and Satan. It was thought that these creatures survived by sucking blood from the body of the witch to whom they were assigned. The place where blood was drawn was referred to as a witch's teat or witch's mark. Finding such marks on the body of a suspected witch was one of the few types of tangible evidence available to the court. When women were physically examined, it was usually done by a committee of midwives in the company of a doctor. A report declaring their findings was then presented to the court indicating whether the accused bore the requisite witch's teat indicating the presence of a familiar and possible guilt of witchcraft. The following is one such examination.

1692 Salem June 2nd about ten in Morning

We whose names are under written being commanded by Captain George Corwin Esquire Sherriff of the County of Essex this 2nd day of June 1692 for to view the bodies of Bridget Bishop alias Oliver, Rebecca Nurse, Elizabeth Proctor, Alice Parker, Susannah Martin, Sarah Good.

The first three, namely Bishop, Nurse, Proctor, by diligent search have discovered a preternatural excrescence of flesh between the pudendum and anus much like to teets and not usual in women and much unlike to the other three that had been searched by us and that they were in all the three women near the same place.

*J Barton Surgeon
Alice Pickering
her mark

Jane Woolings
her mark

Marjery Williams
her mark

Anna Stephens
her mark

Elizabeth Hill
her mark

Elanor Henderson
her mark

Rebecca Sharpe
her mark

Lydia Pickman

*Hannah Kezer

Sworn in Court June 2nd 169
*Attest * Step: Sewall Cle*

Source: Essex County Court Archives, vol. 1, no. 136, Massachusetts Supreme Judicial Court, Judicial Archives, on deposit James Duncan Phillips Library, Peabody Essex Museum, Salem, MA.

Document 60

REBECAH SHARPE ET AL., "PHYSICAL EXAMINATION OF BRIDGET BISHOP, REBECCA NURSE, ELIZABETH PROCTOR, AND SUSANNAH MARTIN, NO. 2," JUNE 2, 1692

Again, the physical examination of a part of the same group of women suspected of witchcraft resulted in a report made by the examiners to the court. The report noted that between the morning exam and the afternoon inspection several of the suspected witches had physical features which dramatically changed in their physical appearance in a very short interval. The implication in the second report infers that these physical changes had occurred in an unnatural manner, implying a supernatural intervention.

Salem, about 4 in the afternoon June 2nd, 1692

We whose names are subscribed to the within mentioned, upon a second search about 3 or 4 hours distance, did find the said Brigett Bishop alias Oliver in a clear and free state from any preturnaturall Excrescence, as formerly seen by us. Also Rebecah Nurse instead of that Excrescence within mentioned it appears only as a dry skin without sense, & as for Elizabeth Proctor, which Excrescence like a teet, red and fresh, not anything appears, but only a proper [procedeulia ani], and as for Susannah martin, whose breast in the morning search appeared very full; the nibbs fresh and starting, now at this searching all lancke and pendant, which is all at present from the within mentioned subscribers, and that the piece of flesh of Goodwife Nurse's formerly seen is gone and only a [piece of] dry skin nearer to the anus in another place.

    Rebecah Sharpe marke
    the marke of Elizabeth Hill
    Lidia Pickman
    Elanor Henderson her marke
    J. Barton, Surgeon
    Alice Pickering marke
    Hannah Kezer
    Marjery Williams marke
    Anna Stephens
    Jane Wollings marke
    Sworne in Court, June 2nd 1692
    (Reverse) Jury of Women's Return

Source: Essex County Court Archives, vol. 1, no. 136, Massachusetts Supreme Judicial Court, Judicial Archives, on deposit James Duncan Phillips Library, Peabody Essex Museum, Salem, MA.

Document 61

UNKNOWN, "DEPOSITION OF JOHN BLY, SR. AND REBECCA BLY V. BRIDGET BISHOP," JUNE 2, 1692

In addition to the commonplace spectral evidence presented during the trials by the afflicted children, another form of evidence often presented was testimony to what were perceived as "supernatural malefic events," often closely following a disputation between the deponent and the accused witch. Usually, these occurrences involved a coincidental form of accident, harm, or damage done to deponent, his family, his property, or his livestock. The purpose of such a deposition was to place blame for damage or loss on the suspected witch in the hope of harming them, or in expectation of reimbursement or compensation. The sheer number of such accounts of damage attributed to Bridget Bishop indicates that, while not a witch, she certainly had, over the course of her life, alienated many of her neighbors.

John Bly Sr. and Rebecca Bly his wife of Salem, both testify and say that said John Bly bought a sow off Edward Bishop of Salem Sawyer and by agreement with said Bishop was to pay the price agreed upon, unto Lt. Jeremiah Neale of Salem, and Bridget the wife of said Edward Bishop because she could not have the money or deponents in Salem and quarreled with them about it. Soon after which the sow having pigged, she was taken with strange fits jumping up and knocking her head against the fence and seemed blind and deaf and would not eat neither let her pigs suck but foamed at the mouth, which Goody Hinderson hearing of said she believed she was over-looked, and that they had their cattle ill in such a manner at the Eastward when she lived there, and used to cure them by giving of them red ocre and milk. Which we also gave the sow. Quickly after eating of which she grew better and then for the space of near two hours together she getting into the street did set of jumping and running between the house of said deponents and said Bishop's as if she were stark mad; and after that was well again and we did then apprehend or judge and do still that said Bishop had bewitched said sow.

Jurat in Curia

Source: Essex County Court Archives, vol. 1, no. 150, Massachusetts Supreme Judicial Court, Judicial Archives, on deposit James Duncan Phillips Library, Peabody Essex Museum, Salem, MA.

Document 62

UNKNOWN, "DEPOSITION OF JOHN BLY, SR. AND WILLIAM BLY V. BRIDGET BISHOP," JUNE 2, 1692

This next deposition from the Bly family is one of the most curious of all those presented against Bridget Bishop in that it implies that actual tangible evidence of malefic witchcraft using poppets, similar to those used by Goody Glover in the Goodwin case in Boston, was being employed by Bishop to harm certain unknown individuals. Sadly, Bridget did not seem to have a reasonable explanation to refute this testimony except to assert her innocence in claiming she did "not even know what a witch is."

June 2nd 1692 John Bly Senior aged about 57 years and William Bly aged about 15 years both of Salem testify and say that being employed by Bridget Bishop Alias Oliver of Salem to help take down the cellar wall of the old house she formerly lived in we, the said deponents, in holes of the said old wall belonging to the said cellar found several poppets made up of rags and hog's bristles with headless pins in them with the points outward and this was about seven years last past.

Jurat Curia

Papers against Bridget Bishop no. 16 John Bly and William Bly Court of Oyer and Terminer held at Salem 2nd June. 92. Poppets Oliver

Source: Essex County Court Archives, vol. 1, no. 147, Massachusetts Supreme Judicial Court, Judicial Archives, on deposit James Duncan Phillips Library, Peabody Essex Museum, Salem, MA.

Document 63

UNKNOWN, "DEPOSITION OF JOHN COOK V. BRIDGET BISHOP," JUNE 2, 1692

A goodly amount of spectral evidence was presented against Bridget Bishop as represented in the following testimony offered by John Cook, one of many who testified that they saw Bridget's specter in their house at all times of the day. Usually, the narrative indicates that she made her spiritual visits to work a spell or harm the residents in some way, and often in retribution for a perceived disputation with the deponents.

John Cook aged about 18 years testifies that about five or six years ago one Morning about sun rising as I was in bed before I rose I saw Goodwife Bishop alias Oliver standing in the chamber by the window and she looked on me and grinned on me and presently struck me on the side of the head which did very much hurt me and then I saw her go out under the end window at a little crevice about so big as I could thrust my hand into. I saw her again the same day, which was the Sabbath Day, about noon walk and cross the room and having at the time an apple in my hand it flew out of my hand into my mother's lap who sat six or eight-foot distance from me and then disappeared and though my mother and several others were in the same room yet they affirmed they saw her not.

John Cook appeared before us the Jury of inquest and did own this to be his testimony on the oath that he hath taken this 2nd day of June 92.

Jurat in Curia

John Cook Witness

Source: Essex County Court Archives, vol. 1, no. 148, Massachusetts Supreme Judicial Court, Judicial Archives, on deposit James Duncan Phillips Library, Peabody Essex Museum, Salem, MA.

Document 64

UNKNOWN, "DEPOSITION OF JOHN LOUDER V. BRIDGET BISHOP," JUNE 2, 1692

The following document contains one of the most vivid and elaborate narratives offered against Bridget Bishop and accepted by the court as admissible evidence. It again involves a disputation of Bridget with a neighboring family. As in the previous deposition, Bridget is seen within the home of the deponent in a spectral form doing harm, but later sends her familiar, or a satanic minion, into Louder's house to both tempt and afflict him.

John Louder of Salem aged about thirty-two years Testifies and says that about seven or eight years since I then living with Mr. John Gedney in Salem and having had some controversy with Bridget Bishop the wife of Edward Bishop of Salem Sawyer about her fowls that used to come into our orchard or garden. Some little time after which, I going well to bed; about the dead of the night felt a great weight upon my breast and awakening look and it being bright moon; light did clearly see said Bridget Bishop—or her likeness sitting upon my stomach and putting my arms off of the bed to free myself from that great oppression she presently laid hold of my throat and almost choked me and I had no strength or power in my hands to resist or help myself; and in this condition she held me to almost day. Sometime after this, my Mistress Susannah Gedney was in our orchard and I was then with her and said Bridget Bishop being then in her orchard which was next adjoining to ours my Mistress told said Bridget that I said or affirmed that she came one night and sat upon my breast as aforesaid which she denied and I affirmed to her face to be true and that I did plainly see her upon which discourse with her she threatened me. And some time after that I being not very well stayed at home on a Lord's day and on the afternoon of said day the doors being shut I did see a black pig in the room coming towards me so I went towards it to kick it and it vanished away.

Immediately after I sat down in a narrow bar and did see a black thing jump into the window and came and stood just before my face, upon the bar the body of it looked like a monkey only the feet were like a cocks feet with claws and the face somewhat more like a man's than a monkey and I being greatly affrighted not being able to speak or help myself by reason of fear I suppose, so the thing spoke to me and said I am a messenger sent to you for I understand you are troubled in mind, and if you will be ruled by me you shall want for nothing in this world upon which I endeavored to clap my hands upon it, and said you devil I will kill you. But could feel no substance and it jumped out of the window again and immediately came in by the porch although the doors were shut and said you had better take my council, where upon I struck at it with a stick but struck the groundsill and broke the stick, but felt no substance, and that arm with which I struck was presently disenabled, then it vanished away and I opened the back door and went out and going towards the house end I espied said Bridget Bishop in her orchard going towards her house. And seeing her, I had no power to set one foot forward but returned in again and going to shut the door. I again did see that or the like creature that I before did see within doors, in such a posture as it seemed to be ageing to fly at me, upon which I cried out; the whole armor of God be between me and you. So it sprang back and flew over the apple tree flinging the dust with its feet against my stomach, upon which I was struck dumb and so continued for about three days' time—and also shook many of the apples off from the tree which it flew over.

John Louder appeared before me this 2nd day of June 1692 and one the oath that he had taken did own this testimony to be the truth before us the Jury of Inquest.

Jurat Curia On her trial Bridget Bishop alia Oliver denied that she knew this deponent though the orchard of this deponent and the orchard of said Bishop joined and they often had difference of some years together.

Source: Essex County Court Archives, vol. 1, no. 145, Massachusetts Supreme Judicial Court, Judicial Archives, on deposit James Duncan Phillips Library, Peabody Essex Museum, Salem, MA.

Document 65

JOHN HATHORNE, "DEPOSITION OF RICHARD COMAN V. BRIDGET BISHOP," JUNE 2, 1692

The following deposition is similar in some respects to that of John Louder in that both testify that Bridget Bishop, or her specter, mysteriously enters their houses, appears in their respective bedchamber, and proceeds to lie upon their chests, almost suffocating them. One possible explanation for this phenomenon offered recently by Dr. Emerson Baker is that both Coman and Louder were suffering from "sleep paralysis," which is often accompanied by "a feeling of weight on the chest" during rapid eye movement (REM) phase of sleep. What is more difficult to explain is why both men were dreaming about Bridget Bishop.

Richard Coman aged about 32 years testifies that sometime about eight years since I then being in bed with my wife at Salem. One fifth day of the week at night either in the latter end of May the beginning of June. And alight burning in our room I being awake, did then see Bridget Bishop of Salem alias Olliver come into the room we lay in and two women more with her. Which two women were strangers to me I knew them not. But said Bishop came in her red paragon bodice and the rest of her clothing that she then usually did were, and I knowing of her well also the garb she did use to go in did clearly and plainly know her, and testifies that as he locked the door of the house when he went to bed so he found in afterwards when he did rise; and quickly after they appeared the light was out, and the curtains at the foot of the bed opened where I did see her presently came and lay upon my breast or body and so oppressed him that he could not speak nor stir no not so much as to awake his wife although he endeavored much so to do it. The next night they all appeared again in like manner and she said Bishop alias Oliver took hold of him by the throat and almost hauled him out of the bed. The Saturday night following I having been that day telling of what I had seen and how I suffered the two nights before, my Kinsman William Coman told me he would stay with me and lodge with me and see if they would come again and advised me to lay my sword on top my body. Quickly after we went to bed that said night and both well awake and discoursing together in came all the three women again and said Bishop was the first as she had been the other two nights, so I told him; William here they be all come again and he was immediately struck speechless and could not move hand or foot and immediately they got hold of my sword and strived to take it from me but I held so fast as they did not get it away; and I had then liberty of speech and called William also my wife and Sarah Phillips that [lay with] my wife. Who all told me [afterwards they heard] me, but had not power to speak [or stir] afterwards and the first that spoke was Sarah Phillips and said in the name of God Goodman Coman what is the matter with you, so they all vanished away.

Sworn Salem June 2'd 1692.
Jurat in Curia
Before me
*John Hathorne

Source: Essex County Court Archives, vol. 1, no. 146, Massachusetts Supreme Judicial Court, Judicial Archives, on deposit James Duncan Phillips Library, Peabody Essex Museum, Salem, MA.

Document 66

STEPH SEWALL, "DEPOSITION OF SAMUEL AND SARAH SHATTUCK V. BRIDGET BISHOP," JUNE 2, 1692

What sets the following deposition apart from nearly all other testimonies of malefic witchcraft against Bridget Bishop is the simple fact that both Samuel and Sarah Shattuck were Quakers and not affiliated in any way with the Puritan faith, or either the Salem, Beverly, or Salem Village congregations. As members of the Society of Friends, Quakers up until the 1680s were generally persecuted as an unwanted religious minority group in Massachusetts Bay Colony. It was not until the Act of Toleration of 1689 that religious dissenters were allowed to freely practice their faith in the Massachusetts theocracy. Despite the persecution and intolerance faced by Quakers, the Shattucks sincerely believed that Bridget was responsible for placing a malefic curse upon their previously normal son resulting in both his mental and physical disability.

Samuel Shattuck aged 41 years testifies that in the year 1680.

Bridget Oliver formerly wife to old Goodman Oliver now wife to Edward Bishop did come to my house pretending to buy an old hogshead which though I asked very little for and for all her pretended want she went away without it and sundry other times she came in a smooth flattering manner in very slightly errands we have thought since on purpose to work mischief at or very near this time our eldest child who promised as much health and understanding both by countenance and actions as any other children of his years was taken in a very drooping condition and as she came oftener to the house he grew worse and worse as he would be standing at the door would fall out and bruise his face upon a great step stone as if he had been thrust out by an invisible hand often times falling and hitting his face in a very miserable manner. After this the above-said Oliver brought me a pair of sleeves to dye and after that sundry pieces of lace some of which were so short that I could not judge them fit for any use she paid me 2 d for dying them which 2 d I gave to Henry Williams which lived with me he told me put it in a purse among some other money which he locked up in a box and that the purse and money was gone out of the box he could not tell how and never found it after just after the dying of these things this child taken in a terrible fit; his mouth and eyes drawn aside and gasped in such a manner as if he was upon the point of death. After this he grew worse in his fits; and out of them would be almost always crying that for many months he would be crying till natures strength was spent and then would fall asleep and then awake and fall to crying and moaning that his very countenance did bespeak compassion; and at length we perceived his understanding decayed so that we feared (as it has since proved) that he would be quite bereft of his wits; for ever since he has been stupefied and void of reason his fits still following of him. After he had been in this kind of sickness some time he has gone into the garden and has got upon a board of an inch thick which lay flat upon the ground and we have called him; he would come to the edge of the board and hold out his hand and make as if he would come but could not till he was helped off the board; other times when he has got upon a board as aforesaid my wife has said she has offered him a cake and money to come to her and he has held out his hand and reached after it but could not come till he has been helped off the board; by which I judge some enchantment kept him on about 17 or 18 months after, the first of this illness there came a stranger to my house and pitied this child and said among other words we are all borne some to one thing and some to another. I asked him and what do you say this child is borne too he replied he is born to be bewitched and is bewitched I told him he did not know; he said he did know and said to me you have a neighbor that lives not far of that is a witch. I told him we had no neighbor but what was honest folk; he replied you have a neighbor that is a witch and she has had a falling out with your wife and said in her heart your wife is a proud woman and she would bring down her pride in this child. I paused in myself and did remember that my wife had told me that Goodwife Oliver had been at the house and spoke to her to beat Henry Williams, that lived with us and that she went away muttering and she thought threatening, but little before our child was taken ill; I told the aforesaid stranger that there as such a woman as spoke of; he asked where she lived for he would go and see her if he knew how I gave him money and bid him ask her for a pot of cider away he went and I sent my boy with him who after a short time both returned; the boy's face bleeding and I asked what the matter they told me the man knocked at the door and Goody Oliver came to the door and asked the stranger what he would have he told her a pot of cider she said he should have none and bid him get out and took up a spade and made him go out she followed him and when she came without the porch she saw my boy and ran to him and scratched his face and made it bleed saying to him though rogue why did you bring this fellow here to plague me; now this man did say before he went out he would fetch blood of her and ever since this child hath been followed with grievous fits as if he would never recover more his head and eyes drawn aside so as if they would never come to rights more lying as if he were in a manner dead falling anywhere either into fire or water if he be not constantly looked to, and generally in such an uneasy and restless frame almost always running to and fro acting so strange that I cannot judge otherwise but that he is bewitched and by these circumstances do believe that the aforesaid Bridget Oliver now Called Bishop is the cause of it and it has been the judgement of doctors such as lived here and foreigners that he is under and evil hand of witchcraft.

Samuel Shattuck and Sarah Shattuck

Affirmed upon the oath they have taken to the truth of what is above written. Jurat in Curia June 2nd 92

*Attest *Steph Sewall Clerk*

Source: Essex County Court Archives, vol. 1, no. 144, Massachusetts Supreme Judicial Court, Judicial Archives, on deposit James Duncan Phillips Library, Peabody Essex Museum, Salem, MA.

Document 67

UNKNOWN, "DEPOSITION OF SUSANNAH SHELDON V. BRIDGET BISHOP," JUNE 2, 1692

Between late April and June, Susannah Sheldon provided an enormous body of testimony and deposition documents calculated to accuse and convict a large number of individuals ranging from the extremely poor to the extremely rich. Among the targets of her depositions were: Reverend George Burroughs, Goody Buckley, Bridget Bishop, Martha Corey, Lydia Dustin, Mary English, Sarah Good, John and Elizabeth Proctor, and John Willard. Of these accused, six would be hanged for witchcraft.

The Deposition of Susannah Sheldon aged about 18 years who testifies and said that on this 2nd June 1692 I saw the apparition of Bridget Bishop and immediately appeared to little children and said that they were Thomas Green's two twins and told Bridget Bishop to her face that she had murdered them in setting them into fits whereof they died.

Source: Essex County Court Archives, vol. 1, no. 149, Massachusetts Supreme Judicial Court, Judicial Archives, on deposit James Duncan Phillips Library, Peabody Essex Museum, Salem, MA.

Document 68

WILLIAM STOUGHTON, "DEATH WARRANT FOR BRIDGET BISHOP," JUNE 10, 1692

Bridget Bishop's death by hanging on June 10, 1692, marks a pivotal moment in the Salem witch trial episode. Up to the time of her execution, the entire incident might have remained as a minor footnote of social crisis in an era of social crisis. Once Bridget Bishop was hanged, the incident began to gain ever increasing momentum. "The Return of Several Ministers" was written and circulated five days later, cautioning the court about their future use of spectral evidence and superstitious tests that were difficult to admit and apply in a real court of law. Despite this warning, Chief Justice Stoughton proceeded without hesitation to follow his preordained course in apprehending and prosecuting without restraint or reason. In this sense, the execution of Bridget Bishop set a dangerous legal and moral precedent for all those cases that would follow. The addendum at the close of the warrant explains the procedure followed by Sheriff Corwin in all future cases, that being transportation from the Salem jail, execution by hanging followed by immediate burial at the place of execution. The only two individuals who were, in all probability removed following their execution by their families were the bodies of Rebecca Nurse and George Jacobs Sr. Both these victims were believed to be buried on their respective family farms in unmarked graves.

To George Corwin gentleman High Sheriff of the County of Essex Greeting
Whereas Bridget Bishop alias Olliver the wife of Edward Bishop of [Salem] in the County of Essex Sawyer at a special Court of Oyer and Terminer [held at] Salem the second day of this instant month of June for the Counties of Essex, Middlesex, and Suffolk before William Stoughton Esquire and his Associates Justices of the said court was indicted and arraigned upon five several [seal] indictments for using, practicing, and exercising [on the nineteenth day of April] last past and diverse other days and times [before and after certain acts of] witchcraft in and upon the bodies of Abigail Williams, Anne Putnam Jun'r, Mercy Lewis, Mary Walcott, and Elizabeth Hubbard of Salem Village single-women, whereby their bodies were hurt, afflicted, pined, consumed, wasted, and tormented contrary to the form of the statute in that case [made and] provided to which indictments the

said Bridgett Bishop pleaded no[t guilty] and for trial thereof put herself upon God and her Country, where[upon] she was found guilty of the felonies and witchcrafts whereof she stood indicted and sentence of death accordingly passed against her as the law directs, execution whereof yet remains to be done. These are therefore in the name of their Majesties William and Mary now King and Queen [over] England and to will and command you that upon Friday next being the tenth day of this instant month of June between the hours of eight and twelve in the afternoon of the same day you safely conduct the said Bridgett Bishop alias Olliver from their Majesties jail in Salem aforesaid to the place of execution and there cause her to be hanged by the neck until she be de[ad] and of your doings herein make return to the clerk of the said Court and precept. And hereof you are not to fail at your peril. And this shall be [your] sufficient warrant given under my hand and seal at Boston the eighth day of June in the fourth year of the reign of our Sovereign Lord and [Lady] William and Mary now King and Queen over England. Anno Dom 1692.

*William Stoughton

June 10th—1692

According to the within written precept I have taken the body of the within named Bridget Bishop of their Majesties jail in Salem and safely conveyed her to the place provided for her execution and caused the said Bridget to be hanged by the neck until she was dead [and buried in the place] all which was according to the time within required and so I make return by me.

George Corwin Sheriff

Source: Essex County Court Archives, vol. 1, no. 71, Massachusetts Supreme Judicial Court, Judicial Archives, on deposit James Duncan Phillips Library, Peabody Essex Museum, Salem, MA.

Document 69

REVEREND COTTON MATHER ET AL., "THE RETURN OF SEVERAL MINISTERS CONSULTED BY HIS EXCELLENCY AND THE HONORABLE COUNCIL UPON THE PRESENT WITCHCRAFTS IN SALEM VILLAGE," JUNE 15, 1692

Perhaps one of the most overlooked and underappreciated documents to be issued in an effort to guide the newly established Court of Oyer and Terminer was the following report generated by 12 Boston ministers under the guidance of Reverend Cotton Mather. In it, the conservative pastors strongly advocated that the special court exercise great caution in using spectral evidence, and indeed any superstitious methods such as "the touch test" as a means of convicting persons suspected of witchcraft. There is little doubt that the court was remiss in not taking this document more seriously and following the good advice of the several ministers. What hurt the document was the concluding paragraph penned by Reverend Cotton Mather encouraging the court to pursue their present course toward "the speedy and vigorous prosecution" of those who have *"rendered themselves obnox-ious"* to the Laws of God. This, as far as Chief Justice Stoughton and the other justices were concerned, was the *"green light"* to stay the course and continue the policies that had led to the hanging of Bridget Bishop.

June 15, 1692

I. The afflicted state of our poor neighbors, that are now suffering by molestations from the invisible world, we apprehend so deplorable that we think their condition calls for the utmost help of all persons in their several capacities.

II. We cannot but will all thankfulness acknowledge the success which the merciful God has given unto the sedulous and assiduous endeavors of our honorable rulers to detect the abominable witchcrafts which have been committed in the country, humbly, praying that the discovery of these mysterious and mischievous wickednesses may be perfected.

III. We judge that in the prosecution of these and all such witchcrafts, there is need of a very critical and exquisite caution, lest by too much credulity for things received only upon the Devil's authority, there be a door opened for a long train of miserable consequences and Satan get an advantage over us, for we should not be ignorant of his devices.

IV. As in complaints upon witchcrafts there may be matters of enquiry which do not amount unto matters of presumption, and there may be matters of presumption which yet may not be reckoned matters of conviction; so 'tis necessary that all proceedings thereabout be managed with an exceeding tenderness towards those that may be complained of, especially if they have been persons formerly of unblemished reputation.

V. When the first enquiry is made into the circumstances of such as may lie under any just suspicion of witchcrafts, we could wish that there may be admitted as little as is possible of such noise, company, and openness as may too hastily expose them that are examined; and that there may nothing be used as a test for the trial of the suspected, the lawfulness whereof may be doubted among the people of God; but that the directions given by such judicious writers as [William] Perkins and [Richard] Bernard be consulted in such a case.

VI. Presumptions whereupon persons may be committed, and much more convictions whereupon persons may be condemned as guilty of witchcrafts, ought certainly to be more considerable than barely the accused person being represented by a specter unto the afflicted; inasmuch as 'tis an undoubted and a notorious thing that a demon may, by God's permission, appear even to ill purposes in the shape of an innocent, yea, and a virtuous man. Nor can we esteem alterations made in the sufferers by a look or touch of the accused to be an infallible evidence of guilt, but frequently liable to the abused by the Devil's legerdemains.

VII. We know not whether some remarkable affronts given to the devils by our disbelieving of those testimonies, whose whole force and strength is from them alone, may not put a period unto the progress of the dreadful calamity begun upon us in the accusation of so many persons, whereof we hope some are yet clear from the great transgression laid unto their charge.

VIII. Nevertheless, we cannot but humbly recommend unto the government the speedy and vigorous prosecution of such as have rendered themselves obnoxious, according to the direction given in the laws of God and the wholesome statutes of the English nation for th detection of witchcraft.

Source: "The Return of Several Ministers," in Increase Mather. *Cases of Conscience Concerning Evil Spirits Personating Men.* Boston: Printed, and Sold by Benjamin Harris, 1693, postscript, pages not numbered.

Document 70

BENJ'A WALKER ET AL., "RETURN OF THE CORONER'S JURY ON THE DEATH OF ROGER TOOTHAKER," JUNE 16, 1692

Dr. Roger Toothaker was arrested on May 28, 1692, and sent to the Boston jail where he died of natural causes on or about June 16, 1692. Since only five persons, including one infant, died in prison, coroner's reports of this type were rare during the trials. This document is an important acknowledgment of one of the Salem witch trial victims who lost his life as a result of prison conditions.

We whose names are underwritten being summoned by virtue of a Warrant from Mr. Edward Williss one of their Majesties Coroners of the County of Suffolk to view the Body of Roger Toothacker who dyed in the Goal of Boston, in obedience, to which we have viewed the same and obtain'd the best Information we can from the persons near and present at his death & doe find he came to his end by a natural death as witness our hands this 16 of June 1692

The s'd Toothacker was an Inhabitant of the Town of Bellricky in the County of Essex

    *Benj'a Walker fore man
    *Enoch Greenleafe
    *Thomas Barnard
    *Dan'll Powning
    *Roger Gubberidg
    *James Thornberei
    *William Paine
    *Andrew Cunningham
    *William Man
    *John Kilby
    *John Roulston
    *Abraham Blith
    *John Riggs
    *Sam'll Wentworth
    *francis Thresher

Source: Suffolk County Court Records, vol. 32, Case No. 2690. James Duncan Phillips Library, Peabody Essex Museum, Salem, MA.

Document 71

REBECCA NURSE, "PETITION OF REBECCA NURSE TO THE COURT," JUNE 28, 1692

The following petition was submitted by Rebecca Nurse in an effort to persuade the court to allow her to be reexamined by a new team of inspectors for witch's marks, since she claimed that she was clean of such bodily evidence of witchcraft, and only bore the normal physical marks of old age. It is noteworthy that Rebecca does not attempt to refute the belief in witch's familiars who allegedly create these marks by nursing blood from the witch to whom they are assigned. Rather she asserts that she is a Christian woman who is innocent of the charge of witchcraft and that her unblemished body is testimony to that fact.

To the honored Court of Oyer and Terminer now sitting in Salem, this 28 of June Anno 1692

The humble petition of Rebecca Nurse of Salem Village humbly show that whereas some women did search your petitioner at Salem, as I did then conceive for some supernatural Mark, and then one of the said women which is known to be, the most ancient, skillful, prudent person of them all as to any such concerned did express herself to be of a contrary opinion from the rest and did then declare, that she saw nothing in or about your Honors poor petitioner but what known reason as to myself of the moving cause thereof which was by exceeding weaknesses descending partly from an overture of nature and difficult exigencies that have befallen me in the times of my travels. And therefore your petitioner humbly prays that your Honors would be pleased to admit of some other women to inquire into this great concern, those that are most grand, wise, and skillful namely Mrs. Higginson, senior, Mrs. Buckstone, Mrs. Woodbery, two of them being midwives, Mrs. Porter together with such others, as may be Chosen, on that account before I am brought to my trial all which I hope your Honors will take Into your prudent consideration, and find it requisite so to do for my life lies now in your hands under God and being conscious of my own innocence—I humbly beg that I may have liberty to manifest it to the world partly by the means abovesaid and your poor petitioner shall evermore pray as in duty bound.

Rebecca Nurse
Her mark

Source: Essex County Court Archives, vol. 1, no. 88, Massachusetts Supreme Judicial Court, Judicial Archives, on deposit James Duncan Phillips Library, Peabody Essex Museum, Salem, MA.

Document 72

ROBERT PAYNE, "INDICTMENT NO. 1 V. CANDY, FOR AFFLICTING MARY WALCOTT," JULY 2, 1692

While it is commonly acknowledged by historians that Tituba and her husband, John Indian, were actually Native American slaves of Reverend Samuel Parris, it is important to acknowledge that some of the accused were African slaves brought into the colony from the West Indies as a result of the profitable West Indies molasses trade. One such witch-craft suspect was Mary Black, and another was Candy, the slave of Margaret Hawkes of Salem. She is accused of hurting one of the central members of the group of afflicted girls, Mary Walcott.

Essex in the Province of the Massachusett Bay in New England\s-\Ss
Anno R R's & Reginae Gulielmi & Mariae &c quarto Anoq'e Dom 1692
The Jurors for o'r Sov'r: lord & lady the King & Queen doe present
That Candy. A Negro Woman Servant of Margarett Hawkes of Salem in & Upon the
Second day of July last in the Yeare 1692 and divers other days & times as well before
as after Certaine detestable Arts Called Witchcrafts & Sorceries Wickedly Mallitiously
& felloniously hath Used practised & Exercised in the Towne of
Salem afors'd Upon and Against One Mary Wallcot of Salem Single
Woman by which Wicked Arts The Said Mary wallcot the day
& Yeare aforesaid & Divers other times as well before as after was
& is Tortured Aflicted Consumed Wasted pined & Tormented
Contrary to the peace of our Sov'r lord & lady the King & Queen their
Crowne & dignity & The laws in that Case made & provided

(Reverse) Candy Negro: for bewitching Mary Wallcott Billa Vera,
*Robert Payne foreman. Ponet Se. The juery find the person here
inditted not gilty of this indittement.

Source: Massachusetts State Archives, vol. 135, no. 31.1.

Document 73

ROBERT PAYNE, "INDICTMENT NO. 2 V. CANDY, FOR AFFLICTING ANN PUTNAM JR.," JULY 2, 1692

In this second indictment of the West Indian slave, Candy, 12-year-old Ann Putnam Jr. is identified as the victim. As with the Andover cases, it is doubtful that Ann Putnam or any of the afflicted girls would have been familiar with Candy on a personal level, so the question is: why is she accused?

Essex In the province of the Massachusetts Bay in New England\s-\Ss
Anno R R's Reginae Gulielmi & Mariae Angliae &c Quarto Anoq'e Dom 1692

The Jurors for o'er Sovereign lord and lady the King and Queen present
That Candy A Negro Woman Servant to Margaret Hawkes of Salem
in the County of Essex aforesaid, In & Upon the Second day of July last in
the Year 1692 And divers other days & times as well before as after certain detestable
Arts Called Witchcrafts & Sorceries,
wickedly maliciously and feloniously hath used practices & exercised
in the Town of Salem aforesaid Upon & Against One An Putnam of
Salem Single Woman: By which wicked Arts The Said Ann Putnam
the day & Year aforesaid & divers other days & times both before
& after Was & is Tortured afflicted Consumed Wasted pined and tormented
Contrary to the peace of our Sovereign lord & Lady the King
& Queen Their Crown & dignity and the laws in that Case made
& provided

(Reverse) Candy Negro: for bewitching Ann Putnum Billa Vera,
*Robert Payne foreman Ponet Se. The jury find the person here
indicted not guilty of this indictment

Source: Massachusetts State Archives, vol. 135, no. 31.2.

Document 74

JOHN HATHORNE, "EXAMINATION OF CANDY," JULY 4, 1692

In this examination on July 4, we discover that Candy is originally from the Island of Barbados, and claims that she never practiced witchcraft there, but her mistress in Salem, Margaret Hawkes, is identified as the person who made her sign the Devil's Book. *What is fascinating, like the 1689 case of confessed witch Goody Glover in Boston, is the court asks Candy, using cloth poppets, to perform acts of malefic witchcraft in order to observe the harmful effects upon the afflicted. Not surprisingly, the afflicted respond exactly as one would expect. Strangely, witness Rev. Noyes did not stop the proceedings by explaining that asking a suspected witch to perform an act of witchcraft was, for a gathering of Christians, inherently wrong on many levels, not the least of which would be the possible harm pinching, fire, and water might do to the afflicted girls.*

SALEM, Monday, July 4, 1692. The examination of Candy, a negro woman, before Bartholomew Gedney and John Hathorne Esqrs. Mr. Nicholas Noyes also present.

Q. Candy ! are you a witch?

A. Candy no witch in her country.

Candy's mother no witch. Candy no witch, Barbados. This country, mistress give Candy witch.

Q. Did your mistress make you a witch in this country?

A. Yes, in this country mistress give Candy witch.

Q. What did your mistress do to make you a witch?

A. Mistress bring

book and pen and ink, make Candy write in it.

Q. What did you write

in it?—She took a pen and ink and upon a book or paper made a mark.

Q. How did you afflict or hurt these folks, where are the pup- pets you did it with?—
She asked to go out of the room and she would shew or tell; upon which she had
liberty, one going with her, and she presently brought in two clouts, one with two
knots tied in it, the other one; which being seen by Mary Warren, Deliverance
Hobbs and Abigail Hobbs, they were greatly affrighted and fell into violent fits,
and all of them said that the black man and Mrs. Hawkes and the negro stood by
the puppets or rags and pinched them, and then they were afflicted, and when the
knots were untied yet they continued as aforesaid. A bit of one of the rags being set
on fire, the afflicted all said they were burned, and cried out dreadfully. The rags
being put into water, two of the aforenamed persons were in dreadful fits almost
choaked, and the other was violently running down to the river, but was stopped.

Attest.   John Hathorne, Just. Peace.

Source: T.B. Howell, comp. *A Complete Collection of State Trials*, vol. VI. London:
T.C. Hansard, 1816, 661–662.

Document 75

WILLIAM STOUGHTON, "DEATH WARRANT FOR SARAH GOOD, REBECCA NURSE, SUSANNAH MARTIN, ELIZABETH HOW, AND SARAH WILDS," JULY 19, 1692

*Bridget Bishop was the first and only victim to be hanged in June 1692. By July, the Court
of Oyer and Terminer had gathered five more victims, all women. All would be executed
on the same day, July 22, 1692, at the same location, Proctor's Ledge, a rocky, outcropping situated between present-day Gallow's Hill and Boston Street in Salem.*

To Georg: Corwin Gentleman High Sheriff of the County of Essex Greeting
    Whereas Sarah Good Wife of William Good of Salem Village Rebecka Nurse
wife of Francis Nurse of Salem Villiage Susanna Martin of Amesbury Widow Elizabeth
How wife of James How of Ipswich Sarah Wild Wife of John Wild of Topsfield
all of the County of Essex in their Majesties' Province of the Massachusetts Bay
in New England At A Court of Oyer & Terminer held by Adjournment for Our
Sovereign Lord & Lady King William & Queen Mary for the said County of
Essex at Salem in the said County on the 29th day of June [torn] were Severally
arraigned on Several Indictments for the horrible Crime of Witchcraft by them

practiced & Committed On Several persons and pleading not guilty did for their Trial put themselves on God & Their Country whereupon they were Each of them found & brought in Guilty by the Jury that passed On them according to their respective Indictments and Sentence of death did then pass upon them as the Law directs Execution whereof yet remains to be done:

Those are Therefore in their Majesties name William & Mary now King & Queen over England &ca: to will & Command you that upon Tuesday next being the 19th day of [torn] Instant July between the hours of Eight & [torn] in [torn] forenoon the same day you Elizabeth How & Sarah Wild From their Majesties' Goal in Salem aforesaid to the place of Execution & there Cause them & Every of them to be hanged by the Neck until they be dead and of the doings herein make return to the Clerk of the said Court & this precept and hereof you are not to fail at your peril and this Shall be your Sufficient Warrant Given under my hand & seal at Boston the 12'th day of July in the fourth year of the Reign of our Sovereign Lord & Lady Wm & Mary King and Queen &ca:

*Wm Stoughton

Annoq Dom. 1692—

(Reverse)

Salem July 19th 1692

I caused the within mentioned persons to be Executed according to the Tenour of the with [in] warrant

*George Corwin Sherif

Source: MS Am 48, Rare Books & Manuscripts, Boston Public Library. Courtesy of the Trustees of the Boston Public Library/Rare Books.

Document 76

ASSORTED FRIENDS AND NEIGHBORS OF MARY BRADBURY, "PETITION FOR MARY BRADBURY," JULY 22, 1692

Mary Bradbury was the wife of Captain Thomas Bradbury, one of the leading citizens of Salisbury, Massachusetts, near the New Hampshire boundary. As with Rebecca Nurse and John and Elizabeth Proctor, the following deposition document is a collective testimonial signed by 118 friends and neighbors confirming their opinion that 70-year-old Mary was indeed "a lover of the ministry in all appearance and a diligent attender upon God's holy ordinances."

Concerning m's Bradburies life & conversation

We the Subscribers doe testifie; that it was such as became the
gospel she was a lover of the ministrie in all appearance & a diligent,
attender upon gods holy ordinances, being of a courteous, & peaceable

disposition & cariag: neither did any of us (some of whom have
lived in the town w'th her above fifty yeare) ever heare or know that
shee ever had any difference or falling oute w'th any of her neighbors man woman or child- but was always, readie & willing to does
for them w't laye in her power night & day, though w'th hazard of
her health: or other danger: more might be spoken in her commendation
but this for the pr'sent

Martha Pike

William Buswell

Sarah Buswell

Samuell Felloes sen'r

Rodger Easman

Sarah Easman

Joseph Fletcher &

his wyfe

Joseph French

John French sen'r

Nathanel Stevens & his

wyfe

Ephraim Severans

Lidia Severans

Sam'll Felloes jun'r

Abigail Felloes

Phoeboe Morrill

Elizabeth Easman

Joseph Eaton

Mary Eaton his wife

Robert Downer

Sarah Downer

Richard Long & his

wyfe

Richard Smith & his wyfe

Joseph True, & his wyfe

Andrew Greley & his

wyfe

Sam'l Easman

Mary French his wyfe

Abigayl French

John Allin

Mary Allin

William Carr

Elizabeth Carr

Sam'll Colby

Samuell French & his wyfe

Henry Ambros & his wyfe

Philip Grele and his wyfe

Richard Hubbard

Martha [?] Hubbard his wyfe

Daniell Moody

Elizabeth Moody

Isaac Morrill

John Clough & his wyfe

John Maxfeild

Jarves Ring

Hannah Ring

Nathanel Whitter

Mary Whitther

Jacob Morrill

Susannah Morrill

Elizabeth Maxfeild

Hanah Stevens widdow

John Stevens

Dorethie Stevens

William Hooke

Elizabeth Hooke

Benjamin Allin and Rachel

his wyfe

Benj Allin and Rachell

his wyfe

Isaac Buswell, & his

wyfe

William Allin

Ephraim Eaton

Ephraim Winsley

Mary Winsley his wyfe

Nathaniel Eastman

Elizabeth Easman

John Eastman &

Mary Eastman his wife

Sarah Shepherd

Willi: Osgood

Abigayl osgood

Susanah Severance

Onesiphris Page & his

wyfe

Sam'll Bill & his wyfe

Joanna Stevens

Sarah Hacket

Marthe Carter

Elizabeth Gettchell

Benj: Eastmen

Ann Easman

Benony Tucker

Ebenezer Tucker

Nathanel Brown

Hannah Brown

Tho: Evens

Hannah Evens

Abraham Brown & his wyfe

Tho. Clough & his wyfe

Sarah Conner widow

John Tomson

John Watson & his wyfe

Steven Tongue & his wyfe

John Connor & his wyfe

Joseph Page

Meres Tucker & his wyfe

Henry Brown Sen'r &

his wyfe

Source: Essex County Court Archives, vol. 2, no. 83, Massachusetts Supreme Judicial Court, Judicial Archives, on deposit James Duncan Phillips Library, Peabody Essex Museum, Salem, MA.

Document 77

UNKNOWN, "INDICTMENT V. MARY BRADBURY, FOR AFFLICTING TIMOTHY SWAN," JULY 26, 1692

This is a completely unique deposition whereby a young man, Timothy Swan, claims to be the victim of Mary Bradbury's witchcraft. Timothy Swan, a resident of Andover seems to be, by July, a frequent male sufferer as the trials reach beyond Salem Village and touch residents of northern and more distant communities of Essex County like Andover and Salisbury.

Essex in the province of the Massachusetts Bay in New England

Anno R R's & Reginae Gulielmi & Mariae Angliae &c Quarto Annoq'e Domini 1692

Ss/ The Juriors for our Sov'r Lord and Lady the King and Queen doe present That Mary Bradbury Wife of Capt Thomas Bradbury of Salisbury—In the County of Essex Gent upon the Twenty Sixth day of July

In the yeare aforesaid and divers other dayes and times as well before as after Certaine Detestable arts called Witchcraft & Sorceries Wickedly Maliciously and feloniously hath used practiced and Exercised

At and in the Township of Andover in the County of Essex aforesaid in upon & against one Timothy Swann of Andivor In the County Aforesaid Husbandman— by which said Wicked Acts the said Timothy Swann upon the 26th day of July Aforesaid and divers other days & times both before and after was and is Tortured Afflicted Consumed Pined Wasted and Tormented, and also for Sundry other Acts of Witchcraft by the said Mary Bardbury Comitted and done before and since that time against the peace of our Sov'r Lord & Lady the King and Queen their Crowne and dignity And the forme Of the Statute In that case made and Provided.

Wittness:

Mary Walcott

Ann Puttnam

(Reverse) Indictm't vs Bradbury for Bewitching Swan bila vera

Source: Essex County Court Archives, vol. 2, no. 69, Massachusetts Supreme Judicial Court, Judicial Archives, on deposit James Duncan Phillips Library, Peabody Essex Museum, Salem, MA.

Document 78

THOMAS BRADBURY, "TESTIMONY OF THOMAS BRADBURY FOR MARY BRADBURY," JULY 28, 1692

The following testimonial is both touching and poignant. It is the statement of elderly Captain Bradbury in support of his wife of 55 years. In this document is clearly stated all those qualities which marked the ideal housewife, mother, and wife. Such a woman could hardly be considered a suspect of witchcraft. Seventy-year-old Mary Bradbury was found guilty in early September 1692, and condemned by the court. What saved her was a temporary reprieve from Governor Phips, similar to the one presented in favor of Rebecca Nurse. Taking advantage of this opportunity, Captain Bradbury and her friends "organized an escape from jail and placed her into hiding" (Baker, A Storm of Witchcraft, p. 38).

July the 28, 1692

> Concerning my beloved wife Mary Bradbury this is that I have to
> say: we have been married fifty five years: and she hath bin a
> loving & faithful wife to me, unto this day she hath been wonderfull
> laborious diligent & Industrious in her place and employment,
> about the bringing up our family (which have been eleven children of
> our own, & four grand-children: she was both prudent, & provident:
> of a cheerful Spirit, liberal, Charitable: She being now very
> aged & weak, & grieved under her affliction may not be able to
> speak much for herself, not being so free of Speech as some others
> may be: I hope her life and conversation hath been such amongst
> her neighbors, as gives a better & more real Testimony of her,
> then can be expressed by words.

> owned by me
> *Thomas Bradbury
> (Reverse) Capt. Bradburys testimony of his wife

Source: Essex County Court Archives, vol. 2, no. 73, Massachusetts Supreme Judicial Court, Judicial Archives, on deposit James Duncan Phillips Library, Peabody Essex Museum, Salem, MA.

Further Reading

Baker, Emerson W. *A Storm of Witchcraft: The Salem Trials and the American Experience.* Oxford, UK: Oxford University Press, 2015.

Demos, John Putnam. *Entertaining Satan: Witchcraft and Culture in Early New England.* Oxford, UK: Oxford University Press, 1982.

Godbeer, Richard. *The Salem Witch Hunt: A Brief History with Documents.* Boston and New York: Bedford/St. Martin's, 2011.

Goss, K. David. *The Salem Witch Trials: A Reference Guide.* Westport, CT: Greenwood Press, 2008.

Hoffer, Peter Charles. *The Salem Witchcraft Trials: A Legal History.* Lawrence, Kansas: The University Press of Kansas, 1997.

Levin, David. *What Happened in Salem?* New York: Harcourt, Brace and Co., 1960.

Reis, Elizabeth. *Damned Women: Sinners and Witches in Puritan New England.* Ithaca, NY: Cornell University Press, 1997.

Rosenthal, Bernard. *Salem Story: Reading the Witch Trials of 1692.* Cambridge, UK: Cambridge University Press, 1993.

Upham, Charles W. *The History of Witchcraft and Salem Village, Volumes 1 and 2.* Boston: Wiggin and Lunt, 1867.

Chapter 3

August to December 1692

The culmination of the witch trial episode takes place between August and December 1692. It is during this period that the only male suspects would come to trial and be condemned, most especially Reverend George Burroughs, George Jacobs Sr., John Willard, John Proctor, and in September, Samuel Wardwell Sr., all of whom stand out as unusual examples of witch trial victims. This is not to forget the September 19 pressing of Giles Corey who is likewise unique in being the only individual to be pressed to death by a legitimate court in American history. Two more episodes of hanging would also take place during this period on the dates of August 19 and September 22, respectively, where a total of 13 victims would be hanged. What truly sets this period apart, aside from the extensive loss of human life as the trials reach their culmination, is the growing public unrest and anxiety concerning the methods employed by Chief Justice Stoughton and his Court of Oyer and Terminer, which begin to come under severe criticism by critics such as Thomas Brattle and Robert Calef of Boston.

Late September begins to see the first appearance of written critiques calling the court and its findings into question. Finally, social pressure from the Boston elite and persons of high standing begin to influence the royal governor, Sir William Phips, to take steps to close the court by late October, reopening a new Superior Court of Judicature that was instructed to ignore spectral evidence. Following this, the trials continued until early 1692/1693, but while a few were condemned by the court, none were executed in large part due to the leniency of Governor Phips who was by this time facing severe criticism from both home and abroad about the poor managing of the episode during his administration. The following documents are some of the last narratives to emerge from the trials as they decline including depositions, testimonials, petitions from convicted witches, pardons and notices of bail-postings, whereby certain individuals awaiting trial were allowed to post a bond and return home promising to come if and when summoned to court. Most interesting are letters from Thomas Brattle, excerpts from the writings of Robert Calef and from Sir William Phips, all portraying the witch trials in a very critical and more objective light.

Document 79

EXAMINATION COMMITTEE, "THE PHYSICAL EXAMINATIONS OF GEORGE BURROUGHS AND GEORGE JACOBS, JR.," AUGUST 4, 1692

The search for witch's marks was not limited to female suspects, but males were similarly inspected for any indication of the presence of familiars. The following undated document illustrates how men suspects were likewise examined by a committee of men in search of any unusual discoloration or skin growths which might serve to feed blood to a demonic creature.

Wee whoes names are under written, having received an order from the sheriff for to search the bodies of George Burroughs and George Jacobs; wee find nothing upon the body of the above said Burroughs what is natural; but upon the body of George Jacobs we find 3 tetts which according to the best of our judgements we think is not natural for wee run a pin through 2 of them and he was not sensible of it; one of them being within his mouth; upon the inside of his right shoulder blade; and a 3rd upon his right hipp.

> Ed Weld sworne
> Will Gill sworne
> Tom Flint Jurat
> Tom West sworne
> Zeb Hill Jurat
> Sam Morgan sworne
> John Bare Jurat (Reverse) Jury men Return about Jacobs and Burroughs

Source: Essex County Court Archives, vol. 2, no. 23, Massachusetts Supreme Judicial Court, Judicial Archives, on deposit James Duncan Phillips Library, Peabody Essex Museum, Salem, MA.

Document 80

SAMUEL SIBLEY, "SAMUEL SIBLEY AGAINST JOHN PROCTOR," AUGUST 5, 1692

The following document presented by Samuel Sibley provides an important insight into the thinking of some Salem Village citizens, including John Proctor concerning the actions of the afflicted children. Indeed, this document marks the beginning of Proctor's troubles with those providing spectral evidence in that he publicly calls into question their veracity. The incredulous Proctor had decided that his servant girl ("his jade") Mary Warren needed to be separated from the other afflicted girls, physically disciplined (whipped) and put to work ("kept close to the wheel"). He goes on to suggest that not only was such harsh treatment effective with his own servant girl, but that it should be applied to all the others. If the girls were allowed to continue unchecked, he predicted, "we should all be devils and witches quickly" as a result of their accusations. The afflicted girls were left unchecked, and both Proctor and his wife Elizabeth would be convicted; Proctor hanging for witchcraft on August 19, 1692.

August 5, 1692

The morning after the examination of Goody Nurse, Samuel Sibley met John Proctor about Mr. Phillips['s house] who called to said Sibley as he was going to said Phillips and asked how the folks did at the village. He answered he heard they were very bad last night but he had heard nothing this morning. Proctor replied he was going to fetch home his jade. He left her there last night and had rather given 40s [shillings] than let her come up. Said Sibley asked why he talked so. Proctor replied, if they were let alone, so we should all be devils and witches quickly; they should rather be had to the whipping post, but he would fetch his jade home and thrash the Devil out of her, and more to the like purpose, taken with fits, he kept her close to the wheel and threatened to thrash her, and then she had no more fits till the next day he was gone forth, and then she much have her fits again, forsooth, etc.

Proctor owns [that] he meant Mary Warren.

Source: Essex County Archives, vol. 1, no. 52, from the Records of the Court of Oyer and Terminer, 1692, Property of the Supreme Judicial Court, Division of Archives and Records Preservation, on deposit at the Peabody Essex Museum, Salem, MA.

Document 81

REVEREND JOHN WISE, "PETITION FOR JOHN PROCTOR AND ELIZABETH PROCTOR NO. 1," AUGUST 5, 1692

Both John Proctor and his wife Elizabeth were accused by their servant girl Mary Warren, who began as one of the afflicted girls, then eventually confessed to witchcraft as a means of saving her own life, when the girls turned upon Mary. As the number of accusations against John and Elizabeth increased, it appeared that a testimonial petition might be necessary to help counteract the spectral evidence being amassed against them. In this effort, Reverend John Wise of Ipswich became the prime mover, collecting 32 signatures from respectable neighbors and friends living nearer to the Ipswich side of the Proctor Farm boundary. The testimonial assumes that the Court of Assistants will be willing to intervene on John and Elizabeth Proctor's behalf with the deliberations of the Court of Oyer and Terminer responsible for conducting the witch trials. The Court of Assistants was unwilling to interfere in the activities of Stoughton's court, and both John and Elizabeth were condemned. John was hanged on August 19, 1692. Elizabeth was reprieved as a result of her pregnancy.

August 5, 1692

The humble and sincere declaration of us subscribers, inhabitants in Ipswich, on the behalf of our neighbors John Proctor and his wife, now in trouble and under suspicion of witchcraft

To the Honorable Court of Assistants now sitting in Boston:

Honored and Right Worshipful:

The foresaid John Proctor may have great reason to justify the divine sovereignty of God under these severe remarks of Providence upon his peace and honor under a due reflection upon his life past. And so the best of us have reason to adore the great pity and indulgence of God's Providence, that we are not as exposed to the utmost shame that the Devil can invent under the permissions of sovereignty though not for that sin forenamed, yet for our many transgressions; for we do at present suppose that it may be a method within the severer but just transaction of the infinite majesty of God that he sometimes may permit Satan to [im]personate, dissemble, and thereby abuse innocents and such as do in the fear of God defy the Devil and all his works. The great rage he is permitted to attempt holy Job with, the abuse he does the famous Samuel, in disquieting his silent dust, by shadowing his venerable person in answer to the charms of witchcraft, and other instances from good hands may be argued, besides the unsearchable footsteps of God's judgments that are brought to light every morning that astonish our weaker reasons, to teach us adoration, trembling, and dependence, etc. But-

We must not trouble your honors by being tedious. Therefore, we being smitten with the notice of what hath happened, we reckon it within the duties of our charity that teacheth us to do as we would be done by to offer thus much for the clearing of our neighbor's innocence, viz. that we never had the least knowledge of such a nefarious wickedness in our said neighbors since they have been within our acquaintance; neither do we remember any such thoughts in us concerning them, or any action by them or either of them directly tending that way, no more than might be in the lives of any other persons of the clearest reputation as to any such evils. What[ever] God may have left them to, we cannot go into God's pavilions clothed with clouds of darkness round about.

But as what we have ever seen or heard of them, upon our consciences we judge them innocent of the crime objected. His breeding hath been amongst us and was of religious parents in our place; and by reason of relations and properties within our town hath had constant intercourse with us.

We speak upon our personal acquaintance and observations, and so leave our neighbors, and this our testimony on their behalf, to the wise thoughts of your honors, and subscribe, etc.

John Wise	Nathaniel Perkins	Benjamin Marshall
William Story, Sr.	Thomas Lovkin	John Andrews, Jr.
Reginald Foster	William Cogswell	William Butler
Thomas Choate	Thomas Varney	William Andrews
John Burnham, Sr.	John Fellows	John Andrews
William Thompson	William Cogswell, Sr.	John Choate, Sr.
Thomas Low, Sr.	Jonathan Cogswell	Joseph Proctor
Isaac Foster	John Cogswell, Jr.	Samuel Gidding
John Burnham, Jr.	John Cogswell	Joseph Euleth
William Goodhugh	Thomas Andrews	James White
Isaac Perkins	Joseph Andrews	

Source: Essex County Court Archives, vol. 1, no. 60, Massachusetts Supreme Judicial Court, Judicial Archives, on deposit James Duncan Phillips Library, Peabody Essex Museum, Salem, MA.

Document 82

NATHANIEL FELTON SR. AND OTHERS, "PETITION FOR JOHN PROCTOR AND ELIZABETH PROCTOR NO. 2," AUGUST 5, 1692

The following petition is signed by neighbors and friends of John and Elizabeth Proctor in a fruitless attempt to persuade the court that they were respectable people with an unblemished reputation. Most of those listed on this second petition were residents of the Salem Village side of the Proctor property.

August 5, 1692

We whose names are underwritten, having several years known John Proctor and his wife, do testify that we never heard or understood that they were ever suspected to be guilty of the crime now charged upon them; and several of us, being their near neighbors, do testify that to our apprehension they lived Christian life in their family and were ever ready to help such as stood in need of their help.

Nathaniel Felton Sr. and Mary, his wife	Samuel Frail and Ann, his wife
Samuel March and Priscilla, his wife	Samuel Endicott and Hannah, his wife
James Holton and Ruth, his wife	Samuel Stone
John Felton	George Locker
Samuel Gaskell and Provided, his wife	George Smith
Nathaniel Felton Jr.	Edward Gaskell
Zachariah Marsh and Mary, his wife	

Source: Essex County Court Archives, vol. 1, no. 110, form the Records of the Court of Oyer and Terminer, 1692, Property of the Supreme Judicial Court, Division of Archives and Records Preservation, on deposit at the Peabody Essex Museum, Salem, MA.

Document 83

ABRAHAM HASELTINE, "INDICTMENT V. MARY BRIDGES, JR. FOR AFFLICTING ROSE FOSTER, NO. 1," AUGUST 25, 1692

The following indictment accuses Mary Bridges Jr. of acts of witchcraft against Rose Foster of Andover. Rose Foster was one of three Andover girls who by August were accusing their neighbors of witchcraft in ways similar to the afflicted girls of Salem

Village. This small group of Andover's afflicted children included Rose Foster, Martha Sprague, and Abigail Martin. It appears that all of these accusers were around 16 years of age. While Martha Sprague testified against several suspects who eventually were hanged, Rose Foster "testified against none that were executed" (Rosenthal, Salem Story, p. 54).

1st Paper
Province of the Massathusets Bay in New England, Essex County
Anno RR's & Reginae Gulielmi & Mariae Angliae & Quinto Annoq'e Dom 1693
The Jurors for our Sov'r Lord and Lady the King & Queen present
That Mary Bridges of Andover Junior On or about the Twenty fifth Day of August
last in the Yeare 1692 [aforesaid]—and Divers
other Days & times as well before as after Certaine Detestable Arts
called witchcrafts and Sorceries wickedly Mallishiously and felloniously
hath used Practised and Exercised at and in the Towne of
Salem in the County of Essex aforesaid Upon and against one Rose foster of
Andov'r aforesaid Single Woman by which wicked Arts the
said Rose Foster—The Day and year aforesaid and Diverse other
Dayes and times as well before as after, was and is Tortured afflicted
Tormented Consumed Pined and wasted against the Peace of
our Sovereigne Lord and Lady the King and Queen their Crowne
and Dignity and ag't the Lawes in that case made & Provided
Wittness his Confession

Martha Sprague Alle Tyler
& Rose foster hir selfe
(Reverse)
Billa Verra
Abraham Haseltine
foreman of the
Grand Jury
not Guilty

Source: Suffolk County Court Files, vol. 32, docket 2729, p. 72.

Document 84

HON. WILLIAM STOUGHTON, "VERDICT AND DEATH SENTENCE FOR ABIGAIL FAULKNER," SEPTEMBER 17, 1692

Abigail Dane Faulkner was the daughter of Reverend Francis Dane, pastor of the congregation in Andover, Massachusetts. Like Reverend George Burroughs, the accusation of a minister, or a direct relation of a minister did not dissuade or discourage the afflicted girls. *Some historians have actually seen a pattern in that of the total 172 persons cried out against, 20 were ministers or close relatives to ministers. Only two of these persons would actually be condemned—Reverend George Burroughs and Abigail Dane Faulkner. While she was condemned by the Court of Oyer and Terminer, she also was found to be pregnant and escaped the hangman in September 1692 remaining in jail until the birth of her child. By the end of October, Governor Phips had shut down the Court of Oyer and Terminer, and ultimately saw the sense of setting her free, but without declaring her innocent of the crime of witchcraft. This act, though beneficial, left the taint of criminality upon those that were freed without a reversal of the verdict of guilty proclaimed by the court. As a result, on June 13, 1700, Abigail Faulkner began the process of a "reversal of attainder" whereby she would have her conviction for witchcraft reversed by the Colony of Massachusetts. Ultimately, her petition was approved by the House of Representatives, but was never approved by the Governor's Council or by Governor Bellomont himself. Abigail Faulkner's innocence was finally acknowledged in a bill that passed the General Court in 1703, stating that she, Sarah Wardwell, and Elizabeth Proctor had been wrongfully accused "by certain possessed persons."*

At a Court of Oyer and Terminer holden at Salem by adjournment September 1692—

Abigail Faulkner of Andover indicted and arraigned for the crime of felony by witchcraft committed on the bodies of Martha Sprague evidences being called and sworn in open Court matter of fact committed the Jury.

The Jury find Abigail Faulkner wife of Francis Faulkner of Andover guilty of the felony by witchcraft committed on the body of Martha Sprague also on the body of Sarah Phelps.

Sentence of death passed on Abigail Faulkner.

Copia Vera

Source: Massachusetts State Archives, vol. 135, no. 49.

Document 85

STEPHEN SEWELL, "SUMMONS FOR WITNESSES V. MARY BRADBURY," SEPTEMBER 5, 1692

Mary Bradbury, one of the leading citizens of Salisbury, Massachusetts, is being accused of witchcraft. The following document is a summons demanding that certain specific individuals known to be involved in her case be required to attend her hearing.

Wm & Mary by the Grace of God of England Scotland France
& Ireland King & Queen defend'rs of the faith &c. a
To Thomas Ring of Amesbury or Salsbury Timothy Swann of
Andover Richard Carr & James Carr of Salsbury.
Greeting Wee Comand you all Excuses Set apart to be and personaly

appear at the Next Court of Oyer & Terminer holden at Salem On
Tuesday Next at Twelve of the Clock or as soon after as possible
There to Testify the truth on Severall Indictments to be Exhibited
against mrs Mary Bradbury & other prisoners to be Tried for the
horrible Crime of Witchcraft, hereof Make return fail not dated in
Salem Sep'r 5'th 1692 & in the fourth year of Our Reign

To the Sheriff of Essex or
Constables of Andover Haverill
Salsbury Amesbery, Bradford or Newbury.
*Stephen Sewall Cle[rk]
(Reverse)
Zerub. Endecot
Sam. Endecot
James Carr
Rich'd Carr
Timo: Swan
Jos: Ringg

Source: Essex County Court Archives, vol. 2, no. 74, Massachusetts Supreme
Judicial Court, Judicial Archives, on deposit James Duncan Phillips Library,
Salem, MA.

Document 86

STEPHEN SEWELL, "SUMMONS FOR MARY TOWNE AND REBECCA TOWNE," SEPTEMBER 8, 1692

Individual private citizens who were thought by members of the court to have informa-
tion relevant to a specific case could be summoned to testify at a court session. This was
a mandatory order, even if those summoned did not wish to involve themselves in the
proceedings, as in the case of the two Topsfield women mentioned in the following docu-
ment who were family relations of Rebecca Nurse and her sisters Sarah Cloyce and Mary
Easty.

William and Mary by the Grace of God of England, Scotland, France, and Ireland
King and Queen defenders of the faith.
    To Mary Towne widow and Rebecca Towne her daughter greeting.
    We command you all excuses set apart to be and appear at the Court of Oyer
and Terminer holden at Salem tomorrow morning at eight of the clock precisely
there to testify the truth to the best of your knowledge on several indictments
exhibited against Mary Easty hereof fail not at your utmost peril.
    Dated in Salem September 8th 1692 and in the fourth year of our reign.
    Stephen Sewall Cler
To the Constable of Topsfield hereof make return fail not.

I have warned the widow town and her daughter to appear at the court according to time spoken of in the warrant as attested.

By me *Ephraim Wildes constable of Topsfield

Source: Essex County Court Archives, vol. 1, no. 288, Massachusetts Supreme Judicial Court, Judicial Archives, on deposit James Duncan Phillips Library, Peabody Essex Museum, Salem, MA.

Document 87

ANN PUTNAM, "ANN PUTNAM JR. V. MARY BRADBURY," SEPTEMBER 8, 1692

Interestingly, although having no personal familiarity with either Andover or Salisbury, Ann Putnam Jr. claimed in the following deposition that she had witnessed Mary Bradbury's specter harming Andover resident Timothy Swan as well as being harmed by Mary Bradbury's specter herself. It should be observed that this document was generated quite late in the trials, yet Ann Putnam is still endeavoring to further expand the number of suspects by accusing persons in distant towns and communities well beyond the environs of Salem Village.

The deposition of Ann Putnam who testifieth and saith that
I being at Andevour on the 26 day of July 1692 I saw there Mis Mary Bradbery the wife of Capt Tho: Bradbery of Salisbury or
hir Apperance most grevious afflecting and tormenting of Timothy Swan of Andevor allmost Redy to kill him also severall times before
and sence that time I have seen mist. Bradbery or hir Apperance
most greviously afflecting Timothy Swan and I beleve that Mis Bradbery
is a most dreadfull witch for sence she has been in prison she
or hir Apperance has com to me and most greviously afflected me
Ann Putnam owned before the grand Inquest this her evidens to be
the truth one the oath that she hath taken: this: 8 day of September 1692

(Reverse) Ann Putnam

Source: Essex County Court Archives, vol. 2, no. 77, Massachusetts Supreme Judicial Court, Judicial Archives, on deposit James Duncan Phillips Library, Peabody Essex Museum, Salem, MA.

Document 88

MARY WARREN, "DEPOSITION OF MARY WARREN V. MARY BRADBURY," SEPTEMBER 9, 1692

Once again, a deposition is submitted against Mary Bradbury of Salisbury, a prominent and well-loved member of that community. In this document, submitted by Mary

Warren, Mrs. Bradbury's specter is accused of committing acts of witchcraft against the entire central group of afflicted girls. Just so that there could be no mistaking the identity of the harmful specter, Mary Warren claims that before committing acts of physical affliction, Bradbury identifies herself by name.

The Deposition of Mary Warren who testifieth and saith that I
have been along time afflected by a woman which tould me hir name
was Mis Bradbery and that she came from Salisbury but on the 2'th day of July 1692:
being the day of the examination of mis Mary Bradbery I then saw that she was the very
same woman which tould me hir name was mis Bradbery and she did most greviously
Afflect and torment me dureing the time of hir examination for
if she did but look upon me she would strike me down
or almost Choak me also on the day of her examination I saw
mis Bradbery or hir Apperance most greviously afflect and torment Mary Wallcott, Sarah Vibber, Eliz Hubbard and Ann Putnam
and I beleve in my heart that mis Bradbery is a witch & that she
has very often afflected and tormented me and several others by
hir acts of witchcraft.

Mary Warrin owned this har testimony one the oath which she hath taken before the grand Inquest this. 9th of September 92
(Reverse)
Mary Warren, Deposition

Source: Essex County Court Archives, vol. 2, no. 78, Massachusetts Supreme Judicial Court, Judicial Archives, on deposit James Duncan Phillips Library, Peabody Essex Museum, Salem, MA.

Document 89

MERCY LEWIS, "DEPOSITION OF MERCY LEWIS V. GILES COREY," SEPTEMBER 9, 1692

Mercy Lewis was the 19-year-old servant of the Thomas Putnam family. She like several others of the afflicted girls was a victim of the Indian war on the Maine frontier where she had lost her parents in a raid during the summer of 1689. As a resident of the Putnam household, she soon became a confidant of Ann Putnam Jr., thus also became one of the central figures in the circle of girls responsible for providing spectral evidence to the court against a wide number of suspects including: Bridget Bishop, Mary Lacey Sr., Susannah Martin, John Willard, Nehemiah Abbot Jr., Sarah Wildes, Reverend Burroughs, and Giles Corey.

The Deposition of Mercy Lewis aged about 19 years who testifies and says that on the 14'th April 1692 I saw the apparition of Giles Corey come and afflict me urging me to write in his book and so he continued most dreadfully to hurt me by times beating me and almost breaking my back till the day of his examination being the 19th April and then also during the time of his examination he did afflict and torture me most grievously and also several times since urging me vehemently to write in his book and I verily believe in my heart that Giles Corey is a dreadful wizard for since he had been in prison he or his appearance has come and most grievously tormented me.

Mercy Lewis affirmed to the Jury of Inquest that the above written evidence is the truth upon the oath she has formerly taken in the Court of Oyer and Terminer. September 9th, 1692.

Mercy Lewis against Giles Corey.

Source: Essex County Court Archives, vol. 2, no. 85, Massachusetts Supreme Judicial Court, Judicial Archives, on deposit James Duncan Phillips Library, Peabody Essex Museum, Salem, MA.

Document 90

ROBERT PAYNE, "INDICTMENT NO. 3 V. SARAH CLOYCE, FOR AFFLICTING REBECCA TOWNE," SEPTEMBER 9, 1692

Rebecca Towne was the niece of Sarah Cloyce and a resident of Topsfield. By the time of this deposition, one sister, Rebecca Nurse was already hanged, and a second sister, Mary Easty, was awaiting execution on September 22. This document is part of an attempt to eliminate all three of the Towne sisters. And although Sarah Cloyce was condemned, she was never executed, languishing in jail until her release in January 1692/1693. Sarah was known for her willingness to challenge the afflicted girls and stand firm in the face of a hostile court.

Essex County in the Province of the Massachusetts Bay in New England
Anno RR's & Reginae Gulielmi & Mariae Angliae &c Quarto Annoq'e Domini 1692
The Jurors for our Sover' Lord and Lady the King & Queen doe
present that Sarah Cloyce Wife of Peter Cloyce of Salem—In the
County of Essex Husbandman—In & upon the Ninth Day of the Instant September—
In the yeare aforesaid and Divers other Days and
times as well before as after Certaine Detestable arts called Witchcraft and Sorceries Wickedly Mallitiously and felloniously hath used
practised and Exercised At and in the Towne of Salem in the County
of Essex—aforesaid in upon and against one Rebeckah Towne of
Topsfeild in the County of Essex aforesaid Single Woman—by which
said Wicked Acts the said Rebeckah Towne the Day & yeare—aforesaid
and divers other Days and times both before and after was and
is Tortured Aflicted Consumed Pined Wasted and Tormented, and
also for sundry other acts of Witchcraft by the said Sarah Cloyce—
Comitted and done before and Since that time against the Peace of

our Sov'rn Lord and Lady the King & Queen theire Crowne and
Dignity and the form of the Statute In that case made and Provided.

(Reverse)
Ignoramus
*Robert Payne
foreman

Source: Suffolk County Court Records Case No. 2677, p. 8.

Document 91

MARY EASTY, "PETITION OF MARY EASTY,"
C. SEPTEMBER 9 TO 21, 1692

Another remarkable and unique document is the following petition of Mary Easty, sister of Rebecca Nurse and Sarah Cloyce. Once again, the incredibly impartial petitioner does not call into question the necessity of the court's mission to hunt down and execute witches, or question the reality of witchcraft in general. All it stresses is that she is aware that she knows herself to be innocent of the crime, and that if the court does not correct the errors of its methods and procedures, more innocent blood will be shed. In order to prevent further innocent deaths, Mary Easty offers some helpful suggestions so that the court might do a better job witch hunting. First, check out the truthfulness of some of the confessed witches who she suspects may have committed perjury to save their lives. Second, keep the afflicted person apart from each other, and simply question them individually. Such an approach, she thinks, would be more effective in discovering the truth or falsehood of their testimony. The court never harkened to her advice, and she was hanged on September 22, 1692.

The humble petition of Mary Easty unto his Excellency Sir William Phips to the honored Judge and bench now sitting in Judicature in Salem and the reverend ministers humbly show that whereas your poor and humble petition being condemned to die do humbly beg of you to take it into your judicious and pious considerations that your poor and humble petitioner knowing my own innocence blessed be the Lord for it and seeing plainly the wiles and subtlety of my accusers by myself cannot but judge charitably of others that are going the same way of myself if the Lord steps not mightily in I was confined a whole month upon the same account that I am condemned for and then cleared by the afflicted persons as some of your honors know and in two days' time I was cried out upon by them and have been confined and now am condemned to die the Lord above knows my innocence then and likewise does now as at the great day will be known to men and angels—I petition to your honors not for my own life for I know I must die and my appointed time is set but the Lord he knows it is that if it be possible no more Innocent blood may be shed which undoubtedly cannot be avoided In the way and course you go in I question not but your honors does to the utmost of your powers in the discovery and detecting of witchcraft and witches and would not be guilty of innocent blood for the world but by my own innocence I now you are in the wrong way the Lord in his infinite mercy direct you in this great work if it be his blessed will that no more innocent blood be shed I would humbly beg of you that your honors would be pleased to examine these afflicted persons strictly and keep them apart some time and likewise to try some of these confessing witches I being confident there is several of them has belied themselves and others as will appear if not in this world I am sure in the world to come whither I am now agoing and I question not but you'll see an alteration of these things they say myself and others having made a league with the Devil we cannot confess I know and the Lord knows as will shortly appear they belie me and so I question not but they do others the Lord above who is the searcher of all hearts knows that as I shall answer it at the tribunal seat that I know not the least thing of witchcraft therefore I cannot I dare not belie my own soul I beg your honors not to deny this my humble petition from a poor dying innocent person and I question not but the Lord will give a blessing to your endeavors.

To his Excellency Sir William Phipps Governor and to the honored Judge and Magistrates now setting in Judicature in Salem.

Mary Easty Petition

Source: Essex County Court Archives, vol. 1, no. 295, Massachusetts Supreme Judicial Court, Judicial Archives, on deposit James Duncan Phillips Library, Peabody Essex Museum, Salem, MA.

Document 92

STEPHEN SEWELL AND JAMES SMITH, "SUMMONS FOR WITNESSES AGAINST WILMOT REDD," SEPTEMBER 13, 1692

Wilmot Redd (or Reed) was a resident of Marblehead with a reputation for quarreling and obstinacy. Her nickname was "Mammy" Redd, and she lived a destitute life with her equally impoverished fisherman husband Samuel Redd. Their residence was a shanty located on the banks of Redd's pond. During her lifetime she built a reputation for herself as independent and cantankerous, capable of harming babies in their cradles, and curdling fresh milk. When asked what she thought of the afflicted girls, she responded bluntly, "they are in a sad condition."

Essex ss. W'm & Mary by the Grace of God. of England Scotland france & Ireland King & Queen defend'rs of the faith &c'a

To the Sheriff of Essex Or deputy or Constable of Marblehead

Greeting

Wee Comand you to Warne & give Notice unto the wife & daughter of Thomas Dodd the Wife & daughter of Thomas Ellis John Caley David Shapley Wife & daughter John Chinn. Marthah Beale, Elias Henly jun'r & wiffe. Benjamin Gale,

Joane Bubbee, Charity Pittman, & Jacob Wormwood, That they & Every of them be and personaly appear at the Court of Oyer and Terminer holden at Salem tomorrow at Eight of the Clock in the Morning tomorrow there to Testify the Truth to the best of your knowledge on Severall Indictments Exhibited against Wilmot Redd hereof Make return fail not dated in Salem Sep'r 13'th 1692. & in the fourth yeare of Our Reign:

*Stephen Sewall Clerk, Wilmot Redd

(Reverse)

I have warned & summoned all the persons within mentioned accordingly except John Calley & Ellis Henly who are at sea, & Beni. Gale who is not well. Sept'ber the 14'th by 7 o'clock in the morning.

P mee *James Smith Cons't in Marblehead

(Reverse) Wilmot Redd/

Source: Essex County Court Archives, vol. 2, no. 7, Massachusetts Supreme Judicial Court, Judicial Archives, on deposit James Duncan Phillips Library, Peabody Essex Museum, Salem, MA.

Document 93

MARY WARREN, "MARY WARREN V. WILMOTT REED," SEPTEMBER 14, 1692

This first deposition of one of the several key members of the circle of afflicted girls against Marblehead's Wilmot "Mammy" Reed (or, Redd), contains a contradiction. Interestingly, in the narrative the deponent says, "I cannot say that Willmot Rett ever hurt me," while at the end of the document, the court officer wrote: September 14, 1692, and "this day, she (Wilmot Reed) hath afflicted this deponent (Mary Warren) most grievously."

The deposition of Mary Warren who testified and saith that I cannot say that (or I cannot say that) Willmott Rett ever hurt me but I saw Willmott Redd on the 31 may 1692 most: grievously affected and torment Mary Walcott Abigail, Williams and Elizabeth Booth & Elizabeth Hubbard and Ann Putnam and I verily believe in my heart that Wilmott Rett is a witch and that she has often hurt the above said parsons by accounts of witchcraft

Mary: Where in upon oath: affirmed to the grand Inquest: to the truth of the above written evidence: Sept 14'th 1692 & this day, she hath afflicted this deponant most grievously

Jurat in Curia

(Reverse) Mary Warren deponent against Wilmot Redd.

Source: Essex County Court Archives, vol. 2, no. 10, Massachusetts Supreme Judicial Court, Judicial Archives, on deposit James Duncan Phillips Library, Peabody Essex Museum, Salem, MA.

Document 94

ANN PUTNAM JR., "ANN PUTNAM, JR. V. WILMOTT REED," SEPTEMBER 14, 1692

Known as the ringleader of the afflicted girls, Ann Putnam Jr. continued to accuse victims of witchcraft up to the very end of the trials, in this case, mid-September 1692. The difference with this deposition is that, although she did not known "Mammy" Redd personally, she knew her by reputation—which was scandalous and odious. With that knowledge alone, the bold Ann Putnam felt safe in her inclusion of "Mammy" Redd into the list of suspects.

The deposition of Ann Putnam who testifieth and saith that I was for a considerable time affected by a woman that told me her name was Redd and that she came from Marblehead but on the 31 May 1692 being the day of the Examination of Wilmott Redd then I saw that she was the very same woman that told me her name was Redd and she did most grievously torment me during the time of her Examination for if she did but look on me she would strike me down or almost choke me: also on the day of her examination I saw Willmott Redd or her Appearance most grievously afflict and torment Mary Walcott Elizabeth Hubburd Elizabeth Booth and Abigail Williams: and I very believe that Willmott Redd is a witch and that she has often afflicted me and the aforesaid persons by acts of witchcraft

    Ann Putnam owned the truth of the above written evidence: to the grand Inquest: Sept'r: 14: 1692 upon oath

    Jurat in Curia

    (Reverse) An Puttnam Evidence Against Willmott *Redd*

Source: Essex County Court Archives, vol. 2, no. 13, Massachusetts Supreme Judicial Court, Judicial Archives, on deposit James Duncan Phillips Library, Peabody Essex Museum, Salem, MA.

Document 95

SARAH DODD, "SARAH DODD V. WILMOTT REED," SEPTEMBER 14, 1692

The following deposition is presented against the Marblehead resident Wilmot "Mammy" Redd by Sarah Dodd, who testified that she understood that "Mammy" Redd had placed a curse upon a Mrs. Syms (Simms) that she might never urinate or defecate, so that she "continued many months during her stay in the town and was not cured while she tarried." This is probably what is meant in the deposition as to Mammy Redd's "misdemeanures" that [Mrs.] "Simse might never, any ways ease nature."

Sarah Dod: Affirmed: upon her oath to the grand Inquest: that: she heard: M'rs Simse threatned to have Wilmot Redd: before a Majestrate. for some of s'd Redds misdemeanures. s'd Redd. wisht s'd Simse might never any wayes ease nature before she did it: & soon after; to this deponan'ts knowledge it fell out with: M'rs Simse: according s'd Redds wish

    this she ownd before: s'd Jury of inquest: Sept'r 14: 1692

    (Reverse) Sarah Dodd evidence agst Willmott Redd

Source: Essex County Court Archives, vol. 2, no. 15, Massachusetts Supreme Judicial Court, Judicial Archives, on deposit James Duncan Phillips Library, Peabody Essex Museum, Salem, MA.

Document 96

AMBROSE GALE, "AMBROSE GALE V. WILMOTT REED," SEPTEMBER 14, 1692

Women were not the only persons to have disputations with Wilmot "Mammy" Redd; Ambrose Gale presented a deposition confirming that the aforementioned Mrs. Simms was indeed constipated at the hands of Marblehead's notorious witch suspect.

Mr. Ambros Gale: Affirmed that Mrs. Simse was: about that time: or soon after: so: afflicted: as was then Reported & upon that: September 14: 1692

    Jurat in Curia

Source: Essex County Court Archives, vol. 2, no. 15, Massachusetts Supreme Judicial Court, Judicial Archives, on deposit James Duncan Phillips Library, Peabody Essex Museum, Salem, MA.

Document 97

CHARITY PITMAN, "CHARITY PITMAN V. WILMOTT REED," SEPTEMBER 14, 1692

The following deposition presented against "Mammy" Redd submitted by Charity Pitman gives insight into the kind of argument which often led to accusations of witchcraft. Mrs. Simms, as mentioned in the deposition of Sarah Dodd, claimed that the servant of Wilmot Redd had stolen some linen from her and confronted "Mammy" Redd, threatening to take the matter to Judge Hathorne. Redd's response was to curse Mrs. Simms with the inability to urinate and defecate for many months.

"The Testimony of Charity Pitman of Marblehead"

    This deponent aged twenty nine years affirms, that about five years agoe, M'rs Syms of the Towne having lost some linen which she suspected Martha Laurence the girle which then lived with Wilmott Redd had taken up, desired the deponent to goe with her to Wilmott Redds, and demanding the same, having many words about the same, M'rs Syms told her, that if she would not deliver them she would go to Salem to Mr. Hathorne, and get a special warrant for her servant girl; upon which the s'd Redd told her in my hearing, that she wished that she might never mingere [urinate], nor cacare [defecate], if she did not goe, and some short time after the deponent observed that the s'd M'rs Syms was taken with the distemper of the dry Belly=ake, and so continued many moneths during her stay in the Towne, and was not cured whilst she tarryed in the Countrey,—

Jurat in Curia

(Reverse) Charity Pittman against Willmott Redd

Source: Essex County Court Archives, vol. 2, no. 14, Massachusetts Supreme Judicial Court, Judicial Archives, on deposit James Duncan Phillips Library, Peabody Essex Museum, Salem, MA.

Document 98

MARY WALCOTT, "MARY WALCOTT V. WILMOTT REED," SEPTEMBER 14, 1692

While most of the hard evidence against "Mammy" Redd was testimony presented by local, Marblehead people, providing anecdotal evidence against their feisty neighbor, the afflicted girls would not be denied the opportunity to also present depositions against her as well. Mary Walcott, one of the primary ringleaders of the afflicted accusers of Salem Village, provides in this deposition a vague and fairly typical testimony of how an anonymous specter approached her, identified itself as the specter of Wilmot Redd, and then proceeded to choke and strike her, causing her to "believe in my heart that Willmott Redd is a witch."

The deposition of Mary Walcott who testifieth and saith I was for a considerable time afflicted by a woman which tould me hir name was Redd: and that she came from marblehead but on the 31: may 1692 being the day of the Examination of willmott Redd then I saw that she was the very same woman that tould me hir name was Redd: and she did most dreadfully afflect and tormet me dureing the time of hir Examination. for if she did but look upon me she would strick me down or almost choak me: also on the day of hir Examination I saw willmott Redd: or hir Ap (Eliz: Booth) Ann putnam and I beleve in my heart that willmott Redd is a wicth and that she has often affleted and tormented me & the aforesad persons by acts of wicthcraft.

Jurat in Curia

Mary: Walcot: upon her oath: Affirmd to the grand Inquest that the above written evidence is the truth: Sep'r 14: 1692

(Reverse) Mary Walcott Evidence against *Willmott Redd*

Source: Essex County Court Archives, vol. 2, no. 11, Massachusetts Supreme Judicial Court, Judicial Archives, on deposit James Duncan Phillips Library, Peabody Essex Museum, Salem, MA.

Document 99

ELIZABETH HUBBARD, "ELIZABETH HUBBARD V. WILMOTT REED," SEPTEMBER 14, 1692

Since the Salem Village afflicted girls were allowed to attend pretrial hearings and listen to the testimony of other cases from beyond the boundaries of their community, they often felt obliged to join in and provide additional incriminating evidence themselves—even if they were not familiar with the person being questioned by the court. Such is the case with the following deposition submitted by Elizabeth Hubbard. She hearkens back to the first examination of "Mammy" Redd in May 1692 and provides a description of an encounter with the specter of "Mammy" Redd, which occurred at that time. Curiously, she waited until Redd's trial in September to come forward with the details in a formal deposition.

The deposition of Eliz: Hubburd who testifieth and saith that I was a considerable time afflected by a woman w'ch tould me hir name was Redd: and that she came from marblehead; but on the 31 may 1692 being the day of the Examination of willmott Redd then I saw that she was the very same woman that tould me hir name was Redd: and she did most greviously afflect and torment me dureing the time of her Examination for if she did but look upon me she would strick me down or almost choake me: also on the day of hir examination I saw Willmott Redd or hir Apperance most dreadfully afflect and torment Mary Walcott Abigail Williams, Eliz: Booth and Ann Putnam and I believe that Willmott Redd is witch and that she hath often afflicted me and the affore-said parsons by acts of wicthcraft

  Eliz Hubbert: upon her oath: to the grand Inquest: to the truth of the above written: evidence:; Sep'r 14: 1692 Jurat in Curia

  (Reverse) Eliz'a Hobert depo Agst.: Willmott Redd

Source: Essex County Court Archives, vol. 2, no. 12, Massachusetts Supreme Judicial Court, Judicial Archives, on deposit James Duncan Phillips Library, Peabody Essex Museum, Salem, MA.

Document 100

THOMAS BRATTLE, "THE LETTER OF THOMAS BRATTLE TO A REVEREND GENTLEMAN," OCTOBER 8, 1692

Boston merchant Thomas Brattle (1658–1713) was a businessman and intellectual. He was the son of one of Boston's wealthiest maritime merchants, Captain Thomas Brattle. He graduated from Harvard College with a bachelor's degree in science and mathematics, and held the position of treasurer at Harvard College until his death. Besides his great wealth, he was noted for his intellectual abilities, and for his writings on astronomy and mathematics, he was elected to the prestigious Royal Society of London. His involvement in the Salem witch trial episode was strictly that of an observer and commentator. As is evidenced by his "letter to a reverend gentleman," he was highly critical of the Court of Oyer and Terminer and in particular the willingness of court officers to allow spectral evidence and other unverifiable proofs and actions performed by the afflicted children. The letter was circulated to members of Boston's political and business elite, and its commonsense reasoning did much to influence public opinion against the trials and against the royal governor's mishandling of the episode in general. In this way, Thomas Brattle may be seen as having a positive impact in helping to bring the Salem episode to a close.

Reverend Sir,

Yours I received the other day, and am very ready to serve you to my utmost. I should be very loath to bring myself into any snare by my freedom with you. . . . Obedience to lawful authority I evermore accounted a great duty; and willingly I would not practice anything that might thwart and contradict such a principle. . . . Far, therefore, be it from me, to have anything to do with those men your letter mentions, whom you acknowledge to be men of a factious spirit, and never more in their element than when they are declaiming against men in public place, and contriving methods that tend to the disturbance of the common peace. . . . However, Sir, I never thought Judges infallible; but reckoned that they, as well as private men, might err; and that when they were guilty of erring, standers by, who possibly had not half their judgement, might, notwithstanding, be able to detect and behold their errors. . . .

First, as to the method which the Salem Justices do take in their examinations, it is truly this: A warrant being issued out to apprehend the persons that are charged and complained of by the afflicted children, (as they are called); said persons are brought before the Justices, (the afflicted being present.) The Justices ask the apprehended why they afflict those poor children; to which the apprehended to look upon the said children, which accordingly they do; and at the time of that look, (I dare not say by that look, as the Salem Gentlemen do) the afflicted are cast into a fit. The apprehended are then blinded, and ordered to touch the afflicted; and at that touch, though not by the touch, (as above) the afflicted ordinarily do come out of their fits. The afflicted persons then declare and affirm, that the apprehended have afflicted them; upon which the apprehended persons, though of never so good repute, are forthwith committed to prison, on suspicion for witchcraft. One of the Salem Justices was pleased to tell Mr. Alden, (when upon his examination) that truly he had been acquainted with him these many years; and had always accounted him a good man; but indeed now he should be obliged to change his opinion. This, there are more than one or two did hear, and are ready to swear to, if not in so many words, yet as to its natural and plain meaning. He saw reason to change his opinion of Mr. Alden, because that at the time he touched the poor child, the poor child came out of her fit. I supposed his Honor never made the experiment, whether there was not as much virtue in his own hand, as there was in Mr. Alden's, to cure by a touch. I know a man that will venture two to one with any Salemite whatever, that let the matter be duly managed, and the afflicted person shall come out of her fit upon the touch of the most religious hand in Salem. It is worthily noted by some, that at some times the afflicted will not presently come out of their fits upon the touch of the suspected; and then, forsooth, they are ordered by the Justices to grasp hard, harder yet, etc. insomuch that at length the afflicted come out of their fits; and the reason is very good, because that a touch of nay hand, and process of time, will work the cure; infallibly they will do it, as experience teaches.

I cannot but condemn this method of Justices, of making this touch of the hand a rule to discover witchcraft; because I am fully persuaded that it is sorcery, and a superstitious method, and that which we have no rule for, either from reason or religion. The Salem Justices, at least some of them, do assert, that the cure of the afflicted persons is a natural effect of this touch; . . .

I would fain know of these Salem Gentlemen, but as yet could never know, how it comes about, that if these apprehended persons are witches, and, by a look of the eye, do cast the afflicted into their fits by poisoning them, how it comes about, I say, that, by a look of their eye, they do not cast others into fits, and poison others by their looks; and in particular, tender, fearful women, who often are beheld by them, and as likely as any in the whole world to receive an ill impression from them. This Salem philosophy, some men may call the new philosophy; but I think it rather deserves the name of Salem superstition and sorcery, and it is not fit to be named in a land of such light as New-England is. I think the matter might be better solved another way; but I shall not make any attempt that way, further than to say, that these afflicted children, (as they are called,) do hold correspondence with the devil, even in the esteem and account of the S[alem]. G[entlemen]., for when the black man, *i.e.* (say these gentlemen,) the Devil, does appear to them, they ask him many questions, and accordingly give information to the inquirer; and if this is not holding correspondence with the devil, and something worse, I know not what is.

But furthermore, I would fain know of these Salem Justices what need there is of further proof and evidence to convict and condemn these apprehended persons, than this look and touch, if so be they are so certain that this falling down and arising up, when there is a look and a touch, are natural effects of the said look and touch, and so a perfect demonstration and proof of witchcraft in those persons. What can the Jury or Judges desire more, to convict any man of witchcraft, than a plain demonstration, that the said man is a witch? Now if this look and touch, circumstanced as before, be a plain demonstration, (as their Philosophy teaches,) what need they seek for further evidences, when, after all, it can be but a demonstration?

But let this pass with the S.G. for never so plain and natural a demonstration; yet certain is it, that the reasonable part of the world, when acquainted herewith, will laugh at the demonstration, and conclude that the said S.G. are actually possessed, at least with ignorance and folly. . . .

Secondly, with respect to the confessors, (as they are improperly called,) or such as confess themselves to be witches, (the second thing you inquire into in your letter), there are now about fifty of them in Prison; many of which I have again and again seen and heard; and I cannot but tell you, that my faith is strong concerning them, that they are deluded, imposed upon, and under the influence of some evil spirit; and therefore unfit to be evidences either against themselves, or anyone else. I now speak of one sort of them, and of others afterward.

These confessors, (as they are called,) do very often contradict themselves, as inconsistently as is usual for any crazed, distempered person to do. This the S.G. do see and take notice of; and even the Judges themselves have, at some times, taken these confessors in flat lies, or contradictions, even in the Courts; By reason of which, one would have though, that the Judges would have frowned upon the said confessors, discarded them, and not minded one tittle of anything that they said; but instead thereof, (as sure as we are men,) the Judges vindicate these confessors, and salve their contradictions, by proclaiming, that the Devil takes away their memory, and imposes upon their brain. If this reflects anywhere, I am very sorry for it: I can but assure you, that, upon the word of an honest man, it is truth, and that I can bring you many credible persons to witness it, who have been eye and ear witnesses to these things.

If the Devil does actually take away the memory of them at some times, certainly the Devil, at other times, may very reasonably be thought to affect their fancies, and to represent false ideas to their imagination. But now, if it be thus granted, that the Devil is able to represent false ideas (to speak vulgarly) to the imaginations of the confessors, what man of sense will regard the confessions, or any of the words, of these confessors?

In the next place, I proceed to the form of their indictments, and the Trials thereupon.

The Indictment runs for sorcery and witchcraft, acted upon the body of such an one, (say M. Warren), at such a particular time, (say April 14, '92,) and at divers other times before and after, whereby the said M. W. is wasted and consumed, pined, etc.

Now for the proof of the said sorcery and witchcraft, the prisoner at the bar pleading not guilty.

1. The afflicted persons are brought into Court; and after much patience and pains taken with them, do take their oaths, that the prisoner at the bar did afflict them: And here I think it very observable, that often, when the afflicted do mean and intend only the appearance and shape of such an one, (say G[oodwife]. Proctor) yet they positively swear that G. Proctor did afflict them; and they have been allowed so to do; as though there was no real difference between G. Proctor and the shape of G. Proctor. This, methinks, may readily prove a stumbling block to the Jury, lead them into a very fundamental error, and occasion innocent blood, yea the innocentest blood imaginable, to be in great danger. Whom it belongs unto, to be eyes unto the blind, and to remove such stumbling blocks, I know full well; and yet you, and everyone else, do know as well as I who do not [i.e., the judges].

2. The confessors do declare what they know of the said prisoner; and some of the confessors are allowed to give their oaths; a thing which I believe was never heard of in this world; that such as confess themselves to be witches, to have renounced God and Christ, and all that is sacred, should yet be allowed and ordered to swear by the name of the great God! This indeed seemeth to me to be a gross taking of God's name in vain. I know the S.G. do say, that there is hope that the said Confessors

have repented; I shall only say, that if they have repented, it is well for themselves; but if they have not, it is very ill for you know who. But then,

3. Whoever can be an evidence against the prisoner at the bar is ordered to come into Court; and here it scarce ever fails but that evidences, of one nature or another, are brought in, though, I think, all of them altogether alien to the matter of indictment; for they none of them do respect witchcraft upon the bodies of the afflicted, which is the alone matter of charge in the indictment.

4. They are searched by a Jury; and as to some of them, the Jury brought in, that [on] such or such a place there was a preternatural excrescence. And I wonder what person there is, whether man or woman, of whom it cannot be said but that, in some part of their body or other, there is a preternatural excrescence. The term is a very general and inclusive term.

In short, the prisoner at the bar is indicted for sorcery and witchcraft acted upon the bodies of the afflicted. Now, for the proof of this, I reckoned that the only pertinent evidences brought in are the evidences of the said afflicted.

It is true, that over and above the evidences of the afflicted persons, there are many evidences brought in, against the prisoner at the bar; either that he was at a witch meeting, or that she sold butter to a sailor, which proving bad at sea, and the seamen exclaiming against her, she appeared, and soon after there was a storm, or the like. But what if there were ten thousand evidences of this nature; how do they prove the matter of indictment! And if they do not reach the matter of indictment, then I think it is clear, that the prisoner at the bar is brought in guilty, and condemned, merely from the evidences of the afflicted persons.

The S.G. will by no means allow, that any are brought in guilty, and condemned, by virtue of specter Evidence, (as it is called,) i.e. the evidence of these afflicted persons, who are said to have spectral eyes; but whether it is not purely by virtue of these specter evidences, that these persons are found guilty, (considering what before has been said,) I leave you, and any man of sense, to judge and determine. When any man is indicted for murdering the person of A.B. and all the direct evidence be, that the said man pistolled the shadow of the said A.B. though there be never so many evidences that he said person C.D., E.F. and ten more persons, yet all this will not amount to legal proof, that he murdered A.B.; and upon that indictment, the person cannot be legally brought in guilty of the said indictment; it must be upon this supposition, that the evidence of a man's pistoling the shadow of A.B. is a legal evidence to prove that the said man did murder the person of A.B. Now no man will be so much out of his wits as to make this a legal evidence; and yet this seems to be our case; and how to apply it is very easy and obvious.

As to the late executions, I shall only tell you, that in the opinion of many unprejudiced, considerate and considerable spectators, some of the condemned went out of the world not only with as great protestations, but also with as good shows of innocency, as men could do.

They protested their innocency as in the presence of the great God, whom forthwith they were to appear before: they wished, and declared their wish, that their blood might be the last innocent blood shed upon that account. With great affection they entreated Mr. C[otton]. M[ather]. to pray with them: they prayed that God would discover what witchcrafts were among us; they forgave their accusers; they spoke without reflection on Jury and Judges, for bringing them in guilty, and condemning them: they prayed earnestly for pardon for all other sins, and for an interest in the precious blood of our dear Redeemer; and seemed to be very sincere, upright, and sensible of their circumstances on all accounts; especially Proctor and Willard, whose whole management of themselves, from the Jail to the Gallows, and whilst at the Gallows, was very affecting and melting to the hearts of some considerable Spectators, whom I could mention to you-but they are executed and so I leave them.

Many things I cannot but admire and wonder at, an account of which I shall here send you.

1. I do admire that some particular persons, and particularly Mrs. Thatcher of Boston, should be much complained of by the afflicted persons, and yet that the Justices should never issue out their warrants to apprehend them, when as upon the same account they issue out their warrants for the apprehending and imprisoning many others.

1. This occasions much discourse and many hot words, and is a very great scandal and stumbling block to many good people; certainly distributive Justice should have its course, without respect to persons; and although the said Mrs. Thatcher be mother in law to Mr. [Jonathan] Corwin, who is one of the Justices and Judges, yet if Justice and conscience do oblige them to apprehend others on the account of the afflicted their complaints, I cannot see how, without injustice and violence to conscience, Mrs. Thatcher can escape, when it is well known how much she is, and has been, complained of.

3. If our Justices do think that Mrs. C. Mr. E. and his wife, Mr. A. and others, were capital offenders, and justly imprisoned on a capital account, I do admire that the said Justices should hear of their escape from prison, and where they are gone and entertained, and yet not send forthwith to the said places, for the surrendering of them, that Justice might be done them. In other Capitals this has been practiced; why then is it not practiced in this case, if really judged to be so heinous as is made for?

4. I cannot but admire, that they should go with their distempered friends and relations to the afflicted children, to know from what their distempered friends ail; whether they are not bewitched; who it is that afflicts them, and the like. . . .

    A person from Boston, of no small note, carried up his child to Salem, (near 20 miles,) on purpose that he might consult the afflicted about his child; which accordingly he did; and the afflicted told him, that his child was afflicted by Mrs. Cary and Mrs. Obinson. The man returned from Boston, and went forthwith to the Justices for a warrant to seize the said Obinson, (the said Cary being out of the way); but the Boston Justices saw reason to deny a warrant. The Rev. Mr. I[ncrease]. M[ather]. of Boston, took occasion severely to reprove the said man; asking him whether there was not a God in Boston, that he should go to the Devil in Salem for advice; warning him very seriously against such naughty practices; which, I hope, proved to the conviction and good of the said person; if not, his blood will be upon his own head.

5. I cannot but admire that the Justices, whom I think to be well-meaning men, should so far give ear to the Devil, as merely upon his authority to issue out their warrants, and apprehend people. Liberty was evermore accounted the great privilege of an Englishman; but certainly, if the Devil will be heard against us, and his testimony taken, to the seizing and apprehending of us, our liberty vanishes, and we are fools if we boast of our liberty. Now, that the Justices have thus far given ear to the Devil, I think may be mathematically demonstrated to any man of common sense: And for the demonstration and proof hereof, I desire, only, that these two things may be duly considered, *viz.*

1. That several persons have been apprehended purely upon the complaints of these afflicted were perfect strangers, and had not the least knowledge of imaginable, before they were apprehended.

2. That the afflicted do own and assert, and the Justices do grant, that the Devil does inform and tell the afflicted the names of those persons that are thus unknown unto them. Now these things being duly considered, I think it will appear evident to any-one, that the Devil's information is the fundamental testimony that is gone upon in the apprehending of the aforesaid people.

If I believe such or such an assertion as comes immediately from the Minister of God in the pulpit, because it is the word of the everlasting God, I build my faith on God's testimony: and if I practice upon it, this my practice is properly built on the word of God: even so in the case before us,

If I believe the afflicted persons as informed by the Devil, and act thereupon, this my act may properly be said to be grounded upon the testimony or informa-tion of the Devil. And now, if things are thus, I think it ought to be for a lamenta-tion to you and me, and all such as would be accounted good Christians.

The chief Judge is very zealous in these proceedings, and says, he is very clear as to all that hath as yet been acted by this Court, and, as far as ever I could per-ceive, is very impatient in hearing anything that looks another way. I very highly honor and reverence the wisdom and integrity of the said Judge, and hope that this matter shall not diminish my veneration for his honor; however, I cannot but say, my great fear is, that wisdom and counsel are withheld from his honor as to this matter, which yet I look upon not so much as a Judgment to his honor as to this poor land.

But although the Chief Judge, and some of the other Judges, be very zealous in these proceedings, yet this you may take for a truth, that there are several about the Bay, men for understanding, Judgment, and Piety, inferior to few, (if any) in N.E. that do utterly condemn the said proceedings, and do freely deliver their Judgment in the case to be this, *viz.* that these methods will utterly ruin and undo poor N.E. I shall nominate some of these to you, *viz.* The hon'ble Simon Brad-street, Esq. (our late Governor); the hon'ble Thomas Danforth, Esq. (our late Dep-uty Governor); the Rev'd Mr. Increase Mather, and the Rev'd Mr. Samuel Willard. Major N. Saltonstall, Esq. who was one of the Judges, has left the Court, and is very much dissatisfied with the proceedings of it. Excepting Mr. Hale, Mre. Noyes, and Mr. Parris, the Rev'd Elders, almost throughout the whole Country, are very much dissatisfied. Several of the late Justices, viz. Thomas Graves, Esq. N. Byfield, Esq. Francis Foxcroft, Esq. are much dissatisfied; also several of the present Justices; and in particular, some of the Boston Justices, were resolved rather to throw up their commissions than be active in disturbing the liberty of their Majesties' subjects, merely on the accusations of these afflicted, possessed children.

Finally; the principal Gentlemen in Boston, and thereabout, are generally agreed that irregular and dangerous methods have been taken as to these matters.

Nineteen persons have now been executed, and one pressed to death for a mute: seven more are condemned; two of which are reprieved, because they pretend their being with child; one, viz. Mrs. Bradbury of Salisbury, from the intercession of some friends; and two or three more, because they are confessors.

The Court is adjourned to the first Tuesday in November, then to be kept at Salem; between this and then will be [the] great assembly [the General Court], and this matter will be a peculiar matter of their agitation. I think it is matter of earnest supplication and prayer to almighty God, that he would afford his gracious presence to the said assembly, and direct them aright in this weighty matter. Our hopes are here; and if, at this Juncture, God does not graciously appear for us, I think we may conclude that N.E. is undone and undone.

I am very sensible, that it is irksome and disagreeable to go back, when a man's doing so is an implication that he has been walking in a wrong path: however, nothing is more honorable than, upon due conviction, to retract and undo, (so far as may be,) what has been amiss and irregular.

Many of these afflicted persons, who have scores of strange fits in a day, yet in the intervals of time are hale and hearty, robust and lusty, as though nothing had afflicted them. I Remember that when the chief Judge gave the first Jury their charge, he told them, that they were not to mind whether the bodies of the said afflicted were really pined and consumed, as was expressed in the indictment; but whether the said afflicted did not suffer from the accused such afflictions as naturally tended to their being pined and consumed, wasted, etc. This, (said he,) is a pining and consuming in the sense of the law. I add not.

Furthermore: These afflicted persons do say, and often have declared it, that they can see Specters when their eyes are shut, as well as when they are open. This one thing I ever more accounted as very observable, and that which might serve as a good key to unlock the nature of these mysterious troubles, if duly improved by us. Can they see Specters when their eyes are shut? I am sure they lie, at least speak falsely, if they say so; for the thing, in nature, is an utter impossibility. It is true, they may strongly fancy, or have things represented to their imagination, when their eyes are shut; and I think this is all which ought to be allowed to these blind, nonsensical girls; and if our officers and Courts have apprehended, imprisoned, condemned, and executed our guiltless neighbors, certainly our error is great, and we shall rue it in the conclusion. There are two or three other things that I have observed in and by these afflicted persons, which make me strongly suspect that the Devil imposes upon their brains, and deludes their fancy and imagination; and that the Devil's book (which they say has been offered them) is a mere fancy of theirs, and no reality: That the witches' meeting, the Devil's Baptism, and mock sacraments, which they oft speak of, are nothing else but the effect of their fancy, depraved and delude by the Devil, and not a Reality to be regarded or minded by any wise man. And whereas the Confessors have owned and asserted the said meetings, the said Baptism, and mock Sacrament, (which the S.G. and some others, make much account of) I am very apt to think, that, did you know the circumstances of the said Confessors, you would not be swayed thereby, any otherwise than to be confirmed, that all is perfect Devilism, and an Hellish design to ruin and destroy this poor land: For whereas there are of the said Confessors 55 in number, some of them are known to be distracted, crazed women, something of which you may see by a petition lately offered to the chief Judge, a copy whereof I may now send you; others of them denied their guilt, and maintained their innocency for above eighteen hours, after most violent, distracting, and dragooning methods had been used with them, to make them confess. Such methods they were, that more than one of the said confessors did since tell many, with tears in their eyes, that they thought their very lives would have gone out of their bodies; and wished that they might have been cast into the lowest dungeon, rather than be tortured with such repeated buzzings and chuckings and unreasonable urgings as they were treated withal.

They soon recanted their confessions, acknowledging, with sorrow and grief, that it was an hour of great temptation with them; and I am very apt to think, that as for five or six of the said confessors, if they are not very good Christian women, it will be no easy matter to find so many good Christian women in N.E. But, finally, as to about thirty of these fifty-five Confessors, they are possessed (I reckon) with the Devil, and afflicted as the children are, and therefore not fit to be regarded as to anything they say of themselves or others. And whereas the S.G. do say that these confessors made their Confessions before they were afflicted, it is absolutely contrary to universal experience, as far as ever I could understand. It is true, that some of these have made their confession before they had their falling, tumbling fits, but yet not absolutely before they had any fits and marks of possession, for (as the S.G. know full well) when these persons were about first confessing, their mouths would be stopped, and their throats affected, as though there was danger of strangling, and afterward (it is trued) came their tumbling fits. So that, I say, the confessions of these persons were in the beginning of their fits, and not truly before their fits, as the S.G. would make us believe. . . .

What will be the issue of these troubles, God only knows; I am afraid that ages will not wear off that reproach and those stains which these things will leave behind them upon our land. I pray God pity us, Humble us, Forgive us, and appear mercifully for us in this our mount of distress: Herewith I conclude, and subscribe myself,

Reverend Sir, your real friend and humble servant,

T.B. (Thomas Brattle)

October 1692

Source: George Lincoln Burr, ed. *Narratives of the Witchcraft Cases, 1648–1706.* New York: Charles Scribner's Sons, 1914.

Document 101

JOHN OSGOOD, "PETITION OF JOHN OSGOOD AND EIGHT OTHERS," OCTOBER 1692

Mary Osgood was one of a number of accused witches languishing in prison awaiting trial. Her husband was the captain of the Andover militia, and held a responsible and respected place in that community. Sadly, Andover was a place, like Salem Village, where a significant number of individuals were "cried out against" arrested and imprisoned. The following petition, headed by Captain John Osgood and signed by eight other Andover area citizens on behalf of their imprisoned relatives and wives, seeks relief of a humanitarian nature. Up to this point, several victims had died due to poor prison conditions, and the court is being asked here to provide those unfortunates in prison with the basic necessities to deal with "the coldness of the winter season," otherwise that they "be returned home to us" that "they may be more tenderly cared for."

To the Honored Generall Court Now sitting in Boston this 12 of October 1692

Right honored Gentlemen and fathers We your humble petitioners whose Names are under written petition as followeth: viz: We would Not Trouble Your honours w'th a Tedious diversion: but briefly spread open our distressed Condition and beg your honors favor and pity in affording what Relieff may be thought Convenient as for the matter of our Trouble: it is the distressed Condition of our wives and Relations in prison at Salem who are a Company of poor distressed creatures as full of inward grief and Trouble as they are able to bear up in life with all and besides That the aggravation of outward Troubles and hardships they undergo: wants of food Convenient: and the coldness of the winter season that is coming may soon dispatch such out of the way That have Not been used to such hardships: and besides that The exceeding great Charges and expenses that we are at upon many accounts which will be two Tedious to give a particular account of which will fall heavy upon us especially in a time of so great charge and expense upon a general account in the Country which is expected of us to bear a part as well as others which if put all together our families and estates will be brought to Ruin: if it Cannot in time be prevented: having spread open our Condition: we humbly make our address To your honors to Grant that our wives and Relations being of such That have been approved as penitent Confessors might be Returned home to us upon what bond your honors shall see good we do not petition to take them out of the hands of Justice but to Remain as prisoners under bond in their own familys where thay may be more tenderly Cared for: and may be ready to appear to Answer farther when the honored Court shall Call for them: we humbly Crave Your Honors favour and pity for us and ours herein. having let down our Troubled state before you. We heartily pray for your honors.

   petitioners: *John Osgood in behalf of his wife
John Frey in behalf of his wife
John Maston. in behalf of his wife: Mary Maston

*Christopher Osgood in behalf of his daughter Mary Maston
*Joseph Willson: in behalf of his wife & children
John Bridges: in behalf of his wife and children Hope Tiler: in behalf of his wife and daughter
*Ebenezer Barker: for his wife
*Nathaniel Dane for his wife
(In left margin)
John Osgood et al.
Petition

Source: Essex County Court Archives, vol. 2, no. 170, Massachusetts Supreme Judicial Court, Judicial Archives, on deposit James Duncan Phillips Library, Peabody Essex Museum, Salem, MA.

Document 102

REVEREND TIMOTHY OSGOOD AND OTHERS, "PETITION OF THE ANDOVER MINISTERS AND TWENTY-TWO OTHERS," OCTOBER 18, 1692

The following is yet another address to Governor Phips and the Governor's Council in Boston from Andover's clergy and church members begging that the imprisoned women of Andover, at least those who are not freely confessed witches, be released and sent home to their families. The petition coincides with the closing of the Court of Oyer and Terminer in Salem, so the timing of such a request seems quite fortuitous.

To his Excellency the Governour, and Councill, & Representatives, now Assembled at Boston. The Humble Address of the ministers, and of some of the Inhabitants of Andover.

We being deeply sensible of the heavy judgment that the Righteous God hath brought upon this place, thought it our duty (after our earnest prayers to the God of Heaven, to give us help from our trouble) to lay before this Honourable Assembly, our present distressed estate, and to crave a redress of our grievances. It is well known that many persons of this Town, have been accused of witchcraft, by some distempered persons in these parts and upon complaint made have been apprehended and committed to prison. Now though we would not appear as Advocates for any who shall be found guilty of so horrid a crime, but we heartily desire that this place, and the whole land, may be purged from that great wickedness: yet if any of our friends and neighbours have been misrepresented, as tis possible some of them have been; we would crave leave (if it might be without offence) to speak something in their behalf, having no other design therein, then that the truth may appear. We can truly give this Testimony of the most of them belonging to this Town, that have been accused, that they never gave the least occasion (as we hear of) to their nearest relations or most intimate acquaintance, to suspect them of witchcraft. Severall of the women that are accused were members of this church in full Communion, and had obtained a good report, for their blameless conversation, and their walking as becometh women professing godliness. But whereas it may be alledged, that the most of our people that have been apprehended for witchcraft, have upon Examination confessed it. To which we Answer that we have nothing to plead for those that freely and upon conviction own themselves guilty; but we apprehend the case of some of them to be otherwise. for from the information we have had and the discourse some of us have had with the prisoners, we have reason to think that the extream urgency that was used with some of them by their friends and others who privately examined them, and the fear they were then under, hath been an inducement to them to own such things, as we cannott since find thay are conscious of; and the truth of what we now declare, we judge will in time more plainly appear. And some of them have exprest to their neighbours that it hath been their great trouble, that they have wronged themselves and the truth in their confessions.

We are also very sensible of the disstressed condition of severall poor familyes, on whom this great trouble is fallen; some of our neighbors are like to be impoverished & ruin'd by the great charge they are at to maintain such of their familyes as are in Prison, and by the fees that are demanded of them, whose case we pray may be considered.

Our troubles which hitherto have been great, we foresee are like to continue and increase, if other methods be not taken then as yet have been, for there are more of our neighb'rs of good reputation & approved integrity, who are still accused, and complaints have been made against them, And we know not who can think himself safe, if the Accusations of children and others who are under a Diabolicall influence shall be received against persons of good fame.

We thought meet also to Signifye that not only persons of good creditt among ourselves, but some Honorable & worthy men of other places, do suffer in their names by the acusations of afflicted people in this Town

Thus haveing given your Honors some account of our present troubles, we crave pardon for our boldness in this Address, and humbly pray this Honored Court to take into their serious consideration our low and distressed estate: And that the only wise God may bless yo'r counsels & Endeavors for the welfare of his people, shall be the prayer of Dated at Andov'r 18'th Oct. 1692.

Your Humble Petitioners
*Timothy Osgood
*Samuel Osgoode
*Samuel Martin
*William Chandler
*William Abbutt
*Thomas Chandler
*Christopher Osgood
*Ebenezer Barker
*Stephen Barnott
*Joseph Marble

*Ephraim Daviss
*Andrew Peeters
*Walter Rice
*Hooker Osgood
*Francis Dane Sen'r
*Thomas Barnard
*John Osgood
*Thomas Johnson
*Nathaniel Dane
*Hopestil Tiler
*Ephraim Steevens
*John Aslebee
*James Frie
*Joseph Willson
*Joseph Steevens
*Thomas Chandler Jun'r

Source: Massachusetts State Archives, vol. 135, no. 61.

Document 103

GOV. WILLIAM PHIPS, "LETTER ONE OF GOVERNOR WILLIAM PHIPS," OCTOBER 12, 1692

By October 1692, the Salem trials had reached their height and were in decline. Over 20 persons had lost their lives through the actions of the Court of Oyer and Terminer established by Governor Phips. Public criticism of Reverend Cotton Mather and Governor William Phips made it increasingly difficult to continue without fear of serious repercussions from England as negative reports began to filter back. On October 8, skeptical public observer, Thomas Brattle wrote a widely circulated letter severely criticizing the Court of Oyer and Terminer, the Mathers, and the royal governor in mishandling the trials and for allowing questionable testimony and spectral evidence. Added to this was Reverend Increase Mather's new book, Cases of Conscience *(1692), which called into question the use of spectral evidence, upon which so many of the convictions had been based. Sir William Phips knew that all this activity was drawing attention among his superiors in England. A letter needed to be written to explain the Salem trials placing the blame and fault on those who deserved punishment but made Phips appear to have done the best he could under the circumstances. The following document is Phips's first attempt to explain the Salem trials to his superiors, in particular, Sir William Blathwayt. In light of later action taken by the foreign office, it does not appear that Phips's letter had the desired effect.*

When I first arrived I found this Province miserably harassed with a most horrible witchcraft or possession of devils which had broke in upon several towns, some scores of poor people were taken with preternatural torments some scalded with brimstone some had pins stuck in their flesh others hurried into the fire and water and some dragged out of their houses and carried over the tops of trees and hills for many miles together; it had been represented to me much like that of Sweden about thirty years ago, and there were many committed to prison upon suspicion of Witchcraft before my arrival. The loud cries and clamors of the friends of the afflicted people with the advice of the Deputy Governor and many others prevailed with me to give a commission of Oyer and Terminer for discovering what witchcraft might be at the bottom or whether it were not a possession. The chief judge in this commission was the Deputy Governor and the rest were persons of the best prudence and figure that could then be pitched upon. When the Court came to sit at Salem in the County of Essex they convicted more than twenty persons of being guilty of witchcraft, some of the convicted were such as confessed their guilt, the Court as I understand began their proceedings with the accusations of the afflicted and then went upon other humane evidences to strengthen that. I was almost the whole time of the proceeding abroad in the service of their Majesties in the eastern part of the County and depended upon the judgment of the Court as to a right method of proceeding in cases of witchcraft but when I came home I found many persons in a strange ferment of dissatisfaction which was increased by some hot spirits that blew up the flame, but on enquiring into the matter I found that the Devil had taken upon him the name and shape of several persons who were doubtless innocent and to my certain knowledge of good reputation for which I cause I have now forbidden the committing of any more that shall be accused without unavoidable necessity, and those that have been committed I would shelter from any proceedings against them wherein there may be the least suspicion of any wrong to be done unto the innocent. I would also wait for any particular directions of commands if their Majesties please to give me any for the fuller ordering this perplexed affair. I have also put a stop to the printing of any discourses one way or the other, that may increase the needless disputes of people upon this occasion, because I saw a likelihood of kindling an inextinguishable flame if I should admit any public and open contests and I grieved to see that some who should have done their Majesties and this Province better service have so far taken Council of Passion as to desire the precipitancy of these matters, these things have been improved by some to give me many interruptions in their Majesties service and in truth none of my vexations have been greater than this, than that their majesties service has been hereby unhappily clogged, and the persons who have made so ill improvement of these matters here are seeking to turn it all upon me, but I hereby declare that as soon as I came from fighting against their Majesties enemies and understood what danger some of their innocent subjects might be exposed to, if the evidence of the afflicted persons only did prevail either to the committing or trying any of them, I did before any application was made unto me about it put a stop to the proceedings of the Court and they are now stopped till their Majesties pleasure be known. Sir I beg pardon for giving you all this trouble, the reason is because I know my enemies are seeking to turn it all upon me and I take this liberty because I depend upon your friendship, and desire you will please to give a true understanding of the matter if anything of this kind be urged or made use of against me. Because the justness of my proceeding herein will be a sufficient defense Sir.

I am with all imaginable respect your most humble servant,
William Phips

Source: William Phips to William Blathwayt, October 12, 1692. In George Lincoln Burr, ed. *Narratives of the Witch Cases, 1648–1706.* New York: Charles Scribner's Sons, 1914, 196–198.

Document 104

ABIGAIL FAULKNER, "PETITION OF ABIGAIL FAULKNER," DECEMBER 3, 1692

The real reason why Abigail Faulkner was successful in her petition was that Governor Phips was, by December 1692, locked in a struggle with Chief Justice Stoughton who wished to proceed with trials and convictions while Phips was concerned that word had reached his superiors in London, that the entire business had been mishandled and allowed to go out of control. Faulkner's release was a calculated first step by Governor Phips that there would be no more executions under his watch of wrongfully accused and convicted suspects. By so-doing, he hoped to mollify his growing number of critics and help reverse the growing criticism that ultimately would lead to his dismissal and recall as governor of the colony.

The humble petition of Abigail Faulkner unto his Excellency Sir William Phipps knight and Governor of their Majesties dominions in America humbly show that your poor and humble petitioner having been this four months in Salem Prison and condemned to die having had no other evidences against me but the specter evidences and the confessors which confessors have lately since I was condemned owned to myself and other and do still own that they wronged me and what they had said against me was false and that they would not that I should have been put to death for a thousand worlds for they never should have enjoyed themselves again in this world; which undoubtedly I should have been put to death had it not pleased the Lord I had been with child. Thanks be to the Lord I know myself altogether Innocent and Ignorant of the crime of witchcraft which is laid to my charge as will appear at the great day of Judgement (May it please your Excellency) my husband about five years ago was taken with fits which did very much impair his memory and understanding but with the blessing of the Lord upon my endeavors did recover of them again but now through grief and sorrow they are returned to him again as bad as ever they were. I having six children and having little or nothing to subsist on being in a manner without a head to do anything for myself or them and being closely confined can see no other ways but we shall all perish. Therefore may it please your Excellency your poor and humble petitioner do humbly beg and implore of your Excellency to take it into your pious and judicious consideration that some speedy course may be taken with me for my releasement that I and my children perish not through means of my close confinement here which undoubtedly we shall if the Lord does not mightily prevent and your poor petitioner shall forever pray for our health and happiness in this life and eternal felicity in the world to come so prays.

Your poor afflicted humble servant petitioner

Abigail Faulkner from **Salem Prison** December the 3rd, 1692

Source: Salem Selections, Massachusetts Box, Essex Co., Manuscripts & Archives, New York Public Library.

Document 105

JOHN OSGOOD AND OTHERS, "PETITION OF JOHN OSGOOD AND SEVEN OTHERS," DECEMBER 1692

In December 1692, Captain John Osgood of Andover submitted a second request in the form of the following petition asking that his wife and the others still held in prison in Boston be released on their own recognizance. The clear and present danger here is death due to poor prison conditions which had already taken five lives.

To his Excellency the Governour, and Council now sitting at Boston. The humble Petition, of severall of the Inhabitants of Andover, Sheweth

That whereas our Wives and severall of our neighbours, sometime since, were committed to Salem Prison, (for what cause your Hon'rs have been informed) and during their imprisonment have been exposed to great sufferrings, which daily increase by reason of the winter comeing on; we had hoped that before this day they would have had a Goal delivery, but since that hath been so long deferred, and we are very sensible of the extream danger the Prisoners are in of perishing, if they are not speedily released: have made bold to make our humble Petition to yo'r Honors, to consider the present distressed and suffering condition of our friends in Prison and grant them liberty to come home, upon such terms as yo'r Honors shall Judge most meet. If we might be allowed to plead their Innocency, we think we have sufficient grounds to make such a plea for them, and hope their Innocency will in time appear to the satisfaction of others, however they are at present under uncomfortable circumstances. So craving pardon for the trouble we have now given your Honors, and humbly requesting that something may be speedily done for the relief of our friends. And yo'r Petition'rs, as in duty bound shall every pray

&c
Andover 6'th Decemb'r 1692
*John Osgood

*Christopher Osgood
*John Frie
*Nathaniel Dane
*Joseph Willson
*Hopestil Tiler
*John Bridges
*Ebenezer Barker
(Reverse) 1692 Andover petition

Source: Massachusetts State Archives, vol. 135, no. 66.

Document 106

GEORGE HERRICK, "THE PETITION OF GEORGE HERRICK," DECEMBER 8, 1692

George Herrick was the marshal and a sheriff of Essex County. The following petition is a request for payment for services rendered to the province in serving warrants, apprehending suspects, and transporting alleged witches of the witch trials to and from prison. He claims that as a result of the unusually busy duty on behalf of the court, he has not had the opportunity to earn any additional funds, and as a consequence, his family is destitute.

To his Excelency S'r William Phipps Knight Capt Gen'll & Governor of their Majesties Teritores & Dominion of the Massachusetts Bay In New England—
    And To: the Hon'ble William Stoughton Esq'r Leut Govern'r of said Province and To: the Rest of the Honored Councell—
    The Petition of yo'r Pore Serv't George Herrick—Most Humbly Sheweth—
    That Whereas your Excellency & Hon'rs Porre Petitionor haveing been imployed as Marshall & dep't Sheriff for the County of Essex for the Terme of nine months & upwards, in Serveing of Warrants and Apprehending many prisoners attending Examinations & Courts of Oyer & Terminer, as likewise by mitimus and writts of habeas Corpus have often conveighed Prisoners unto Prison & from Prison to Prisson it hath taken up my whole time and made me Incapeable to gett anything for the maintainance of my Porre famally, & by that means become so impoverisht that Nesessity hath forcd me to lay downe my Place and must Certainly come to Wante if not in some Measure suplyd Therefore I humbly beseech your Hon'rs to take my case & Condition so fare into Consideration that I may have some supply this hard winter that I and my Porre children may not be destitute of sustenance & so inevitabley Perish for I have been bred A Gent' & not much used To Worke and am become Despicable in thees hard times and that yo'r Excell' & Hon'rs may not immagine that I am Weary of Serving my King & Country were but my habitation Graced with plenty in the Rooms of Pennury; there shall be no servis too dangerous & difficulte but your Pore Petitioner Will Gladly Except & to the best of my Power accomplish: I shall wholely lay my selfe att your Hon'ble feet for Releife & shall

allwayes Pray for yo'r Excell' and Hon'rs health & hapyness and Subscribe my self hopeing for a Gennerus Returne

Dated in Salem this Eigth day of Decemb'r in the year of our Lord 1692
Yo'r Pore & Humble Pettitioner
*George Herrick
(Reverse) Geo: Herrick his Petition 1692

Source: Massachusetts State Archives, vol. 135, no. 67, p. 66.

Document 107

WIDOW PENNY AND OTHERS, "THE PETITION OF TEN PRISONERS AT IPSWICH," C. JANUARY 1692

The incredibly poor prison conditions, including unheated cells and bad food, prompted the following petition, issued during January 1693, on the part of a group of suspected witches—men and women—languishing in the prison at Ipswich desperately in need of relief. They offered to have their families pay bail for their release with the understanding that they would reappear for their appointed trials in the spring.

To the Honourable Governer and Councell and Generall Assembly now sitting at Boston

The humble petition of us whose names are subscribed hereunto now prisoners at Ipswich humbly sheweth, that some of us have Lyen in the prison many monthes, and some of us many weekes, who are charged with witchcraft, and not being consciouse to ourselves of any guilt of that nature lying upon our consciences; our earnest request is that seing the winter is soe far come on that it cannot be exspected that we should be tryed during this winter season, that we may be released out of prison for the present upon Bayle to answer what we are charged with in the Spring. For we are not in this unwilling nor afrayed to abide the tryall before any Judicature apoynted in convenient season of any crime of that nature; we hope you will put on the bowells of compassion soe far as to concider of our suffering condicion in the present state we are in, being like to perish with cold in lying longer in prison in this cold season of the yeare, some of us being aged either about or nere four score some though younger yet being with Child, and one giving suck to a child not ten weekes old yet, and all of us weake and infirme at the best, and one fettered with irons this halfe yeare and all most distroyed with soe long an Imprisonment: Thus hoping you will grant us a releas at the present that we be not left to perish in this miserable condicion we shall allwayes pray &c.

Widow Penny. Widow Vincent. Widow Prince Goodwife Greene of Havarell, the wife of Hugh Roe of Cape Anne, Mehitabel Dowing. the wife of T[h]imothy Day, Goodwife Dicer of Piscataqua Hanah Brumidge of Havarell Rachel Hafield besides thre or foure men.

Source: No. 1740, John Davis Batchelder Autograph Collection, Library of Congress, Washington, DC.

Document 108

REVEREND FRANCIS DANE, "THE STATEMENT BY THE REV. FRANCIS DANE ON THE ANDOVER OUTBREAK," JANUARY 2, 1693

The following statement by Andover's Reverend Francis Dane provides an excellent perspective of where many critics of the Salem trials stood at the end of the episode. He points out the mistakes made in listening to the spectral evidence of the afflicted, the badgering and threatening of witnesses and suspects alike. He plainly states that he believes that "I believe many innocent persons have been accused and imprisoned," and takes a strong public stand against the continuance of the trials.

Reverend Sir; Whereas there have been divers reports raised, how, and, by what hands I know not, of the Towne of Andover, and the Inhabitants, I thought it my bounden duty to give an account to others, so farr as I had the understanding of anything amongst us. Therefore I doe declare, that I believe the reports have been Scandalous, and unjust, neither will bear the light, As for that, of the Sive, and Cisers I never heard of it, till this last Summer, and the Sabboth after I spake publiqly concerning it since which I beleeve it hath not been tryed, As for such things of Charmes, and ways to find their cattle, I never heard, nor doe I know any Neighbour that ever did so, neither have I any grounds to beleeve it. I have lived above Fortie fower yeares in the Towne, and have been frequent among the Inhabitants, and should certainely heard if so it had been. That there was a suspicion of Goodwife Carrier among some of us before she was apprehended, I know. As for any other persons, I had no suspicion of them, and had Charity been put on, the Divel would not have had such an advantage against us, and I beleeve many Innocent persons have been accused, & Imprisoned, the Conceit of Spectre Evidence as an infallible mark did too far prevaile with us Hence we so easily parted with our neighbours of honest, & good report, & members in full Comunion, hence we so easily parted with our Children, when we knew nothing in their lives, nor any of our neighbours to suspect them and thus things were hurried on, hence such strange breaches in families,—severall that came before me, that spake with much sobrietie, professing their innocency, though through the Devils subtilty they were too much urged to Confesse, and we thought we did doe well in so doeing, yet they stood their ground professing they knew nothing, never saw the devil, never made a covenant with him, & the like; & some Children that we have cause to feare that dread has overcome them to accuse themselves in that they knew not. Stephen Johnson Mary Barker the daughters of Lieftenant Barker, and some others by what we had from them with suitable affections we have cause to beleeve they were in the truth, and so held to it, if after many indeavours they had [been dismissed] not been overcome to say w't they never knew.

This hath been a trouble to me, considering how oft it hath been sayd you are a witch, you are guilty, & who afflicts this maid or the like, & more then this hath been sayd, charging persons with witchcraft, and what flatteries have past from: & threats and telling them they must goe to prison & this feare have caused many to fall. our Sinne of Ignorance wherein we thought we did well, will not excuse us when we know we did amisse but what ever might be a stumbling block to others must be removed, else we shall procure divine displeasure, & Evills will unavoidably breake in upon us.

Andover Jan 2. 92 Yours Sr who am though unworthie a friend to them that are friends to Sion.

Concerning my Daughter Elizabeth Johnson I never had ground to suspect her: neither have I heard any other to accuse her, till [by] Spectre evidence she was brought forth, but this I must say, she was weake, and incapacious, fearfull. and in that respect I feare she hath. falsely accused her self & others. Not long before that she was sent for she spake as to her owne particular, that she was sure she was no witch, and for her Daughter Elizabeth, she is but simplish at the best, and I feare the comon speech that was frequently spread among us, of their liberty, if they would confesse, and the like expression used by some, have brought many into a snare, the Lord direct & guide those that are in place, and give us all submissive wills, & let the Lord doe with me, & mine, what seems good in his owne eys.

Source: Essex County Court Archives, vol. 1, no. 319, Massachusetts Supreme Judicial Court, Judicial Archives, on deposit James Duncan Phillips Library, Peabody Essex Museum, Salem, MA.

Document 109

UNKNOWN COURT OFFICER, "RECOGNIZANCE FOR DOROTHY GOOD," DECEMBER 10, 1692

Little and lost, four-year-old Dorothy Good, daughter of Sarah Good remained in prison long after the hanging of her mother on July 19, 1692. By December, her pitiful condition was recognized by Samuel Ray of Salem who paid the cost of her jail bill and posted bail to the amount of £50. This enabled the child to be released.

Memorandum

That on the Tenth day of December 1692 Samuel Ray of Salem. appeared before me Underwritten One of the Councill for their Majtis Province of the Massachusets Bay in New England and acknowledged himselfe Indebted unto Our Soveraign Lord & Lady the king & Queen the Sume of fifty pounds Currant Money of New: England on the Condition that the hereafter Named—

Vid't: That Dorothy Good Daughter of Sarah Good of Salem, Labourer, being Imprisoned on Suspicion of her being Guilty of the Crime of Witchcraft & being Now Let to Bail. that if the Said Good Shall appear at the Next assize & Gener'll

Goal Delivery to be holden at Salem & abide the Courts Judgment then the above Recognisance to be void Else to remain in force & virtue.

(Reverse) Recog'ce not copied

Source: Essex County Court Archives, vol. 2, no. 185, Massachusetts Supreme Judicial Court, Judicial Archives, on deposit James Duncan Phillips Library, Peabody Essex Museum, Salem, MA.

Document 110

REVEREND INCREASE MATHER, "REV. INCREASE MATHER'S REPORT OF HIS CONVERSATION IN PRISON WITH MARY BRIDGES, SR.," JANUARY 1692

Reverend Increase Mather visited some prisoners to discuss their condition and their confessions since he was convinced that some innocent persons had been wrongfully accused and imprisoned. One such prisoner was Mary Bridges of Andover who had confessed to witchcraft, but later retracted her confession claiming that she had been repeatedly told by court officials that she was guilty of witchcraft, and consequently came to believe it to be true. This point addresses the question of why so many—over 50 persons—admitted to being witches.

Goodwife Bridges said that she had confessed against herself
things which were all utterly false; and that she was brought to
her confession by being told that she certainly was a witch, and so
made to believe it,—though she had no other grounds so to believe.

Source: Charles W. Upham. *Salem Witchcraft*, vol. II. Boston: Wiggin and Lunt, 1867, 406.

Document 111

JONATHAN ELATSON, "RECOGNIZANCE FOR MARY BRIDGES, SR.," JANUARY 12, 1692/1693

After Mary's interview with the renowned Reverend Increase Mather, the need for her to remain in jail seemed pointless, and she was allowed to post a £100 bail and return home in January 1693. She would never be condemned or executed.

Memorandum

That on the Twelfth Day of January 1692 In the fourth year of the
Reigne of o'r Soveraigne Lord and Lady William and Mary by the
Grace of God of England &c King and Queen Defenders of the faith

&c Personally appeared before William Stoughton Esq'r Chief Justice
of their Maj'ties Province of the Massachusets Bay in New England
Jno Bridges of Andover in the County of Essex Blacksmith and Jno Osgood of the same
Towne Husbandman and acknowledged them-
selves to be joyntly and Severally Indebted unto o'r said Soveraigne
Lord and Lady and the Survivor of them Their Heires and Successors
in the Sume of One hundred pounds to be levied on their or Either
of their Lands and Tenem'ts Goods and Chatles for [the] use of our
said Soverainge Lord and Lady the King and Queen or Survivor of
them [th] On Condition that Mary Bridges haveing Stood Comitted for
Suspition of Witchcraft shall make her personall apperance Before
the Justices of o'r s'd Lord and Lady the King and Queen at the
next Court of Assizes and Gen'll Goal Delivery to be held for the
County of Essex Then & There to answer to all such matters and
things as shall in their Maj'ties Behalfe be aledged against her and to
doe and receive that w'ch by the said Court shall be then and there
enjoyned her and thence not to depart without license

Attest.
*Jon Elatson Clerk of the bar
(Reverse) Recognizance of John Bridges & John Osgood for Mary Bridges
May: 10th Appears

Source: Massachusetts State Archives, vol. 135, no. 103, p. 94.

Further Reading

Baker, Emerson W. *A Storm of Witchcraft.* Oxford, UK: Oxford University Press, 2015.

Boyer, Paul, and Stephen Nissenbaum. *Salem Possessed: The Social Origins of Witchcraft.* Cambridge, MA: Harvard University Press, 1974.

Demos, John Putnam. *Entertaining Satan: Witchcraft and the Culture of Early New England.* Oxford, UK: Oxford University Press, 1982.

Godbeer, Richard. *The Devil's Dominion: Magic and Religion in Early New England.* Cambridge, UK: Cambridge University Press, 1992.

Norton, Mary Beth. *In the Devil's Snare: The Salem Witchcraft Crisis of 1692.* New York: Random House, 2002.

Reis, Elizabeth. *Damned Women: Sinners and Witches in Puritan New England.* Ithaca, NY: Cornell University Press, 1997.

Roach, Marilyn K. *The Salem Witch Trials: A Day-by-Day Chronicle of a Community Under Siege.* New York: Cooper Square Press, 2002.

Upham, Charles W. *The History of Witchcraft and Salem Village.* Boston: Wiggin and Lunt, 1867.

Weisman, Richard. *Witchcraft, Magic and Religion in 17th Century Massachusetts.* Amherst: University of Massachusetts Press, 1984.

Chapter 4

Post–Salem Witch Trials— The Aftermath

A large number of persons escaped death during the trials either by confession, such as Tituba, or by reprieve or pardon from Sir William Phips. The following documents examine the situations surrounding these other victims of the Salem witch trials. Few persons, especially those who were condemned, but never executed, were able to return to normal lives. For this reason, some of these documents reflect the attempts made by the Province of Massachusetts to pardon those who were condemned—both the executed and those released from jail. Compensation will take the form of reimbursement for items taken by the court, financial restitution for wrongful imprisonment, and a reversal of verdicts by the provincial legislature declaring that all the accused persons were, in fact, innocent.

It is important to note that Tituba was never formally indicted by the Court of Oyer and Terminer in all probability because she was the first to confess and cooperate with the court in providing names and descriptions of witches and witchcraft activity. Why, if the court were interested in gathering and following every clue to ferret out the diabolical witch conspiracy, should they execute their star witness and best source of information? The problem was that by allowing Tituba to live, the court established a dangerous precedent for the Salem trials—that confessed witches would not be executed. In her extensive testimony describing the activities of a coven of nine witches, Tituba lit the fire of paranoia that would burn virulently in Massachusetts for most of 1692.

Document 112

UNKNOWN, "THE INDICTMENT OF TITUBA INDIAN," MAY 9, 1693

The document that follows was prepared at the end of Tituba's long prison stay in May 1693 and issued by a Supreme Judicial Court, not the Court of Oyer and Terminer. When the court finally did hear her case, Governor Phips only wanted the episode to end, and it was decided to drop it, allowing Tituba to be sold to pay the jailer's bill for her incarceration since March of the previous year.

That Tittapa and Indian Woman, servant to Mr. Samuel Parris of Salem village in the County of Essex—aforesaid—upon or about the latter end of the year 1691 in the town of Salem Village aforesaid, wickedly, maliciously and feloniously

A Covenant with the Devill did make and sign the Devill's Book with a marke like A:C by which wicked covenanting with the Devill, she the Said Tittapa, is become a detestable Witch against the Peace of Our Sovereign Lord and Lady, the King and Queen, their Crown and Dignity and the Laws in that case made and provided.

Source: Suffolk County Court Files, vol. 32, docket 2760, p. 102.

Document 113

JONATHAN ELAT, "RECOGNIZANCE FOR MARY BRIDGES, SR.," JANUARY 1692/1693

Both Mary Bridges Sr., wife of Andover blacksmith, John Bridges, and Mary Bridges Jr., their daughter, were accused, imprisoned, tried, and found innocent of the charge of witchcraft. The real ordeal for them, as for most victims subjected to imprisonment, was life in jail. The inhumane prison conditions during the trials were responsible for the deaths of several persons. The following document is one of the rare surviving acknowledgments of posting bail for a witch suspect, Mary Bridges Sr. Here her husband and an associate, John Osgood, posted a £100 bond guaranteeing Mary Bridges Sr.'s return to court to stand trial. This change in policy concerning witch suspects under arrest was instituted by Royal Governor Phips in an effort to show leniency to victims and relieve the pressure on jails by placing them under the care and custody of friends and family, instead of a jailer. This option proved successful and helped minimize the growing public outcry against the government's handling of the trials.

Memorandum

That on the twelfth day of January 1692 In the fourth year of the reign of our Sovereign Lord and Lady William and Mary by the Grace of God of England and King and Queen defenders of the faith and personally appeared before William Stoughton Esquire Chief Justice of their Majesties Province of the Massachusetts Bay in New England John Bridges of Andover in the County of Essex blacksmith and John Osgood of the same town husbandman and acknowledged themselves to be jointly and severally indebted unto our said Sovereign Lord and Lady and the Survivor of them their heirs and successors in the sum of one hundred pounds to be levied on their or either of their lands and tenements goods and chattles for the use of our said Sovereign Lord and Lady the King and Queen or Survivor of them on condition that Mary Bridges having stood committed for suspicion of witchcraft shall make her personal appearance before the justices of our said Lord and Lady the King and Queen at the next Court of Assizes and general jail delivery to be held for the County of Essex then and there to answer to all such matters and things as shall in their Majesties behalf be alleged against her and to do and receive that which by the said Court shall be then and there enjoined her and thence not to depart without license.

Attest
*Jon Elat

Source: Massachusetts State Archives, vol. 135, no. 60.

Document 114

GEORGE JACOBS JR., "A STATEMENT OF LOSS SUBMITTED TO THE COLONY OF MASSACHUSETTS FOR DAMAGES UPON THE ESTATE OF GEORGE JACOBS, SR., VICTIM OF THE SALEM WITCH TRIALS," C. 1693

Among the many injustices suffered by the victims of the trials was the seizure of personal property by officers appointed by the Court of Oyer and Terminer from the families of the condemned. The following inventory document illustrates a typical confiscation and the value of the property seized. Not all persons were compensated for their losses by the Colony of Massachusetts in the years that followed. The following request for compensation was submitted to the Massachusetts Great and General Court on behalf of the Jacobs family, by the son of George Jacobs Sr.

"An account of what was seized and taken away from my Father's Estate, George Jacob's Sr., late of Salem, deceased, by Sheriff Corwin and his Assistants in the year 1692."

"When my father was executed, and I was forced to fly out of the country, to my great damage and distress of my family, my wife and daughter imprisoned,—viz., my wife eleven months, and my daughter seven months in prison,—it cost them twelve (L12) pounds money to the officers, besides other charges."

Five cows, fair large cattle, 3 pounds per cow	L 15	00	0
Eight loads of English hay taken out of the barn, 35 shillings per load	L 14	00	0
A parcel of apples that made 24 barrels cider to halves; viz., 12 barrels of cider, @ 8 shillings per barrel	L 4	16	0
Sixty bushels of Indian corn, @ 2 shillings 6 pence per bushel	L 7	10	0
A mare	L 2	00	0
Two good feather beds, and furniture, rugs, blankets sheets bolsters and pillows	L 10	00	0
Two brass kettles, cost	L 6	00	0
Money, 12 shillings; and a large gold thumb ring, 20 shillings	L 1	12	0
Five swine	L 3	15	0
A quantity of pewter which I cannot exactly know the worth, perhaps	L 3	00	0
	L67	13	0

Besides abundance of small things, meat in the house, fowls, chairs, and other things took clear away ⟶ <u>L 12   00   0</u>

Total ⟶ <u>L 79   13   0</u>

"George Jacobs"

Source: Charles W. Upham. *Salem Witchcraft*, vol. II. Boston: Wiggin and Lunt, 1867, pp. 382–383.

Document 115

HON. SAMUEL SEWELL, "THE PUBLIC APOLOGY OF THE HONORABLE SAMUEL SEWALL," JANUARY 14, 1697

The following document is perhaps the most unique and remarkable of all post-trial, primary-source commentaries because it was written by one of the judges who actually presided at the Court of Oyer and Terminer in Salem, Honorable Samuel Sewell. Sewell was a graduate of Harvard College (1671) with an original expectation to serve as a minister of a New England congregation. His marriage in 1676 to a daughter of John Hull, a wealthy Boston merchant and mintmaster of Massachusetts Bay Colony, drew him into the maritime shipping business instead. He had come to believe that God was punishing him and his family "for the execution of innocent victims." In January 1697, at the order of the colonial government, the entire colony was observing a "fast of repentance" to ask God for forgiveness for having allowed the Salem witch trials. In the Sunday morning service of Boston's Third Church, Sewell took advantage of the opportunity to stand before the attending congregation and have their minister Reverend Samuel Willard read this confession and apology (Baker, A Storm of Witchcraft, pp. 222–223).

January 14, 1697

Copy of the bill [that] I put up on the fast day; giving it to Mr. Willard as he passed by, and standing up at the reading of it, and bowing when finished, in the afternoon:

Samuel Sewall, sensible of the reiterated strokes of God upon himself and family; and being sensible that as to the guilt contracted upon the opening of the late Commission of Oyer and Terminer at Salem (to which the order for this day relates) he is upon many accounts more concerned than any that he knows of, desires to take the blame and shame of it, asking pardon of men, and especially desiring prayers that God, who has unlimited authority, would pardon that sin and all other his sins, personal and relative; and according to his infinite benignity and sovereignty, not visit the sin of him or of any other upon himself or any of his, nor upon the land; but that He would powerfully defend him against all temptations to sin for the future and vouchsafe him the efficacious, saving conduct of his word and spirit.

Source: Nathan Henry Chamberlain. *Samuel Sewall and the World He Lived In.* Boston: De Wolfe, Fiske & Company, 1898, 174.

Document 116

ROBERT CALEF, *MORE WONDERS OF THE INVISIBLE WORLD*, 1700

This is an impartial account of the most memorable matters of fact, touching the supposed witchcraft of New England.

Mr. Parris had been some years a minister in Salem-Village, when this sad calamity (as a deluge) overflowed them, spreading itself far and near:

He was a gentleman of liberal education, and not meeting with any great encouragement, or advantage in merchandizing, to which for some time he applied himself, betook himself to the work of the ministry; this village being then vacant, he met with so much encouragement, as to settle in that capacity among them.

After he had been there about two years, he obtained a grant from a part of the town, that the house and land he occupied, and which had been allotted by the whole people to the ministry, should be and remain to him, etc. as his own estate in fee simple.

This occasioned great divisions both between the inhabitants themselves, and between a considerable part of them and their said minister, which divisions were but as a beginning or praeludium to what immediately followed.

It was the latter end of February 1691, when divers young persons belonging to Mr. Parris's family, and one or more of the neighborhood began to act, after a strange and unusual manner, viz. as by getting into holes, and creeping under chairs and stools, and to use sundry odd postures and antick gestures, uttering foolish, ridiculous speeches, which neither they themselves nor any others could make sense of; the physicians that were called could assign no reason for all this; but it seems one of the, having recourse to the old shift, told them he was afraid they were bewitched: upon such suggestions, they that were concerned applied themselves to fasting and prayer, which was attended not only in their own private families, but with calling in the help of others.

March the 11th

Mr. Parris invited several neighboring ministers to join with him in keeping a solemn day of prayer at his own house; the time of the exercise those persons were for the most part silent, but after any one prayer was ended, they would act and speak strangely and ridiculously, yet were such as had been well educated and of good behavior, the one, a girl of 11 or 12 years old, would sometimes seem to be in a convulsion fit, her limbs being twisted several ways, and very stiff, but presently her fit would be over.

A few days before this solemn day of prayer, Mr. Parris's Indian man and woman made a cake of rye meal, with the children's water, and baked it in the ashes, and as is said gave it to a dog; this was done as a means to discover witchcraft; soon after which those ill affected or afflicted persons name several that they said they saw, when in their fits, afflicting them.

The first complained of, was the said Indian Woman, named Tituba. She confessed that the Devil urged her to sign a Book, which he presented to her, and also to work mischief among the children, etc. She was afterwards committed to prison, and lay there till sold for her fees. The account she since gives of it is, that her master did beat her and otherways abuse her, to make her confess and accuse (such as he called) her sister-witches, and that whatsoever she said by way of confessing or accusing others, was the effect of such usage; her master refused to pay her fees, unless she would stand to what she had said.

Tituba, the woman from the West Indies who helped to start the hysteria, was promised by Parris that she would be freed for her cooperative testimony. He didn't follow through with his promise. She recanted her story, saying that Samuel Parris had beaten her into confessing herself a witch. She said that everything she'd confessed or said to accuse others was a direct result of those beatings. In May of 1693, Tituba was sold to someone else; she would never see the Parris family again.

The children complained likewise of two other women, to be the authors of their hurt, viz. Sarah Good, who had long been counted a melancholy and distracted woman, and one Osburn, an old bed-rid woman; which two were persons so ill thought of, that the accusation was more readily believed; and after examination before two Salem Magistrates, were committed:

March the 19th

Mr. (Deodat) Lawson (who had formerly been a preacher at the said Village) came thither, and hath since set forth in print an account of what then passed, about which time, as he saith, they complained of Goodwife Cory, and Goodwife Nurse, members of the churches at the village and at Salem, many others being by that time accused.

March the 21st

Goodwife Cory was examined before the Magistrates of Salem, at the meetinghouse at the Village, a throng of spectators being present to see the novelty. Mr. Noyes, one of the ministers of Salem, began with prayer, after which the prisoner being called, in order to answer to what should be alleged against her, she desired that she might go to prayer, and was answered by the magistrates, that they did not come to hear her pray, but to examine her.

The number of the afflicted were at that time about ten, viz. Mrs. Pope, Mrs. Putnam, Goodwife Bibber, and Goodwife Goodall, Mary Wolcott, Mercy Lewes (at Thomas Putnam's) and Dr. Grigg's maid, and three girls, viz. Elizabeth Parris, daughter to the minister, Abigail Williams his niece, and Ann Putnam, which last three were not only the beginners but were also the chief among these accusations.

These ten were most of them present at the examination, and did vehemently accuse her of afflicting them, by biting, pinching, strangling, etc. And they said, they did in their fits see her likeness coming to them, and bringing a book for them to sign; Mr. Hathorn, a magistrate of Salem, asked her, why she afflicted those children? She said, she did not afflict them; he asked her, who did then? She said, I do not know. How should I know? She said, they were poor distracted creatures, and no heed to be given to what they said;

Mr. Hathorn and Mr. Noyes replied that it was the judgment of all that were there present, that they were bewitched, and only she (the accused) said they were distracted: she was accused by them, that the Black Men whispered to her in her ear now (while she was upon examination) and that she had a yellow bird, that did use to suck between her fingers, and that the said bird did suck now in the assembly; order being given to look in that place to see if there were any sign, the girl that pretended to see it said, that it was too late now, for she had removed a pin and put it on her head, it was upon search found, that a pin was there sticking upright.

When the accused had any motion of their body, hands or mouth, the accusers would cry out, as when she bit her lip, they would cry out of being bitten, if she grasped one hand with the other, they would cry out of being pinched by her, and would produce marks, so of the other motions of her body, as complaining of being prest, and when she leaned to the seat next her, if she stirred her feet, they would stamp and cry out of pain there.

After the hearing the said Cory was committed to Salem Prison, and then their crying out of her abated.

March the 24th

Goodwife Nurse was brought before Mr. Hathorn and Mr. Corwin (magistrates) in the meetinghouse. Mr. Hale minister of Beverly, began with prayer, after which she being accused of much the same crimes made the like answers, asserting her own innocence with earnestness. The accusers were mostly the same, Thomas Putnam's wife, etc. complaining much. The dreadful shrieking from her and others, was very amazing, which was heard at a great distance; she was also committed to prison.

A child of Sarah Goods was also apprehended, being between four and five years old. The accuser said this child bit them, and would show such like marks; as those of a small set of teeth upon their arms; as many of the afflicted as the child cast its eye upon, would complain they were in torment, which child they also committed.

Concerning those that had been hitherto examined and committed, it is among other things observed by Mr. Lawson that they were by the accusers charged to belong to a company that did muster in arms, and were reported to keep days of fast, thanksgiving and sacraments; and that those afflicted (or accusers) did in the assembly cure each others, even with a touch of their hand, when strangled and otherwise tortured, and would endeavor to go to the afflicted to relieve them thereby (for hitherto they had not used the experiment of bringing the accused to touch the afflicted, in order to their cure) and could foretell one another's fits to be coming, and would say, look to such a one, she will have a fit presently and so it happened, and that at the same time when the accused person was present, the afflicted said they saw her spectre or likeness in other places at the meetinghouse suckling of their familiars.

The said Mr. Lawson being to preach at the village, after the Psalm was sung, Abigail Williams said, 'Now stand up and name your text'; after it was read, she said 'It is a long text.' Mrs. Pope in the beginning of the sermon said to him 'Now there is enough of that.' In sermon, he referring to his doctrine, Abigail Williams said to him, 'I know no doctrine you had, if you did name one I have forgot it.'

Ann Putnam, an afflicted girl, said, there was a yellow bird state on the hat as it hung on the pin in the pulpit.

March 31, 1692.

Was set apart as a day of solemn humiliation at Salem, upon the account of the business, on which day Abigail Williams said, that she saw a great number of persons in the Village at the administration of a mock sacrament, where they had bread as red as raw flesh, and red drink.

April 1st

Mercy Lewis affirmed, that she saw a man in white, with whom she went into a glorious place, viz. In her fits, where was no light of the sun, much less of candles, yet was full of light and brightness, with a great multitude in white glittering robes, who sang the song in 5 rev. 9 and the 110 and 149 Psalms; and was grieved that she might tarry no longer in this place. This White Man is said to have appeared several times to the others of them, and to have given then notice how long it should be before they should have another fit.

April the 3rd

Being Sacrament Day at the village, Sarah Cloys, sister to Goodwife Nurse, a member of one of the churches, was (though it seems with difficulty prevailed with to be) present; but being entered the place, and Mr. Parris naming his text, 6 John 70. Have I not chosen you twelve and one of you is a Devil (for what may cause rest as a doubt whether upon account of her sisters being committed, or because of the choice of that text) she rose up, and went out, the wind shutting the door forcibly, gave occasion to some to suppose she went out in anger, a might occasion a suspicion of her; however she was soon after complained of, examined and committed.

April the 11th

By this time the number of the accused and accusers being much increased, was a publick examination at Salem, six of the magistrates with several ministers being present; there appeared several who complained against others with hideous clamors and screechings. Goodwife Proctor was brought thither, being accused or cryed out against; her husband coming to attend and assist her, as there might be need, the accusers cryed out of him also, and that with so much earnestness, that he was committed with his wife.

About this time besides the experiment of the afflicted falling at the sight, etc., they put the accused upon saying the Lord's Prayer, which one among them performed, except in that petition, deliver us from evil, she expressed it thus, deliver us from all evil.

This was looked upon as if she prayed against what she was now justly under, and being put upon it again, repeated those words, hallowed be thy name, she expressed it hollowed be thy name, this was counted a depraving the words, as signifying to make void, and so a curse rather then a prayer, upon the whole it was concluded that she also could not say it, etc. Proceeding in this work of examination and commitment, many were sent to prison.

Source: Robert Calef. "More Wonders of the Invisible World," reprinted in *The Witchcraft Delusion in New England*, vols. 2 and 3. Edited by Samuel G. Drake. Roxbury, MA: 1866.

Document 117

ANN PUTNAM JR., "THE PUBLIC CONFESSION OF ANN PUTNAM," AUGUST 25, 1706

Of the post–witch trial lives of the so-called afflicted children who testified and demonstrated so vigorously against the many trial victims, comparatively little is known. Mary Warren and Abigail Williams have vanished entirely from the historic record. Elizabeth (aka Betty) Parris, Reverend Samuel Parris's daughter married a shoemaker in 1710, had five children and died at the age of 77 in 1760 in Concord, Massachusetts. Ann Putnam Jr. had already lost both parents by 1700. She was at that time, 20 years of age and responsible for caring for her seven younger siblings on the Putnam family farm in Salem Village. Ann decided to take steps to apply for church membership and met with the new minister of the Salem Village congregation, Reverend Joseph Green, to discuss how she might resolve her interpersonal problems with the family of Rebecca Nurse—who still attended the Salem Village Meeting House. The result of this discussion was the composition of a formal confession and apology which, like that of Judge Samuel Sewell in Boston nine years earlier, would be read by the minister to the entire congregation, while Ann stood, head bowed, in repentance before them.

I desire to be humbled before God for that sad and humbling Providence that befell my father's family in the year about 1692; that I, then being in my childhood, should by such a Providence of God be made an instrument for the accusing of several persons of a grievous crime, whereby their lives were taken away from them, whom now I have just grounds and good reason to believe they were innocent persons; and that it was a great delusion of Satan that deceived me in that sad time, whereby I justly fear [that] I have been instrumental, with others, though ignorantly and unwittingly, to bring upon myself and this land the guilt of innocent blood; though what was said or done by me against any person I can truly and uprightly say, before God and man, I did it not out of any anger, malice, or ill-will to any person, for I had no such thing against [any] one of them; but what I did was [done] ignorantly, being deluded by Satan. And particularly, as I was a chief instrument of accusing Goodwife Nurse and her two sisters,

I desire to lie in the dust and to be humbled for it, in that I was a cause, with others, of so sad a calamity to them and their families; for which I desire to lie in the dust, and earnestly beg forgiveness of God, and from all those unto whom I have given just cause of sorrow and of offence, whose relations were taken away or accused.

Source: Charles W. Upham. *Salem Witchcraft*, vol II. Boston: Wiggin and Lunt, 1867, 510.

Document 118

GOVERNOR JOSEPH DUDLEY, "THE MASSACHUSETTS GENERAL COURT MAKES RESTITUTION," DECEMBER 17, 1711

Thus, in the final analysis, an attempt was made to monetarily compensate victims' families for the wrongful arrest, humiliation, torment, incarceration, and death experienced by their loved ones during the witch trial period. It was a laudable gesture of remorse, but hardly enough.

December 17, 1711

By His Excellency the Governor:
   Whereas the General Assembly in their last session accepted the report of their committee appointed to consider of the damages sustained by sundry persons prosecuted for witchcraft in the year 1692/93, *viz.*

	£	s.	d.
Elizabeth How	12		
John Proctor and wife	15	0	0
George Jacobs	79	0	0
Sarah Wilds	14	0	0
Mary Esty	20	0	0
Mary Bradbury	20	0	0
Mary Parker	8	0	0
Abigail Faulkner	10	0	0
George Burroughs	50	0	0
Abigail Hobbs	10	0	0
Giles Corey and wife	21	0	0
Ann Foster	6	10	0

Rebecca Nurse	25	0	0
Rebecca Eames	10	0	0
John Willard	20	0	0
Dorcas Hoar	21	17	0
Sarah Good	30	0	0
Mary Post	8	14	0
Martha Carrier	7	0	0
Mary Lacey	8	10	0
Samuel Wardwell and wife	36	15	0
	309	1	0
	269	11	0
	578	12	0	TOTAL

I do by and with the advice and consent of Her Majesty's Council hereby order you to pay the above sum of five hundred seventy eight pounds and twelve shillings to Stephen Sewall, Esq., who, together with the gentlemen of the committee that estimated and reported the said damages, are desired and directed to distribute the same in proportion as above to such of the said persons as are living, and to those that legally represent them that are dead, according as the law directs, and for which this shall be your warrant.

Given under my hand at Boston,

Joseph Dudley
Governor of the Province of Massachusetts

Source: Essex County Court Archives, vol. 2, no. 138, from the Records of the Court of Oyer and Terminer, 1692, Property of the Supreme Judicial Court, Division of Archives and Records Preservation, on deposit at the Peabody Essex Museum, Salem, MA.

Further Reading

Baker, Emerson W. *The New England Knight: Sir William Phips, 1651–1695.* Toronto, Canada: University of Toronto Press, 1998.

Baker, Emerson W. *A Storm of Witchcraft.* Oxford, UK: Oxford University Press, 2015.

Boyer, Paul, and Stephen Nissenbaum. *Salem Possessed: The Social Origins of Witchcraft.* Cambridge, MA: Harvard University Press, 1974.

Hoffer, Peter Charles. *The Salem Witch Trials; A Legal History.* Lawrence: University Press of Kansas, 1997.

Konig, David. *Law and Society in Puritan Massachusetts, Essex County, 1629–1692.* Chapel Hill: University of North Carolina Press, 1979.

Norton, Mary Beth: *In the Devil's Snare*. New York: Vintage Books, 2003.

Reis, Elizabeth. *Damned Women: Sinners and Witches in Puritan New England*. Ithaca, NY: Cornell University Press, 1997.

Roach, Marilyn K. *The Salem Witch Trials: A Day-by-Day Chronicle of a Community Under Siege*. New York: Cooper Square Press, 2002.

Rosenthal, Bernard. *Salem Story: Reading the Witch Trials of 1692*. Cambridge, UK: Cambridge University Press, 1993.

Weisman, Richard. *Witchcraft, Magic and Religion in 17th Century Massachusetts*. Amherst: University of Massachusetts Press, 1984.

Conclusion: The Impact of the Salem Trials to the Present

In April 1696, Reverend Samuel Parris, after several years of quarreling with his parishioners, was finally dismissed by his congregation, following the birth of his son Noyes, and the death of his wife, Elizabeth. Parris remained on as a resident of the Salem Village parsonage, however, in lieu of back salary he believed he was owed by the members of his parish. Finally, they sued him for trespass and he countersued for his back pay. The matter was finally resolved in 1697; Parris was paid £79 and he left the parsonage, relinquishing the deed he had been given, to travel to an even more isolated and impoverished parish, Stow, Massachusetts, located about 15 miles west of Concord, Massachusetts. Parris had remarried in 1698 to Dorothy Noyes, a woman from nearby Sudbury. After leaving Stow in 1698, he relocated to several other communities attempting several other professions until finally settling on a small farm in Sudbury, where he died in 1720 at about the age of 67.

In Salem Village, by 1697, the congregation invited a new minister, 22-year-old Reverend Joseph Green, recently graduated from Harvard, to fill the pulpit vacated by Reverend Parris. Under Green, the community began to heal from their wounds. In 1699, Green welcomed the Nurse family back into communion and restructured the seating arrangements in the meetinghouse, placing the Nurses and the Putnams on the same bench. It was Green who "engineered Ann Putnam Jr.'s public apology" in 1706, where she "desired to be humbled before God for [that] sad and humbling providence that befell my father's family in the year about '92" (Baker, *A Storm of Witchcraft*, p. 234). As a result, the Putnams and the Nurses were beginning to put animosities behind them, in large part due to Reverend Green's efforts. As part of this healing process during Reverend Green's tenure at Salem Village, he requested that the congregation repeal their excommunication of Martha Corey.

In nearby Salem town, the impact of the trials was strongly felt for many years. Justice John Hathorne died in 1717 never publicly acknowledging his error, or expressing regret for the role he had played. His legacy of guilt would be handed down to his great-great-grandson, author Nathaniel Hawthorne, who revisited the subject of the Salem witch trials repeatedly in his fictional writing, portraying the actions of the Puritan leadership in a very negative light. Indeed, the negative public image of Puritans from the Victorian era to the present was in large part the result of Hawthorne's perspective of them as a sanctimonious, hypocritical, and judgmental people.

Other participants in the trials reflected soberly upon their actions, and as has been mentioned, the members of the jury publicly expressed regret, and in 1706 even the famous Justice Samuel Sewell felt compelled to stand in church while his apology was read to the congregation. Likewise in 1702, Reverend John Hale published *A Modest Inquiry into the Nature of Witchcraft,* which acknowledges the failures of the Court and admits the harm done to innocent victims of the trials. It should not be surprising that, as time passed, others began to contemplate the manner in which the trials had been conducted and saw them as stain upon the honor and righteousness of the people of God in Massachusetts. Misfortune that followed the trials was soon perceived not as mere coincidence, but as God's judgment for the mishandling of the crisis.

The newly appointed Governor Sir William Phips, who had allowed the trials to proceed in an uncontrolled direction under the virulent and prejudiced hands of Chief Justice William Stoughton, was never able to make amends to his people since he was recalled in 1693 to answer for a variety of bad decisions of which the witch trials was only one. In his absence, now Deputy Governor William Stoughton remained in charge as acting governor of Massachusetts until 1698.

It was William Stoughton, in the role of Chief Justice of both the 1692 Court of Oyer and Terminer and the later, Superior Court of Judicature after December 1692 and into 1693, who pushed for convictions and executions, while Royal Governor William Phips encouraged leniency. Now, after three more years of crop failure, drought, small-pox outbreaks, French and Indian attacks on land and sea, and general misfortune, acting Governor Stoughton issued a proclamation on December 17, 1696, in hopes of alleviating God's displeasure. In this statement, even the harsh chief magistrate begged the people of the Commonwealth that there should be ". . . observed a Day of Prayer with Fasting throughout the Province . . . so that all God's people may put away that which hath stirred God's holy jealousy against this land; that He would help us wherein we have done amiss to do so no more; and especially that whatever mistakes on either hand have been fallen into . . . referring to the Late Tragedy, raised among us by Satan and his instruments, through the awful judgment of God, He would humble us therefore and pardon all the errors and people that desire to love his name . . ." (Governor Stoughton's Proclamation, December 17, 1696, in Hansen, *Witchcraft at Salem,* 207–208).

On this appointed day, the Honorable Captain Samuel Sewell, a former associate justice of the Court of Oyer and Terminer, attended worship services at Boston's South Church. As he stood amid the seated congregation, the pastor, Reverend Samuel Willard, read a document Sewell had written. In it, Sewell declared that he "was sensible of the reiterated strokes of God upon himself and his family . . . that he desires to take the blame and shame of it, asking pardon of men, and especially desiring prayers that God . . . would pardon that sin and all other of his sins." It was a public demonstration of acknowledged guilt and the need for repentance.

In other churches near Salem, the need for repentance was felt. The members of the First Church of Salem stated collectively, "we are, through God's mercy to us, convinced that we were on that dark day, under the powers of those errors which then prevailed in the land." On July 8, 1703, the congregational ministers of Essex County, Massachusetts, produced a collective petition that stated that they believed there was "great reason to fear that innocent persons then suffered, and that God may have a controversy with the land upon that account" (Winfield Nevins, *Witchcraft in Salem Village in 1692*, p. 249).

Finally, on October 11, 1711, the Province of Massachusetts enacted an act of legislation entitled, "A Reversal of Attainder" whereby 22 convicted witches were pardoned, their guilty verdicts reversed to innocent, and their reputations officially restored. In the same year, a more tangible form of compensation for damages suffered by the victims' families came in the form of a cash payment of 578 pounds and 12 shillings to be divided among the heirs of the witchcraft trial victims and others who had been wrongfully accused (David Levin, *What Happened in Salem?* New York: Harcourt, Brace and World, Inc., 1960, p. 140). As a result of these efforts, the people of Salem attempted to put the tragic event behind them and expunge their collective guilt, returning to the more mundane aspects of life in colonial New England.

But New England would never be the same again. The legacy of the witch trials continued to haunt the memories of future generations. Beginning with contemporary critics of the trials, such as Robert Calef and Thomas Brattle, a number of books—particularly Calef's scathing *More Wonders of the Invisible World* (London, 1700)—began to widely circulate. Reverend Cotton Mather is vilified in these accounts as a man of intolerance with a fanatic zeal to condemn innocent persons in the face of reason and common sense. Conversely, Cotton's father, Reverend Increase Mather, President of Harvard College, supported a more moderated position, strongly opposing the use of spectral evidence throughout the trials in his 1692 book: *Cases of Conscience*. As a result, the senior Mather has retained the characterization of a man of moderation who never positioned himself in the camp of the chief prosecutors of the witchcraft trials (Hansen, *Witchcraft in Salem*, pp. 186–187).

Early explanations of the episode, apart from Hale and Mather, were reluctant to place the blame upon real satanic activity. As the Age of the Enlightenment began to dawn in America, skeptics were less inclined to excuse the religious leaders of Salem and Boston, and more inclined to blame them. This does not imply a sudden rejection of religious faith or a complete reversal of a belief in witchcraft. It does imply that the role of community leadership, which once was thoroughly dominated by the Puritan clergy, was shortly undermined by a growing lack of public confidence in the credibility of the Puritan ministers.

As their influence and authority gradually lessened, the political power of the New England merchants continued to rise, and public confidence moved away from religious leaders and toward those whose leadership had proved monetarily successful in the secular world. Royal governors too, anxious to avoid the pitfalls of leaders like Phipps and Stoughton, turned to secular businessmen for advice, and eschewed relying upon the advice of New England's theologians.

This secular shift in Massachusetts's political power base from religion to business, partly accounts for the fact that in such mid-18th-century upheavals as the Seven Years' War and the American Revolution, the merchants of Boston and Salem wielded much greater influence over popular opinion, with little direct input from ecclesiastical leadership (John Putnam Demos, *Entertaining Satan: Witchcraft and the Culture of Early New England*, Oxford, UK: Oxford University Press, 1982, pp. 393–394). In fact, the general decline in the belief in witchcraft did not proceed evenly or equally through all major social ranks in colonial New England. Persons of more than average education and wealth, such as merchants, composed an advanced guard of skeptics—in some individual cases as early as the Salem witch trials.

From a legal perspective, one of the more positive results of the Salem episode was the general reluctance of courts to countenance accusations and trials of witchcraft after 1693. Concerning this, it should be noted that a lesser-known, contemporaneous witch trial episode took place in Fairfield, Stratford, and Wallingford, Connecticut, during the 1692–1693 period. This resulted in five complaints, one formal accusation, one conviction, but no executions (David D. Hall, *Witch-hunting in Seventeenth Century New England*, Boston: Northeastern University Press, 1982, pp. 315–316).

American colonial legal procedures from 1693 onward demanded a change in the process by which suspected capital offenders might be charged and brought to trial. Most important was the complete rejection of the superstitious methods of discovery used in the Salem court—such as the "test of touch," the search for witch's marks, "pressing," and the use of spectral evidence in cases involving witchcraft.

Since the Salem trials were largely conducted by men who lacked formal legal training, there were numerous violations of British court procedure. These judicial errors clearly embarrassed the colonial government and were carefully avoided in later capital trials in New England.

For example, in all later cases, the accused would be offered the right of a defense counsel. Sadly, this benefit was not offered to the accused in Salem in 1692. Similarly, court justices would no longer act as both judge and inquisitor—interrogating the accused in the manner of an attorney for the prosecution. Lastly, persons accused of a crime would be presumed innocent by the court, placing the burden for proof of guilt upon the state. Not surprisingly, there would be no further convictions for the crime of witchcraft in New England. Recent research has, however, uncovered four other incidences of alleged witchcraft in post-1693 New England. Of these cases, none resulted in a condemnation (Demos, *Entertaining Satan*, pp. 408–409).

In the British Isles, the crime of witchcraft would resurface only twice after the Salem incident ended. In 1716, the last episode in England occurred in Huntingdon, Cambridgeshire, when a woman and her nine-year-old daughter were convicted and hanged for raising a storm to endanger shipping and causing harm to their neighbors. The last documented execution in Scotland took place in 1722 when a woman was burned at the stake. Finally, the statute making witchcraft a capital offense in England was repealed in 1736 (Nevins, *Witchcraft in Salem Village in 1692*, Boston: Lee and Shepard, 1892, p. 265).

Public sentiment concerning the Salem trials continued to be shaped, however, and public attitudes changed as the grip of the Puritan religion weakened over New England, and the skepticism of the Age of Reason began to have its full effect. As aforementioned, Governor Thomas Hutchinson, in his mid-18th-century *History of the Commonwealth of Massachusetts Bay*, balked at the notion that those involved may have actually been disturbed by either spiritual or mental disorders, but rather attributed the activities of the afflicted children as those of frivolous seekers of attention "that the whole was a scene of fraud and imposture, begun by young girls." And this opinion continued to gain ground throughout the later 18th and 19th centuries (Thomas Hutchinson, quoted in Hansen, *Witchcraft at Salem*, p. 26).

Without question, the general public's imagination and attitude concerning the Salem witchcraft episode was stimulated and shaped most dramatically by the writings of Nathaniel Hawthorne (1804–1864). More than any other American writer, Hawthorne—in stories such as *The House of the Seven Gables* and *Young Goodman Brown*—popularized the view that the Salem witchcraft trials were the result of Puritan prejudice and social repression.

Hawthorne, as we have noted earlier, wrestled throughout his life with the awareness that he was the great-great-grandson of Justice John Hathorne, a notable actor in the most virulent stage of the trials. Most importantly, in the author's mind, Justice Hathorne was a magistrate who never expressed feelings of guilt or regret for the notorious part he had played in the unjust deaths of 20 fellow citizens. As a result of this, Nathaniel Hawthorne—ever the sentimental and enlightened Victorian intellectual—took every opportunity to cast literary shadows over his Puritan forebears who had showed so little mercy and liberality in the treatment of innocent victims, be they accused of witchcraft or adultery (Hill, from Nathaniel Hawthorne, "Young Goodman Brown" (1835), in *The Salem Witch Trials Reader*, p. 314).

As a result, nearly all of Hawthorne's numerous fictional Puritan authority figures are characterized in his prose as evil men imbued with a fanatic religious zeal to persecute and condemn. In addition, Hawthorne held the view that the religious faith of his Puritan ancestors was rarely sincere. He often depicted Puritan divines, magistrates, and prosperous merchants as hypocritical community leaders using their religious, political, or economic power as a means to accomplish religious, political, or economic objectives. For example, in *The House of the Seven Gables*, the villainous Judge Pyncheon (a character loosely based upon Judge Hathorne), falsely accused Matthew Maule of witchcraft and executes him in order to acquire Maule's land as the location for his new mansion. Thus, from the 1840s onward, Nathaniel Hawthorne's best-selling Gothic fiction negatively shaped the reading public's imagination concerning not only the Salem witchcraft event itself, but Puritans in general (ibid., p. 325).

This image of the Salem Trials would not be helped or altered in any significant way by other authors of the 19th century. Noted New England poets, John Greenleaf Whittier and Henry Wadsworth Longfellow, both come down hard upon the likes of Reverend Cotton Mather and Justice John Hathorne. Whittier's poem, "Calef in Boston," written and published in 1849, depicts Reverend Cotton Mather as a self-righteous teacher of spiritual lies, while "simple tradesman" Robert Calef speaks the honest and simple truth against Mather in words "frank and bold." Similarly, H.W. Longfellow, a friend of Hawthorne's, produced a play in 1868 entitled, "Giles Corey of the Salem Farms." This play explores the superstitions and spectral evidence accepted as truth by Reverend Cotton Mather and Justice John Hathorne in their faulty efforts to ferret out those responsible for witchcraft in Salem Village. As with Hawthorne, these two literary giants had a profound impact upon their own readership. Their published works served only to further erode the reputation of the Puritan leadership of Massachusetts in the late 17th century and elevate the status of those who were victimized by the witchcraft trials. In this way, the public became increasingly more critical of the Puritans in general, while the subject of witchcraft in Salem grew increasingly more popular (ibid., pp. 314, 381–382).

A direct result of this general public skepticism and popularization of the subject of the witchcraft trials was the rise of tourism in Salem. No longer was the subject of witchcraft considered a serious topic of discussion reserved for historians and theologians. By the 1890s, it had already begun to take on a P.T. Barnumesque quality. A local pharmacy occupied the downstairs floor of the Justice Jonathan Corwin House—already a tourist attraction—and produced a brand of cosmetics known simply as "Salem Witch Cream." Local Victorian artist, Tomkins Mattson, produced two powerful and idealized romantic paintings entitled *The Examination of a Witch* and *The Trial of George Jacobs*. The former of these depicts a romantic Victorian heroine modestly attempting to cover her nakedness as she is examined for a "witch's mark" by a clutch of evil-looking crones, while Judge Hathorne and a gathering of other interested male observers look on. The latter painting is the artist's image of alleged witch George Jacobs on his knees pleading for leniency from the merciless Judge Hathorne as Margaret Jacobs testifies against her grandfather. Both of these late Victorian images are more imaginative than accurate, yet they are the two most influential depictions of the Salem witchcraft trials in existence and have shaped public opinion for the past century.

By the turn of the 20th century, far from wishing to avoid the subject, the City of Salem had named its high school sports teams the "Salem Witches." A prominent local jewelry store, Daniel Low's, Inc., produced a line of engraved sterling silver Salem witch spoons with a witch motif for discriminating tourists. For less prosperous visitors, Salem shops were selling tourist guidebooks, post cards, and custom-made Staffordshire plates with witch trial themes. Even the city and its citizens took pride in referring to Salem as "The Witch City," and began a long and profitable association with the Salem witch trials, which has only expanded with the passage of time. The poetic irony of this trend is that "Salem Village"—the hometown of Tituba, the Parris family, the Putnams, the Proctors, the location of the original hearings, the Salem Village Church, Reverend Samuel Parris's Parsonage site, Rebecca Nurse's House and Farm, and many other original locations—is now known as Danvers, Massachusetts. Danvers attracts very little attention from the millions of tourists who now annually flock to the city of Salem in search of the witchcraft trial experience (Rosenthal, *Salem Story*, pp. 204–206).

From the mid-20th century to the present, the public has been nearly overwhelmed with a variety of mass media productions—films, plays, and television documentaries—all of which purport to provide the viewer with a glimpse of the Salem witchcraft trials. Undoubtedly, the most significant of these was Arthur Miller's 1953 play, *The Crucible*, which is generally regarded as one of the greatest plays of the 20th century. In the 1950s and 1960s, it played to millions of Americans as a morality play, warning theatergoers of the dangers of mass hysteria in hunting witches in the same way that Congressman Joseph McCarthy and his House Committee on un-American Activities hunted alleged communists. By 1996, it was transformed to a film directed by Nick Hytner, featuring the acting talents of Daniel Day-Lewis, Winona Ryder, Jean Allen, and Paul Scofield.

While *The Crucible* is an excellent play, it must be regarded as an unfortunate distortion of history. Playwright Arthur Miller conceived of this work in the early 1950s as a means of striking back at those whose power, prejudices, and fanatic zeal against the perceived "Communist threat" had blacklisted many of his colleagues and threatened Miller's career as well. In his attempt to write a good play, Miller took liberties with the facts. For example, he identified as one of the leading causes of the episode, a romantic liaison between Abigail Williams and John Proctor. In actuality, Williams was 11 years old, and Proctor was about 60, an unlikely pair—even by 17th-century standards (ibid., p. 172).

In 1992, the City of Salem and the nearby town of Danvers (Salem Village) commemorated the 300th anniversary of the Salem witchcraft trials with a year-long schedule of events including a conference where scholarly papers on the subject of the Salem episode were presented. Both communities commissioned and created monuments to honor the memory of the victims of the trials. Salem also established an annual award to honor that person who during his or her lifetime had done the most to further the cause of human rights. Most recently, in 2015–2016, a team of historians and archeologists have discovered what is now believed to be the actual site of the execution and burial of the witch trial victims, a now wooded outcropping of rock and shallow soil known as "Proctor's Ledge," situated near the base of Gallows Hill near Boston Street in Salem. Since this property is owned by the City of Salem, at the present time, there are plans to officially recognize the historic significance of the site (Laura Grimaldi, "Researchers Pinpoint Site of Salem Witch Trial Hangings," *Boston Globe,* January 13, 2016).

A commonwealth was humbled, prayers of forgiveness offered, laws were changed, payments were made, histories were written, Gothic tales, documentaries, plays, and films have been produced, and millions of lives have been affected. In spite of it all, however, the true impact of the Salem witchcraft trials has yet to be fully realized (Rosenthal, *Salem Story*, pp. 206–209).

Annotated Bibliography

Primary Sources

Burr, George Lincoln, ed. *Narratives of the Witchcraft Cases, 1648–1706*. New York: Charles Scribner's Sons, 1914.

A marvelous compendium of primary source documents with excellent annotations not otherwise available to researchers contained in one well-organized and convenient volume.

Calef, Robert. *More Wonders of the Invisible World; also called The Wonders of the Invisible World Displayed in Five Parts*. Printed for Nath. Hillar at the Princess—Arms in Leaden-Hall-Street over against Mary-Ax, and Joseph Collier at the Golden Bible on London Bridge, London, 1700.

Robert Calef, a merchant of 17th-century Boston, was also the most outspoken critic of the Salem trials, the actions of the Court of Oyer and Terminer and especially Reverend Cotton Mather. Even the title of Calef's book is a satirical parody of Mather's well-known *Wonders of the Invisible World*. The Mathers prevented this book from being printed in Boston, and Calef was compelled to seek a publisher in London. It provides an excellent counterpoint to other more sympathetic contemporary sources.

Hale, Rev. John. *A Modest Inquiry into the Nature of Witchcraft*, Boston: Town House, 1702.

Reverend Hale, the pastor of the Beverly congregation, uses this book to explain the genuine fear of witchcraft experienced by the Salem community together with a description of the historic precedents for witchcraft commonly known by the local populace. Far from denying the existence of witchcraft, Hale explains why it poses a threat. His greatest objection to the trials is that the methods of evidence gathering, especially the use of spectral evidence, were ill-conceived and misdirected, resulting in a number of innocent deaths.

Hobbes, Thomas. *Leviathan*. Richard Tuck, ed. Cambridge, UK: Cambridge University Press, 1991.

This work, written by English political philosopher Thomas Hobbes in 1660, attempts to describe the means by which a state or commonwealth functions. In the latter chapters of *Leviathan,* he deals with spiritual matters and the importance of religion to the political state as a means of ensuring stability and morality. Although incredulous about the reality of witchcraft per se, Hobbes condemns witchcraft because of its inherently anarchistic and antisocial character, advocating that those claiming to be witches should be executed because of the potential threat they pose to the stability of the state.

The Holy Bible, New King James Version. Nashville: Thomas Nelson Publishers, 1990.

Kramer, Heinrich, and Jacob Sprenger. *The Malleus Maleficarum.* Translated by Montague Summers. Mineola, NY: Dover Publications, 1971.
This work was sponsored by the papacy and produced by two German monks who wished to provide all future witch-finders with a basic guide to identifying and condemning witches. It provides historic examples of actual cases of witchcraft; how witches may be correctly identified from those who are innocent; types of evidences which are reliable in witchcraft cases; and how best to proceed when an outbreak of witchcraft occurs in a particular community or region. Puritan religious leaders like Reverend Cotton Mather were well versed in this publication and gave it credence in the process of dealing with the supernatural.

Lawson, Deodat. *A Brief and True Narrative of Some Remarkable Passages Relating to Sundry Persons Afflicted by Witchcraft, at Salem Village Which Happened from the Nineteenth of March to the Fifth of April, 1692.* Boston: Benjamin Harris, 1692.
Reverend Deodat Lawson had formerly served as pastor to the Salem Village congregation. He traveled to Salem Village from Boston in March, 1692, and remained there through April observing the activities of the afflicted children and especially the actions of the Putnam family. The result of these observations was this 10-page booklet which provides the reader with a first-hand account describing some of the most unusual activities to take place in the village at the very start of the outbreak of witchcraft.

Mather, Rev. Cotton. As reprinted in *The Wonders of the Invisible World: Being an Account of the Tryals of Several Witches Lately Executed in New England.* Printed first at Boston in New England and reprinted at London for John Dunton at the Raven in the Poultry, 1693.
This work was commissioned by Governor Sir William Phips. It provides Reverend Cotton Mather's personal assessment of the Salem witchcraft episode. In his writing of the narrative of the trials, Mather was instructed by Phips to provide a text placing the Salem episode in a reasonable light. As a result, the book focuses upon those witchcraft cases which, in Mather's opinion, made the episode appear most rational to the general public both in New England and in old England. This approach was an attempt to make both Mather and the governor appear less controversial and to divert attention away from some of the harsh criticism raised by people like Thomas Brattle and Robert Calef.

Mather, Rev. Cotton. *Memorable Providences*, Boston: R.P., 1689.
This was a best-selling book in Boston during the years 1689–1690. It provides a first-hand account of Reverend Cotton Mather's experiences in Boston during the previous year dealing with an outbreak of witchcraft involving the children of John Goodwin and an Irish washerwoman, Goody Glover. The behavior of the afflicted Goodwin children is described in detail by Mather and mirrors closely the behavior of the afflicted children of Salem Village three years later. Glover finally confesses to witchcraft and demonstrates her magical abilities to Mather in her prison cell, claiming that other witches will carry on her work after she was gone.

Mather, Rev. Increase. *Cases of Conscience concerning Evil Spirits Impersonating Men.* Boston: Benjamin Harris, 1693.
The author is the respected and venerable father of Cotton Mather attempting to explain the events surrounding the Salem witch episode, published in the same year

as his son's *The Wonders of the Invisible World*. It acknowledges the problems associated with the use of spectral evidence, but stops short of condemning the trials.

Sewall, Samuel. *Diary of Samuel Sewall*, ed. M. Halsey Thomas. 2 vols. New York: Farrar, Straus and Giroux, 1973.
This diary is a vivid perspective on daily life in late 17th-century Massachusetts with intimate thoughts concerning the Salem witch episode as expressed by one of the justices of the Court of Oyer and Terminer. Sewell expresses his reasons for participating and his reasons for apologizing for his involvement in the infamous event.

Secondary Sources

Baker, Emerson W. *A Storm of Witchcraft: The Salem Trials and the American Experience*. Oxford, UK: Oxford University Press, 2015.
Brilliantly conceived and crafted. This is arguably the most comprehensive overview of the Salem witch trials ever written.

Baker, Emerson W., and John G. Reid. *The New England Knight: Sir William Phips*. Toronto: University of Toronto Press, 1998.

Barry, Mary Ann Hester, and Gareth Roberts, eds. *Witchcraft in Early Modern Europe: Studies in Culture and Belief*. Cambridge, UK: Cambridge University Press, 1996.
This is an exhaustively researched academic work providing much evidence of cases of witchcraft during the period from 1400s to the 1700s drawn from court records across Europe. It underscores the long-standing cultural traditions of European common people whose beliefs in witchcraft extend far back into pre-Christian times, yet prevailed until the early modern era.

Bonfanti, Leo. *The Witchcraft Hysteria of 1692*, New England Historical Series. Burlington, MA: Pride Publications, 1979.
This is a two-volume series of booklets, which summarize the Salem witchcraft episode and provide a selection of primary source materials.

Boyer, Paul, and Stephen Nissenbaum, eds. *The Salem Witchcraft Papers: Verbatim Transcripts of the Legal Documents of the Salem Witchcraft Outbreak of 1692*, 3 vols. New York: Da Capo Press, 1977.
This is the most complete collection of legal documents relating to the Salem witchcraft episode currently available. For persons interested in researching the testimony and court proceedings, it is essential reading.

Boyer, Paul, and Stephen Nissenbaum. *Salem Possessed: The Social Origins of Witchcraft*, Cambridge, MA: Harvard University Press, 1974.
This is an excellent study of the demographic details of Salem Village and suggests the strong possibility that there was political, religious, and economic motivation underlying the conflict between bitter factions in the village community.

Burr, George Lincoln, ed. *Narratives of the Witchcraft Cases: 1648–1706*. New York: Charles Scribner's Sons, 1914.
This is an excellent anthology of some of the best-known writings of most of the key figures involved in the Salem witchcraft episode, including Deodat Lawson, Thomas Brattle, William Phips, Cotton Mather, Robert Calef, and John Hale.

Caporeal, Linnda R. "Ergotism: The Satan Loosed in Salem?" *Science*, April 2, 1976.
  A controversial article that discusses the possibility that ergot mold may have been responsible for producing hallucinogenic and physiological symptoms in the afflicted girls of Salem Village in 1692.

Carlson, Laurie Winn. *A Fever in Salem: A New Interpretation of the New England Witchcraft Trials*. Chicago: Ivan R. Dee, 1999.
  This is a work which attempts to attribute the symptoms of the afflicted children to encephalitis lethargica, a disease which produces many similar characteristics such as hallucinations, seizures, fever, and sometimes coma. It is generally regarded as a very controversial theory which exhibits some serious problems in analysis, but provides an even-handed treatment of the Puritan leadership. It is similar to the ergot mold theory in that it identifies a possible physiological rationale for the Salem episode.

Demos, John Putnam. *Entertaining Satan: Witchcraft and the Culture of Early New England*. London: Oxford University Press, 1982.
  This work attempts to find certain common characteristics among the many episodes of witchcraft accusations, which happened in 17th-century New England. It focuses upon what types of individuals might be accused, what personality traits were exhibited by victims, and what social circumstances were frequently present in communities beset by witchcraft outbreaks. It combines an excellent interpretive narrative and biographical details with understandable demographic data.

Godbeer, Richard. *The Devil's Dominion: Magic and Religion in Early New England*. New York: Cambridge University Press, 1992.
  This work examines the dichotomy in New England puritan society which at the popular level embraced practices of English folk magic which at the theological level was condemned from the pulpits of New England's ministers. The Salem episode is mentioned as an example of how practices such as the making of a "witch's cake" could be viewed as an acceptable option by Salem Village parishioners to cure the afflicted children, while being condemned by Reverend Parris. This is an examination therefore of what the author calls the tension between the elite doctrine and folk tradition of early New England culture.

Goss, K. David. *The Salem Witch Trials: A Reference Guide*. Westport, CT: Greenwood Press, 2008.

Goss, K. David. *Daily Life during the Salem Witch Trials*. Santa Barbara, CA: Greenwood Press, 2012.
  A narrative examination of Puritan society in New England during the 1690s.

Goss, K. David, Richard Trask, Bryant F. Tolles, Joseph Flibbert, and James McAllister. *Salem: Cornerstones of a Historic City*. Beverly, MA: Commonwealth Editions, 1999.
  This is a compilation of five essays focusing upon key themes relating to Salem history: maritime history, Salem witchcraft trials, Nathaniel Hawthorne, architecture, and industrial history.

Hall, David D. *Witch-Hunting in Seventeenth Century New England: A Documentary History 1638–1693*. Boston: Northeastern University Press, 1991.
  An examination of all known outbreaks of witchcraft in 17th-century New England other than those at Salem, MA. What distinguishes this work from all others is its attention to primary sources, court records, and verbatim transcripts of testimony

from a wide range of trials. Through these documents, the reader receives a vivid picture of 17th-century daily life and the role of witchcraft in it.

Hansen, Chadwick. *Witchcraft at Salem*. New York: George Braziller, 1969.
An extraordinary analysis of the Salem witchcraft episode with concludes that while the majority of victims were undoubtedly innocent of any wrongdoing, there is reason to suspect that acts of witchcraft, similar to that performed by practitioners of voodoo, were taking place. Dr. Hansen takes an anthropological approach in explaining how the internalized belief in witchcraft can actually produce the expected results in victims who believe they are cursed.

Hill, Frances. *The Salem Witch Trials Reader*. New York: Da Capo Press, 1984.
An excellent and well-written sourcebook for excerpted primary source materials also containing a chronology of the Salem witchcraft episode. Beginning with the *Malleus Malificarum (1486)* by Jacob Sprenger and Heinrich Kramer and concluding with Arthur Miller's 1996 essay, "Why I Wrote the Crucible," Ms. Hill provides an impressive array of witchcraft trial-related materials, including verbatim transcripts and a selection of essays summarizing interpretations by various historians since the 18th century.

Hole, Christina. *A Mirror of Witchcraft*. London: Chatto and Windus, Ltd., 1957.
This is a valuable sourcebook for references to cases involving witchcraft in 17th- and 18th-century England.

Holmes, Thomas J. ed. *Cotton Mather: A Bibliography of His Works*, 3 vols. Cambridge, MA: Crofton Publishing, 1940.
This is a nearly complete collection of the writings of Reverend Cotton Mather.

Johnson, Claudia Durst, and Vernon E. Johnson. *Understanding the Crucible: A Student Casebook to Issues, Sources, and Historical Documents*. Westport, CT: Greenwood Press, 1998.
This is a student casebook that examines Arthur Miller's play, *The Crucible*, and compares Miller's interpretation of the Salem witchcraft trials with the actual event.

Karlsen, Carol F. *The Devil in the Shape of a Woman: Witchcraft in Colonial New England*. New York: W. W. Norton & Co., 1987.
Feminist historian Dr. Carol F. Karlsen analyzes the underlying reasons why certain women in colonial New England were more likely than others to be accused and ultimately convicted of witchcraft. To Karlsen, women in colonial society were categorized into two distinct groups, one that conformed to the expected standards and another that stood at odds with societal expectations. The women of the latter group, identified as "handmaidens of the Devil," could expect to find themselves accused of witchcraft.

Kences, James E. "Some Unexplored Relationships of Essex County Witchcraft to the Indian Wars of 1675 and 1687." Essex Institute Historical Collections (EIHC), July 1984.
This article reflects the theory first suggested in 1984 by Professor James E. Kences that psychological pressure emanating from the frontier wars in Maine had a profound and unsettling impact upon the afflicted children and numerous members of the Salem Village community.

Kors, Alan C., and Edward Peters, eds. *Witchcraft in Europe, 1100–1700: A Documentary History*. Philadelphia: University of Pennsylvania Press, 1972.
This is an important compilation of information relating to the numerous outbreaks of witchcraft in continental Europe down to the end of the 17th century.

Levin, David. *What Happened in Salem?*, 2nd ed. New York: Harcourt, Bruce and World, Inc., 1960.

An excellent, though somewhat dated, student orientation of the Salem witchcraft trials. Dr. Levin provides a good summary overview of the event combined with a selection of primary source testimonies and depositions from the trials. He follows with the evaluations of contemporary observers, Deodat Lawson, Cotton Mather, Increase Mather, and Thomas Brattle. As a point of comparison, Levin concludes with two short stories that deal with the subject of New England witchcraft: Nathaniel Hawthorne's "Young Goodman Brown" and Ester Forbes' "A Mirror for Witches."

Norton, Mary Beth. *In the Devil's Snare*. New York: Vintage Books, 2002.

This is a meticulously researched analysis of the entire Salem episode exploring the viewpoint that New England colonists saw the events of 1692 as a diabolical conspiracy threatening to destroy their society.

Reis, Elizabeth. *Damned Women: Sinners and Witches in Puritan New England*. Ithaca, NY: Cornell University Press, 1999.

Dr. Norton examines the Salem episode in the broader context of Essex County, Massachusetts. She asserts that previous studies have focused on a wide range of issues and possible causes, but have largely ignored the important question: Why was Salem so different from all previous witchcraft outbreaks in New England? Her answer is because of Essex Country's proximity to the Maine frontier and the devastating social and psychological impact of the concurrent frontier Indian wars upon the regional population.

For this she asserts that the Salem episode had the scope it did, focusing upon the entire community of Essex County, Massachusetts.

Roach, Marilynne K. *The Salem Witchcraft Trials: A Day-by-Day Chronicle of a Community Under Siege*. New York: Cooper Square Press, 2002.

A remarkable and exhaustive compendium of detailed Salem witchcraft trial information arranged chronologically from January 1692 to January 1697. For anyone interested in what occurred on a daily basis, this is the ultimate reliable source.

Robinson, Enders A. *The Devil Discovered: Salem Witchcraft 1692*. New York: Hippocrene Books, 1991.

This work explores the interrelationships between accused and accuser in Salem Village. Dr. Robinson suggests that the Salem witchcraft episode had its origins in personal animosities and envy between local residents. It goes on to outline how a conspiracy deprived members of the community of their property by means of accusations for witchcraft.

Rosenthal, Bernard. *Salem Story: Reading the Witch Trials of 1692*. Cambridge, UK: Cambridge University Press, 1993.

This work is dedicated to debunking many of the myths that have sprung up surrounding the Salem witchcraft trials and their participants. Rosenthal is intrigued with questions concerning the need to create an American popular mythology about this event, and why it occupies such a disproportionately large place in our popular culture.

Starkey, Marion. *The Devil in Massachusetts: A Modern Inquiry into the Salem Witch Trials*. New York: Alfred A. Knopf, 1949.

This is an early and entertaining narrative study of the Salem events of 1692–3. Although lacking in the sophisticated interpretive analysis of some more recent works on the subject, Starkey provides the reader with a vivid account of the episode with occasional forays into personal speculation as to the underlying motives of those involved.

Summers, Montague. *The History of Witchcraft and Demonology*. London: Kegan Paul, Trench, Trubner & Co. Ltd., 1926.
This work explores the cases and traditions surrounding witchcraft going back into ancient times.

Taylor, John M. *The Witchcraft Delusion in Colonial Connecticut*. New York: The Grafton Press, 1908.
This work examines the lesser known cases of witchcraft which occurred in Hartford, Stamford, and Fairfield, Connecticut, between 1669 and 1693.

Trask, Richard. *"The Devil Hath Been Raised": A Documentary History of the Salem Village Witchcraft Outbreak of March 1692*. Danvers, MA: Yeoman Press, 1997.
Richard Trask, Town Archivist for Danvers, Massachusetts (Salem Village), has compiled a collection of primary source materials, including depositions, arrest warrants, other legal documents, and letters. These sources, when tied together with an insightful narrative, provide an easy to follow chronological overview of the Salem witchcraft outbreak from its inception to its end.

Upham, Charles. *Salem Witchcraft*, vols. 1 and 2. Boston: Wiggin and Lunt, 1867.
This is one of the best known and most thorough summaries of the events of the trials ever published. Though shallow in analysis and interpretation, the Victorian antiquarian, Charles Upham, provides the reader with an extensive array of details in a well-written narrative that follows the trials from the beginning to the end of the episode.

Williard, Rev. Samuel. *A Brief Account of a Strange and Unusual Providence of God Befallen to Elizabeth Knapp of Groton, Samuel A. Green's, Groton in the Witchcraft Times*. Hartford: Kessinger Publishing, 1883.
This is another, somewhat obscure work which provides information about the lesser known Connecticut witchcraft outbreaks. The story is handled effectively in the more contemporary, *Witch-Hunting in Seventeenth Century New England* by David D. Hall.

Woodward, William E., ed. *Records of Salem Witchcraft, Copied from the Original Documents*, 2 vols. Roxbury, MA: Forgotten Books, 1864.
This is an important compilation of witchcraft trial documents, though it has been in large part superseded by Boyer and Nissenbaum's more recent three-volume collection of transcriptions.

Electronic Resources

Sitecolopedia Network. http://salemwitchtrials.com
Developed by Tim Sutter, this site contains a broad selection of information suitable for the novice researcher of the witch trials at Salem.

University of Virginia. http://etext.lib.virginia.edu/salem/witchcraft
Developed by Professor Benjamin Ray of University of Virginia, this site is without a doubt the *most comprehensive and detailed electronic source* for witch trial document reproductions, texts of trial materials, maps, portraits, and illustrations relating to the event.

Films

Three Sovereigns for Sarah. 1985. Not rated. Running time: 3 hours. Featuring: Vanessa Redgrave, Phillis Thaxter, and Kim Hunter.
A made-for-television film produced by Victor Pisano and Night Owl Productions and televised on PBS. It provides the viewer with a very accurate portrayal of the Salem witchcraft episode, and especially focuses on the case of the three Towne sisters, Rebecca Towne Nurse, Mary Towne Easty, and Sarah Towne Cloyce.

Days of Judgement. 1992. Documentary. Produced in conjunction with the "Days of Judgment Exhibition" by the Essex Institute (Peabody Essex Museum) for the Salem Witchcraft Trial Tercentenary in 1992.
It is the most informative and well-researched program of its kind. Featuring such noted historians of the trials as Stephen Nissenbaum and Richard Godbeer, it provides the most authoritative and accurate interpretation of the episode currently available.

The Crucible, 1996. Directed by Nicholas Hytner, screenplay by Arthur Miller, released and distributed by Twentieth Century Fox Studios, running time: 2 hours, 4 minutes. This film adaptation of Arthur Miller's classic 1950s play is an excellent screen representation of the author's ideas and remains true to the play's original plotline. It is not, however, an accurate representation of the historical events as they happened in Salem in 1692, and should not be viewed as such.

Index

About the Author

K. David Goss, MA, PhD candidate, is professor of history and museum studies at Gordon College, Wenham, MA. His published works include Greenwood's *The Salem Witch Trials: A Reference Guide* and *Daily Life during the Salem Witch Trials*. Goss has received the Marvin Wilson Award for Excellence in Teaching.